YOUTH AND WORK:
TRANSITION TO EMPLOYMENT
IN ENGLAND AND GERMANY

Edited by John Bynner and Ken Roberts

A project of the
Anglo-German Foundation
for the Study of Industrial Society

The Anglo-German Foundation for the Study of Industrial Society was established by an agreement between the British and German governments after a state visit by the late President Heinemann, and incorporated by Royal Charter in 1973. Funds were initially provided by the German government; since 1979 both governments have been contributing.

The Foundation aims to contribute to the knowledge and understanding of industrial society in the two countries and to promote contacts between them. It funds selected research projects and conferences in the industrial, economic and social policy area, designed to be of practical use to policymakers.

Cover: design by Bailey and Kenny

Printed by
Staples Printers Rochester Ltd

Anglo-German Foundation
for the Study of Industrial Society
17 Bloomsbury Square, London WC1A 2LP

Contents

List of Tables

Appendices

List of Figures

ACKNOWLEDGEMENTS

Acknowledgements

The research reported here was supported by a grant from the Anglo-German Foundation for the Study of Industrial Society. Some additional support for cross-national meetings on the project and computing consultancy was provided by Unilever plc. The views expressed in the report, however, are those of the authors alone. We are grateful for the co-operation of the education and training authorities in Bremen, Liverpool, Swindon and Paderborn, and to the young people who participated in the research.

AUTHORS

Authors

Martina Behrens — *University of Bielefeld, Paderborn project*

Alan Brown — *University of Surrey, Swindon project*

John Bynner — *City University, Co-ordinator/General Editor*

Stan Clark — *University of Liverpool, Co-ordinator Liverpool project*

Michelle Connolly — *University of Liverpool, Liverpool project*

Karen Evans — *University of Surrey, Co-ordinator Swindon project*

Walter R. Heinz — *University of Bremen, Co-ordinator Bremen project*

Klaus Hurrelmann — *University of Bielefeld, Co-ordinator Paderborn project*

Peter Kupka — *University of Bremen, Bremen project*

Ken Roberts — *University of Liverpool, Liverpool project/General Editor*

GLOSSARY

Glossary

ABC	*Arbeiterbildungscentrum* Worker Training Centre
ABM	*Arbeitbeschaffungsmaßnahme* Job creation programmes
A-level	Advanced level of the General Certificate of Education - equivalent to the *Abitur* in Germany - taken at 18+
AVJ	*Ausbildungsvorbereitungsjahr* Preparation for training year
BA	*Bundesanstalt für Arbeit* Federal employment office
BFS	*Berufsfachschule* Specialist vocational school
BFS/q	Training scheme leading to qualifications taken exclusively in a vocational school
BVJ	*Berufsvorbereitungsjahr* Vocational preparation year
BGJ	*Berufsgrundbildungsjahr* or *Berufsgrundschuljahr* pre-vocational training year
BIBB	*Bundesinstitut für Berufsbildung* Federal Institute for Training
BMBW	*Bundesministerium für Bildung und Wissenschaft* Federal Ministry for Education and Science
BSc	Bachelor of Science Degree
BTEC	Business and Technical Education Council qualification
CBI	Confederation of British Industry
CGLI	City and Guilds London Institute qualification
CPVE	Certificate of Pre-Vocational Education
CSE	Certification of Secondary of Education (preceded GCSE)
DE	Department of Employment
DES	Department of Education and Science

DTI	Department of Trade and Industry
EC	European Commission
GCSE	General Certificate of Secondary Education
G1, G2, G3	*Grundbildungslehrgang* Vocational preparation (skills) course
HE	Higher education
HMI	Her Majesty's Inspectorate
HND BTEC	Higher National Certificate
IT	Information technology
ITEC	Information Technology Education Council
LEA	Local Education Authority
LINK	Local Industry Network
LVE	*Lehrgang zur Vermittlung und Erweiterung beruflicher Kenntnisse* Course for the training and broadening of vocational skills
MSC	Manpower Services Commission
NCVQ	National Council for Vocational Qualification
NVQ	National Vocational Qualification
O-level	Ordinary level of the General Certificate of Education taken at 16+
ONC BTEC	Ordinary National Certificate
RSA	Royal Society of Arts qualification
TA	Training Agency
TEC	Training and Enterprise Council
TVEI	Technical and Vocational Education Initiative
YTS	Youth Training Scheme

SYNOPSIS

Background

Much has been made in recent years of the importance of a country's education and training system for its economic prosperity. In Britain, the upheavals in the labour market brought about by recession and technological change have focused attention on the lessons to be learned from other countries' approaches to vocational training. In devising the Youth Training Scheme (YTS), British policymakers were strongly influenced by Germany's 'dual system'. On a smaller scale, Germany has adopted some special measures along British lines, such as *Arbeiten und Lernen,* directed at young people who fail to get apprenticeships, or jobs after completing apprenticeships, in areas of high unemployment.

Attempts to transplant elements of an education and training system from one country to another always run the risk of overlooking their quite different underlying cultural traditions. They may also ignore the variations in the way the system works in different regions and the effects of economic conditions. To gain a proper understanding of the working of an education and training system, let alone assess its effectiveness in policy terms, it is necessary to find out how it is experienced. This project examined young people's vocational preparation in two expanding and two contracting labour markets in Britain and Germany. We wanted to find out what it means for a young person to experience equivalent education and training routes in the two countries. How does the experience differ qualitatively and in outcomes? What differences are there between areas with expanding as opposed to contracting labour markets? Finding answers enables us to address a central policy question: what should British and German policymakers be doing to maximise young people's fulfilment and effectiveness in the labour market under different economic conditions? What can each country most usefully learn from the other?

Areas

Our research adopted the novel approach of selecting matched samples of 160 16-19 year-olds from towns twinned on the basis of their contracting or expanding labour markets - Liverpool and Bremen (contracting), and Swindon and Paderborn (expanding). From each town, 160 young people were matched in terms of their career patterns with 160 young people from the twin towns.

Each pair of towns had a similar economic history and current industrial mix. All were coping with major economic changes. New technology was a challenge everywhere, but whereas Liverpool and Bremen, with their contracting maritime industries, had been experiencing economic decline for some time, Swindon and Paderborn had expanding economies that were well stocked with growth businesses. Both Paderborn and Swindon were railway towns in the past and Paderborn still is, but in each place this traditional industry has been overtaken by the growth of new manufacturing and service sector businesses. Swindon has been described as one of the fastest-growing towns in Europe. After the closure of the railway works in the late 1980s, the town soon achieved full employment again and employers had to cope with serious labour shortages. Paderborn appeared to have the greater mismatch problems, with adults who were displaced from older industries finding it more difficult to become re-established. However, by the late 1980s, the Nixdorf computer company was contributing to the town's transformation into an area of relative economic prosperity.

Bremen and Liverpool were both coping with problems of recession and long-term economic decline throughout the 1980s. Each city is a port, and maritime activities were the basis of their one-time prosperity. Liverpool's decline began early in the twentieth century, whereas Bremen remained prosperous until relatively recently, but throughout the 1980s both cities were unemployment blackspots. Each of the locations had a distinct political culture. During the 1980s Liverpool became a Labour city, though previously its politics were strongly influenced by religious sectarianism. Bremen has remained an SPD stronghold with a longer history of radical left politics than Liverpool. Swindon was among the many southern English towns with working-class majorities that elected Conservative Members of Parliament for the first time in the 1980s, though its local Council continued to be run by the Labour Party. Paderborn was also conservative (CDU) politically, but this seemed to owe more to the local influence of religion (most of the population are Catholics) than to social class or economic factors.

Career trajectories

A guiding principle in our research design was the existence of broadly similar routes to employment in the two countries. The term 'career trajectory' reflects the origins of these routes in education and family backgrounds, and the predictability of ultimate destinations in the labour market. As the occupational structures in both countries are similar, it makes good sense to classify the routes leading into them in terms of the same broad career trajectories:

- I: academic mainstream leading towards higher education;

- II: training and education leading to skilled employment: dual system in Germany; work-based training and apprenticeships, or further education college leading to vocational qualifications in Britain;

- III: other forms of education and training leading typically to semi-skilled employment;

- IV: early labour market experience of unskilled jobs, unemployment and 'remedial' training schemes.

The samples

In each area, matched samples of 16-19 year-olds were selected, with equal numbers of boys and girls from each of the four career routes in two cohorts. The younger cohort was one year past compulsory full-time education (16-17 year-olds); the older cohort was two years older (18-19 year-olds). Across the four towns, a total of 640 young people participated in the study. The research was conducted by postal questionnaires, completed in the young people's homes during 1988-89.

Differences in vocational training

Our sample selection was purposely intended to balance the quite different distributions of young people between the career routes in the two countries. In reality, much higher proportions of young people are in trajectories I and II in Germany (academic and skilled) than in Britain, and in Britain far more young people are to be found in trajectory IV (unskilled and unemployed). The advantage of sampling equal numbers from each career route is that cross-national differences in experience within each path to given occupations are brought into much sharper relief. For example, the majority of young people who leave school at 16 in Germany pass into apprenticeship schemes, but we need to know what happens to the minority who do not and how they compare with their British counterparts.

Despite the equating of the distributions across trajectories between the two countries, German respondents were on average two years behind their British counterparts in relation to entry into the labour market. Large numbers of the British sample were in full-time employment, and even when they were on firm-based YTS or apprenticeship schemes, the training and education they were getting were much more likely to be work-based than in Germany. Even on the academic route, completion of degree studies within three years puts British young people well ahead of their German counterparts for entry to full-time employment.

Another major difference was that nearly all the German young people who were based in firms were apprentices with an institutionalised junior status, whereas the majority of the firm-based British respondents were employees. Within German industry there is a clearer division between young trainees on the one hand, and qualified skilled adult workers on the other. Moreover the job of *Meister*, with responsibility for training to which the German worker may aspire, has no direct counterpart in the British system.

Another difference in context was that in Germany the different career routes were more clearly bounded: for example, there was no uncertainty about who was being trained for skilled work under the dual system and who was not. The German apprentices were following prescribed curricula, working towards qualifications that had to be earned before they could become skilled, and their training had a definite duration. However, there were signs that despite the statutory controls on these arrangements, the quality of what was offered was quite variable. An apprentice being trained by a *Meister* in a small building firm of two or three people was receiving qualitatively quite different training from one apprenticed in a large construction company.

In Britain, the division between different routes and in individuals' progress was much less clear cut. The British samples were more likely to have encountered obstacles such as failing examinations and being made redundant. They were also more likely to have changed their career aims recently and to have switched on their own accord, sometimes in an apparently haphazard manner, between training schemes, courses and jobs. Many of the individuals concerned appeared to be constructing their own patterns of career progression.

Academic route

The fluid, and in some ways precarious, nature of the British system was apparent even on this trajectory. Thus, most German students with an *Abitur* were expecting to proceed to higher education or to apprenticeships either as an alternative to, or as a step towards, higher education. In Britain, this progression seemed more affected by the state of the local labour market. About twice the proportion of the Swindon young people with A-levels were being recruited to jobs at 18 compared with those in Liverpool, where employers had fewer employment opportunities to offer.

Route to skilled employment

This route involved a variety of options for young people in Britain with further education college and vocational qualifications at one end, through traditional firm-based apprenticeship schemes, and firm-based YTS at the other. In Germany, the apprenticeship was really the only option. Labour market conditions in both countries affected both the availability of apprenticeships and training schemes, and whether jobs followed them: in Liverpool and Bremen prospects were much poorer for finding and using training than in Swindon and Paderborn. In both of the former towns some credence could be given to the view that apprenticeships and training schemes are sometimes an exploitative form of cheap labour. But a crucial difference was that in Germany every newly-qualified skilled worker had a recognised vocational qualification, whereas there was no such certain outcome from Britain's YTS.

Uncertain routes

Dropouts from apprenticeships and those failing to get them or (in Britain) firm-based training typified this route. The main difference between the two countries was that in Germany the desired outcome was usually a recognised vocational qualification at a later stage; for example through delayed entry to an apprenticeship. In Britain, the typical desired outcome was a job: those staying on at school for one extra year to repeat examinations (GCSE) or to take the Certificate of Pre-Vocational Education (CPVE), or those joining a community-based YTS scheme, saw these as no more than stepping stones to employment. In Britain, these options were more common in Liverpool where jobs were more scarce than they were in Swindon. But even in Liverpool, 75% of the young people on this route expected to be in jobs in a year's time; in Bremen the figure was only 10%.

Routes to nowhere

Those failing to achieve their aims on the previous track were one major source of recruitment to this one. In Britain they were joined by young people who had left school at the minimum age to enter dead-end jobs or unemployment and, in Germany, by dropouts from apprenticeship schemes and those who had failed to obtain places on them. In booming labour markets like Swindon and Paderborn, the availability of casual unskilled work could foster the prospect, however illusory, that a career was being established. In reality, the postponement of entry into proper training made the prospect of getting it later on increasingly unlikely. In Liverpool and Bremen, getting any job was considered a major achievement. In Britain, spells of unemployment had been common for a sizeable proportion of the samples. In Germany, compulsory attendance at a school or on schemes until the age of 18, ensured that all the young people were occupied in education and training through at least some part of the week. But the stigma attached to this experience was likely to make further progress difficult.

Skills and values

The British young people were much closer to the labour market than their German counterparts; indeed many had already entered it, so in many respects the range of work attributes they had acquired, especially job-related skills, was wider than in Germany. More of the British respondents reported being given responsibility, using their initiative, working to deadlines, making decisions, working co-operatively in groups, and taking both written and practical tests. The Germans had less experience of information technology. Also, the British samples were the more likely to report having developed new skills and abilities. In both countries, the academic and skilled career routes were providing the most learning experiences. But the differences between these and the others were widest in the German towns. Within all career tracks the British samples reported the greater breadth of vocational learning.

Perhaps more surprisingly, the British young people held more positive views of their prospects than those in Germany. Though such confidence declined, moving from trajectory I to trajectory IV, the British young people were always ahead of their German counterparts in terms of confidence about getting the jobs they wanted, impressing employers in job interviews, avoiding unemployment and never being dismissed. Even in Liverpool, the most depressed area of all, most young people expected to be in jobs within a year's time. In Germany, the extension of the transition to employment implicit in the dual system, and the accentuated problems for those who failed to get apprenticeships, appeared to be engendering more gloom about the future. In Britain, the possibility of 'a good job', one that paid well, was always just around the corner. Even if it was not, there is a long tradition in depressed areas of coming to terms with unemployment, which sometimes extends across the generations. Community support was reducing the stigma of living on 'welfare' and self-esteem was maintained.

In apparent contrast, the German samples of young people attached the greater value to working hard, making money and getting ahead. They were also the most satisfied with their education, the districts in which they lived, their standard of living and their leisure. The British young people were the more likely to envisage training to work in new occupations sometime in the future and migrating for jobs in different areas.

Nearly all the young people in both countries had very positive self-conceptions and reported good relationships with their families. Quarrels over any issue, including career plans, were exceptional. There appeared to be a broad consensus between the young people and their parents which applied equally in both countries.

In each of the four areas, the young people's political convictions reflected the local political culture. The main international difference was that working-class German youth appeared the most 'detached' from their country's political processes. This detachment showed the same strong relationship to educational level in each country, and was further reflected in career routes and occupational destinations. Thus, the most alienated groups politically were those with the poorest records of educational attainment and extended experience of unskilled work or unemployment. Interest in politics was strongest among the German young people on the academic and skilled routes.

Conclusions

Our research has exposed fundamental differences in the assumptions lying behind the transition to employment in Britain and Germany, which are reflected in the experiences and responses of young people. In Germany, 'vocationalism' is in full flower; it is taken for granted that all young people, whatever the form of employment, must be qualified to enter it. The period of preparation varies from the several years prior to graduation from a German university to the three years for the traditional apprenticeship. In Britain, the persistent assumption of a large proportion of employers, young people and their families is that getting a good job in the minimum possible time is what matters. Even in higher education, graduation generally occurs by age 22, and attempts to extend university courses, such as the four-year degree offered at Keele University, have not caught on elsewhere.

Despite all the initiatives and exhortations by government and business representatives, training as a preliminary to employment has still not penetrated very deeply into the British psyche. The prevailing view still seems to be that whatever you need to know in a job can be taught on the job itself; getting the job is what matters.

To try to draw up a comparative balance sheet of the strengths and weaknesses of the two countries' education and training systems and then to make a judgment about the superiority of one over the other would be invidious. Each type of vocational preparation is a coherent process which can form a clear and, probably for most young people, satisfactory route to adult employment. There is probably no easy way by which a version of the dual system could be established in Britain, despite the Confederation of British Industry's recently expressed hopes.

The German youth who succeeds in getting an apprenticeship in a labour market where the skills acquired are valued, probably has the better all-round preparation for entry to work and adulthood. This is because the mixture of education and training leading to clearly-defined vocational qualifications ensures a degree of breadth in the training experience. For those learning outmoded skills in declining occupations in areas of high unemployment, or for those who fail to gain entry to training in the first place, the prospects can be bleak. In Britain, the far less stringent criteria for entry into jobs means that in a boom economy experience of employment is far easier to get. On the other hand, the kind of generic qualities and educational values demanded by the new technological age are less likely to be present. Job-related training may equip the young person very well to meet the requirements of a particular employer, but may be less suited to the changes in employment that economic transformation brings. In times of slump, this can relegate young people to a pool of under-trained and uneducated labour, ill-equipped to enter the new industries on which the regeneration of the economy depends.

The lessons to be learned concern principally those young people in each of our trajectories for whom the present training system was clearly failing. For Germany, the question is how to build in more flexibility and extended opportunities to gain work experience, qualifications and skilled work itself, especially in areas of high unemployment. For Britain, the issues are how to regulate more effectively, but without destroying, routes into and through training, how to make employers more responsive, and how to make jobs more educative. Both countries may need to look hard again at current discontinuities in the curriculum between 11 and 18. Many successful industrial nations maintain a broader mix of academic and pre-vocational education for longer, and put off employer-based training to later. Both Germany and Britain need to consider this approach as well.

Our research was about experience at the early stages of transition to employment. The next phase will investigate the experience of work itself. Selected young people from our samples will be interviewed, together with their employers and other key people in their lives. This will enable us to relate current performances in jobs and perceptions to the preceding vocational preparation. We suspect that, again, our research will not lead to a judgement that one system is superior to another. Each has its own coherence, matching past assumptions, experience and needs. We conclude that the best way forward for each country is to develop its established training cultures, build upon its existing strengths and work within its historical grain.

CHAPTER I

Background and methods

Rationale

'A hybrid of Europe's best', is how the *Guardian* newspaper described Britain's Youth Training Scheme (YTS). This description indicates a degree of envy for what some continental countries do to equip their young people for employment, and a gap for Britain to make up. Through the 1980s, the belief grew in Britain that one explanation of the country's poor economic performance in comparison with other advanced industrial societies lay in poor work preparation and lack of necessary vocational skills in the workforce. Although originally founded in schemes to combat youth unemployment, YTS came to be targeted at the majority, if not all, 16 and 17 year-old school-leavers (about two-thirds of Britain's young people); the new generation of workers to be equipped with the skills that modern industry needed (DE, 1988). Of all the European models on which Britain has drawn, the West German one has had the most influence. The dual system guarantees, through three-year apprenticeship schemes, a combination of on-the-job and off-the-job training (in schools and colleges), which ensures that virtually all school-leavers become vocationally qualified before entry into a job.

But the unblemished praise that has been heaped in some quarters on the German system, and the mixture of envy and admiration frequently expressed (e.g. Grimond, 1979; Hamilton, 1987; CBI, 1989), may be in some respects misplaced. Germany's apprenticeship system is said to have adapted well to the needs of new technology and has protected young people during the economic changes of recent decades, while Britain's young people have suffered the traumas of unemployment and the series of temporary measures designed to combat it. But such generalisations have never applied in every part of either country. School-leavers' employment prospects have remained buoyant in many parts of Britain in the 1980s (Roberts et al.,

2

1987). Meanwhile, there are parts of Germany, especially in regions whose traditional economic bases have contracted, where young people have found it increasingly difficult to obtain orthodox apprentice training and subsequent employment (Casey, 1986; Heinz, 1985, 1987; Lenhardt, 1977; Roberts, 1986).

Comparative studies have sometimes exaggerated the differences between the British and German treatment of their beginning workers. In Britain, some youth jobs have provided equivalent training to German apprenticeships. Recent government responses to beginning workers' difficulties have made the countries' transitional arrangements more similar than in the past. Like Germany's apprenticeships, at the time of our study, Britain's YTS had become a national but predominantly firm-based scheme. Under the new arrangements for training administered by Training and Enterprise Councils (TECs), this latter principle has been retained. The result is that, in some parts of Britain, two-step transitions have become almost as common as in Germany. Meanwhile, in the latter country, some recently introduced government training schemes, designed for disadvantaged groups of young people in high unemployment areas, have undoubted similarities to Britain's measures based on training workshops, community projects and colleges (Brock et al., 1987).

It is undeniable that each country's provisions for 16-19 year-olds were subjected to new stresses during the 1980s. In both Britain and Germany the 1980s proved to be a decade of massive economic restructuring. In each country, employment shifted from manufacturing to service sectors. The proportions of less-skilled jobs are continuing to decline in the 1990s, while higher-level employment is expanding. And to complicate the picture, the gains and losses are tending to occur in different regions within each country. This makes it unlikely that exactly the same education and training provisions, whether German or British, will operate with similar results and equal effectiveness in every part of either country (Ashton and Maguire, 1986).

3

But in any event, these similarities and the apparent convergence of approaches to vocational preparation in the two countries need to be set against the quite different cultural traditions and assumptions that lie behind them (Lallade, 1989; Rose and Wignanek, 1990). Training in Germany pervades all aspects of work, with the experienced German worker taking on a *Meister* role in relation to junior colleagues. Only in the traditional British apprenticeship scheme is there anything remotely comparable; and that is rapidly disappearing (Rose, 1990).

Moreover, as the British economy picked up in the late 1980s, some employers began reverting to the practice of taking on as many school-leavers as they could find, regardless of any training they might have had. In such a competition for workers, training schemes have increasingly become, in many employers' terms, an unnecessary luxury. This raises the question of how deep the commitment really is to the development in Britain of a 'training culture' on continental lines (DE, 1988). In Germany, such a training culture and the institutional structures which go with it are far more impervious to change in response to economic movements (Rose and Page, 1989). The problem in Germany is more to do with whether the form and content of traditional apprentice training is appropriate to the needs of modern employment. Is it now encompassing a degree of 'time-serving' - the major accusation from British critics of Britain's traditional craft apprenticeships (DE, 1985)? The German response to economic restructuring has tended to be one of reform rather than replacement. The British response has been to drop what no longer seems to be needed and to introduce new measures to tackle new problems, rather than adapt existing measures.

The contrasts and similarities between British and West German policies and experience made a study of vocational preparation in both of them particularly timely. What does it mean for a young person to be equipped for the same job via a similar career track in the two countries? How does the experience differ qualitatively and what differences are there in outcomes: in young people's effectiveness as workers and citizens, and in their attitudes and values? Are these experiences and outcomes the same or different for young people receiving their education and training in areas with contracting as opposed to expanding labour markets? How are they affected by unemployment?

Research plan

The origins of our research lay in contacts between two of the participants, Walter R. Heinz and Ken Roberts, and in a visit to Germany by John Bynner, co-ordinator of the British 16-19 Initiative - a programme of research funded by the Economic and Social Research Council in Britain (Bynner, 1987; Roberts, 1987). Both Walter Heinz in Bremen and Klaus Hurrelmann in Bielefeld had been, or were in the process of, conducting studies of West German young people's transition problems. Britain's 16-19 Initiative includes a core longitudinal study of the economic and political socialisation of approximately 5,000 young people in four contrasting labour markets: Swindon, Sheffield, Liverpool and Kirkcaldy. At the time of Bynner's visit to Germany, data collection was still at an early stage, which raised the possibility of a comparative study - comparing the two most sharply contrasting British areas, Swindon and Liverpool, with two similarly contrasting German cities, Paderborn and Bremen. Both Swindon and Paderborn have expanding labour markets, and Liverpool and Bremen contracting labour markets. By comparing young people's experience in the four cities the intention was not only to display national differences and similarities in the approach to vocational preparation, but to see how these differences might be mediated by local economic circumstances.

Accordingly, a proposal for carrying out a study of vocational preparation in the two countries was submitted to the Anglo-German Foundation for the Study of Industrial Society. Funding was awarded for the period August 1988 to February 1990. In each of the four participating universities - Bremen (Bremen project), Bielefeld

5

(Paderborn project), Surrey (Swindon project) and Liverpool (Liverpool project) - a research fellow was appointed to work on the project. The appointment of bilingual research fellows was an important factor in its success.

A central feature of the research was the use of a common questionnaire (with English and German language versions) to elicit young people's experiences of vocational preparation and attitudes towards it in Britain and Germany. The purpose of the analysis of the responses reported here is to describe the differences and similarities between the two countries and, where differences are evident, to try to elucidate their origins. We look particularly at the concept of 'youth career trajectory', translated into modern conditions in the West German and British labour market contexts. We also consider what policies are required in the two countries for maximising young people's personal fulfilment and success in employment in areas with contrasting economic characteristics. Is there a British solution to youth employment problems? Is there a German one? How can each country learn and benefit from the other's approach? These are the basic questions which this report addresses.

Sample design

In the British 16-19 Initiative two cohorts of young people - those in the last compulsory school year (aged 15-16) and those who were two years ahead of them (aged 17-18) when first contacted - were followed up for two years over the period May 1987 to May 1989. As noted previously, for the purpose of this Anglo-German study, it was decided to take samples from the areas representing the most extreme contrasts in terms of economic prosperity, Swindon and Liverpool, and to select comparable samples from two similarly expanding and contracting labour markets in Germany: Paderborn and Bremen. Both Paderborn and Swindon have capitalised on the growth of new service industries and new technology. Bremen and Liverpool, through their close association with maritime industries

6

(we describe them in detail later), have suffered long-term economic decline.

A second principle in selecting young people for the study was that the full range of vocational preparation in the two countries would be covered. Four distinctive career routes or 'trajectories' could be identified in both countries as set out below:

I - The academic route
Included in this group in the British samples are those either already in higher education or undertaking two or more A-levels (the traditional requirement for entry into higher education). This means, however, that those who were on this track but subsequently went into employment at 18, remain in this category.

Similarly, the German sample includes those who were heading for the *Abitur* or who had completed *Gymnasium*, irrespective of their future directions. Historically, in both Britain and Germany, only a minority, the academic high-achievers, have remained in full-time education until age 18 or later.

Recently, however, each country's staying-on route has widened. In West Germany the proportion of young people taking the *Abitur* has risen to over 30%, alongside a parallel trend towards more of these well-qualified school-leavers seeking and obtaining apprenticeships; this has sometimes meant fewer opportunities for 16 year-old school-leavers, especially in contracting local labour markets. In Britain there has been relatively little change in the proportion of young people gaining the two or more A-levels required for higher education, around 22%, but these are now only half of all who remain full-time students beyond age 16 (Clough, Gray and Jones, 1988a). New courses, often with a technical or vocational bias, such as the Certificate for Pre-Vocational Education (CPVE) in England, and the 16+ Action Plan in Scotland, have been developed specially for these 'new' sixth-formers and college students. Other young people stay on to re-take the 16+ examination, GCSE, or courses leading to well-established pre-vocational qualifications such as RSA

7

(Royal Society of Arts), CGLI (City and Guilds London Institute), and BTEC (Business and Technical Education Council) First. Young people who stay on to take such courses are not included in what we describe as the 'academic route'.

II - Skilled employment or training with vocational qualifications

This route is most easily identified in Germany, where it means serving an apprenticeship with an employer. Over half of all young people in West Germany (600,000 +) obtain apprenticeships under the dual system. This route has been, and remains, the centrepiece in Germany's transitional arrangements, but it has never been the country's sole pathway towards employment. In Britain, a smaller proportion of young people obtain designated apprenticeships, now down from a peak of 120,000 (mostly males) to 40,000 in total. However, it can be argued, convincingly in our view, that all youth jobs in Britain that involve substantial training, formal vocational qualifications and prospects of career progression should be included. The distinction between such employment and apprenticeship is no longer clear cut. Thus this trajectory includes instances where the initial stages of the training are now within firm-based YTS or where vocational qualifications are obtained within education. However, young people who only receive 'on-the-job' training, without any formal qualifications, are not included in this category. Whether opportunities to obtain firm-based training have increased, decreased, or remained stable has varied from place to place in both Britain and Germany, depending on the buoyancy of the local economies and labour markets.

III - Government training schemes, transitional and semi-skilled employment

Government employment schemes were introduced in many parts of Britain and Germany to make good the shortfall in other opportunities. In Britain this route is composed of training schemes that are not employer led, that is, those based on Community Projects, Training Workshops, and Information Technology Centres (ITECs). Germany has a broadly similar range of provisions. In both countries these schemes are most numerous in contracting labour markets, such as Liverpool and Bremen. For our purposes, the category also included both young people who were already undertaking traditional semi-skilled employment (either manual or non-manual) and those who were in a transitional state, meaning that at the time it was unclear where they would end up. Examples included:

- those in semi-skilled employment (including in Britain those performing 'skilled' jobs but without any formal education, training or vocational qualifications; e.g., carpenters learning solely 'on the job');

- those in long-standing specialised vocational education in Germany that does not take place in firms but in a vocational school, such as nursery assistance and paramedical work (the critical point here being to distinguish between those making an educational, but non-academic, transition from those following the firm-based route in apprenticeships);

- those continuing in education, but who were not aiming for qualifications which would place them in trajectories I or II (for example, those repeating earlier qualifications or taking prevocational qualifications);

- those who were moving around in education, training or employment, but who were not so unstable as to be placed in trajectory IV;

- those on government training schemes which were not employer led.

9

IV - Non-skilled employment, underemployment and unemployment

This is less of a route than a residual category. It has always been broader in Britain, but it also exists throughout West Germany. It seems sensible to bracket 16 year-olds who take unskilled jobs with the young unemployed because, in both countries, the same disadvantaged groups of young people are the most likely to experience each. Indeed, young unskilled workers and the young unemployed are often exactly the same individuals at different points in time. With the decline in demand for unskilled labour, even in expanding local labour markets, there has been a general trend towards these young people spending more time unemployed and less time in employment. Also included in this category are those on 'remedial' government schemes which are unlikely to lead to employment or enhance their employment prospects.

Sample selection

In selecting samples for the study, our plan was to fill, in equal numbers, these four categories in each of the four towns, drawing equally from two age groups of young people: those who were one year past compulsory schooling (broadly aged 16-17) and those who were two years ahead of them (broadly aged 18-19).

Needless to say, the sampling had to cope with the fact that in both countries some young people's careers do not fit neatly into any of the four categories. For example, there is much movement between YTS and full-time and part-time jobs in Britain, and there is a steady erosion of numbers on the academic trajectory.

Similarly, in Germany some young people start apprenticeships and then decide to upgrade their qualifications to the *Abitur*. Others decide to gain vocational skills via apprenticeships as a follow-on to academic ones, and may then proceed to higher education.

Consequently, after much debate, we decided to use the four career trajectories as just the first stage in identifying young people who had broadly comparable vocational preparation experiences in the two countries, and then to take into account vocational outcomes. Accordingly, we attempted to 'twin' young people in each pair of cities (Paderborn/Swindon and Bremen/Liverpool).

Thus, a skilled worker, like a heating and ventilation technician in Swindon, was matched with his or her counterpart in Paderborn. Similarly, a trainee hairdresser in Bremen was twinned with his or her counterpart in Liverpool. To achieve such matching between countries, it was initially necessary to draw much larger samples than were originally intended so that a sufficient range of occupations would be encompassed.

The final sample obtained through this matching process comprised 40 young people in each trajectory in each city, equally divided between the two cohorts - in all 160 per city. The total number of young people participating in the study was 640. Full details of the sampling in each city and the matching procedure are given in Appendix I. Profiles of young people in each trajectory in each city are given in Appendix II. Appendix III gives the family social class of the young people, broken down by country, town and career trajectory. More German fathers were in 'skilled' occupational categories and more British fathers were 'partly skilled'. (For a fuller discussion of our comparative methodology, see Bynner and Heinz, 1991.)

Development of the questionnaire

In order to secure sufficient comparability of research questions and procedures, the team decided to develop a standardised questionnaire which had to serve several objectives. It had to cover the most important aspects of transition into work or training in both countries. It had to consider the characteristics, if not peculiarities, of the different systems of education and vocational training, and be precise enough to provide a solid basis for allocating respondents to trajectories. Finally, it had to be sufficiently brief and comprehensible to be completed by young people of all educational levels.

11

The general structure of the questionnaire and the core set of items were taken from the instruments used in the British ESRC 16-19 Initiative. Some of the items for the German version were not included in the British questionnaire because the information had already been collected in the previous surveys of the longitudinal study. (The questionnaire used in Swindon is shown in Appendix IV.)

In addition to seeking 'basic' information about the social class backgrounds and gender of the respondent, the questionnaire covered many topics that were considered to be important for the process of transition:

- experiences over the last two years at school, and in looking for jobs, training schemes or apprenticeships;

- previous work experience and knowledge of information technology;

- plans and expectations for the future;

- attitudes and views about work and training;

- political views;

- self-conception;

- social and family life.

Especially in the area of education and training, it was difficult to develop precisely equivalent questions for the two countries. While the German system of education and vocational training is highly structured, the British system appears comparatively amorphous and unstructured. Thus, it was almost impossible to cover all variations and subdivisions in the two systems without expanding the questionnaire excessively. This meant that we had to compromise, using the minimum number of questions to cover as much common ground as possible. Different approaches had to be used to establish the educational levels of the young people and their parents. While the British questionnaire merely asked for parents' school-leaving ages, it took three items to pin down their status in terms of education and formal qualifications in the German version. Factual questions, and those on work experience, future expectations and work-related attitudes were of a more general nature and posed fewer problems. As a result of extensive discussion, we succeeded in having more than 90% of the total of 147 variables covered by the questionnaire in common.

This lengthy process of question selection and design was vital for the research. The questions were chosen only after a careful comparison of the education and training systems in both countries. The consequence was that the final versions of the questionnaire contained the maximum possible number of items of equivalent meaning for the German and British respondents.

Analysis

The questionnaires were coded for data entry by each of the four teams. They were then compiled into a single data set for computer analysis. After providing the four research teams with the combined data set, consisting of data for 640 young people, two data analysis steps were undertaken.

Quantitative analysis (cross-tabulations) of structural and attitudinal variables within and between the four trajectories

The aim of this step was to ascertain similarities and differences between the four patterns of school-training-employment transition in the two countries related to age, sex and social background. This was followed by a comparative analysis of structural and attitudinal variables by trajectory across the four labour markets and between Britain and Germany. As the samples were constructed on the basis of matching rather than random selection, the differences the figures reveal are not subjected to statistical test and are only used descriptively.

Comparative case analysis

The other part of our comparative analysis was of a qualitative nature, on a case study basis, using the matched pairs.

We are aware of the limitations of cross-cultural analysis based on small numbers of individual cases and groups. However, by focusing on trajectories as they are institutionalised in Britain and Germany, and by selecting closely matched cases, we have a valid frame of reference for comparative study.

CHAPTER II

Labour markets in four cities

Introduction

Each town in this study has its own economic and political history and they all have particular cultural traditions and identities. School-leavers' opportunities depend on the state of their local labour markets, and also, to some extent, on the policies of the government bodies responsible for education and training (CEDEFOP, 1982, 1987). Another reason for sketching each area's political history is that we were interested in the preparation of young people not only as workers, but as citizens.

Britain and Germany are very different political entities. Germany is a federal republic while Britain is a more centralised constitutional monarchy. The division of West Germany into 11 *Länder* has had myriad implications for legislation and administrative provision, including devolved responsibility for education, but in relation to vocational training the national and sectoral levels are more important. The idea of social partnership - between politicians, employers and trade unions - at national and local level is also central to the system. However, even in the more centralised British political system, young people in different parts of the country are exposed to very different local political cultures, as well as contrasting economic conditions. The day-to-day management of education is the responsibility of locally elected Local Education Authorities (LEAs), and since the 1988 Employment Act training, too, has become the responsibility of locally appointed Training and Enterprise Councils (TECs).

Swindon

Swindon is an expanding town in the south of England, experiencing the benefits in terms of jobs, of the growth of new technology industries in the region. In 1988 the town had a population of 133,000 and formed the industrial and commercial heart of the Borough of

16

Thamesdown, its travel-to-work area. Its expansion has been such that, according to the latest European Commission (EC) figures, Swindon is the 'fastest-growing town in Europe'.

From the establishment in the nineteenth century of the Great Western Railway (GWR), up to the 1930s, Swindon grew and developed as a town centred on a single industry - the railway engineering works - which was in regular operation by 1843. At its peak before World War I the works employed 12,000 men out of a population of about 50,000, so the whole town was effectively dependent on the one factory. Postwar decline in the railway workshops accelerated in the 1960s and proceeded to the final shutdown in 1986. In parallel with this decline, a new wave of development in the 1950s began to establish Swindon as a centre for mechanical and electrical engineering and consumer goods manufacture. Expansion of service industries followed in the 1960s, leading to further population growth and diversification of employment.

Overall, the workforce doubled between 1951 and 1981. According to recent studies, new technology jobs accounted for only 6% of employment in the 1980s. Despite Swindon's 'high tech' image, many of the newly created jobs had nothing to do with new technology per se. The relative importance of the main industries up to the beginning of the 1980s is shown in Table 2.1.

Table 2.1: Sectoral classification of those in employment in the Swindon travel-to-work area

	1968 %	1978 %	1981 %
Manufacturing	50	39	29
Construction	7	5	6
Distribution	11	16	18
Services/administration	32	40	47
Total	**100**	**100**	**100**

Source: Department of Employment, Annual Census of Employment, 1981.

17

Important private sector employers in Swindon include Rover, British Telecom, two major finance and insurance companies (Allied Dunbar and Nationwide Anglia), and two major electronics companies (Plessey Semi-Conductors and Thorn EMI). Major public sector employers are Wiltshire County Council, Swindon Health Authority and Thamesdown Borough Council. Honda recently started building a new £300m car-assembly plant to go alongside the existing engine plant, which gives it the facility to produce at least 100,000 cars a year from Swindon.

At the height of the railway engineering industry, Swindon was a typical traditional working-class community, with an economy based on male manual work. The continuing diversification of industries has created new employment and work cultures. Increased demand for temporary and part-time labour and the spread of shift work have increased women's participation in the workforce dramatically, though no more so than in other parts of Britain. In 1981 63% of women aged 16-59 were employed in the locality, close to the national average of 62%.

The arrival of American-controlled firms and other companies in the financial, business and high technology industries brought work cultures which contrasted sharply with the shop-floor management practices of traditional industry in Britain. The influx of new companies seeking to establish themselves in the local community led to widespread innovations in work organisation and management strategies emphasising corporate commitment and discouragement of trade unionism.

The growth of Swindon as án industrial centre can be attributed partly to the expansionist aims of the town's Council. Since 1946, the local authority has played an active part in promoting the industrial and social development of the town away from dependence on the railway workshops. Following the Town Development Act 1952, Swindon participated in 'overspill' schemes from London, and a housing scheme for 'keyworkers' was established as part of a planned expansion and community development strategy. On local government reorganisation in 1974, Swindon Borough Council and Highworth Rural District Council were combined to form Thamesdown Borough Council. This Council adopted corporate planning strategies which aimed to continue the economic development of the Swindon area into the 1990s.

Unemployment in Swindon was above the national average in the 1970s, reflecting the rapid increase in population combined with the effects of recession in manufacturing industry. Subsequently, Swindon benefited from the continuing influx of new industries, leading to unemployment levels lower than the national average. Figures for 1988/89 show a substantial decrease both locally and nationally (reflecting changes in eligibility for social security benefit as well as general decreases in the numbers out of work). New industries took up surplus labour from the manufacturing sector to some extent, though there was some mismatch of skills which has contributed to a residual unemployment problem (Table 2.2).

Table 2.2: Unemployment rate at April of each year, 1985-89

	RATE	
Year	Swindon	UK
1985	10.1	13.1
1986	11.3	13.2
1987	9.6	12.4
1988	7.0	10.0
1989	4.2	7.4

Source: Department of Employment, Annual Census of Employment, 1989.

The youth labour market was affected by the pattern of migration to the Swindon area. With its expanding employment prospects, the town attracted young families from other regions and had proportionately more young people about to enter the labour market than

Liverpool. Despite this, youth unemployment was lower than the national average. Even in the late 1970s and early 1980s, when unemployment throughout Britain reached a postwar peak, there was generally some work available (part-time, temporary or seasonal), such that young people in Swindon would typically spend only a few weeks unemployed. Relatively few young people were continuously unemployed for long spells. However, seasonal and temporary work, although breaking up long-term unemployment, did not always offer young people a route into more stable employment. Those taking such work remained unskilled and at risk of intermittent unemployment. Local manufacturing industry continued to generate vacancies but many of these jobs were relatively short-term, to fulfil particular contracts, reflecting the flexible personnel policies that firms were adopting.

Data on school-leaver destinations in north-east Wiltshire (the smallest local breakdown available) give an indication of the occupations entered by young people in our survey area, given that Swindon young people make up the majority of the age group. Quite a wide spread was in evidence, with clerical jobs taking 43% of females entering work, and manufacturing, construction and engineering taking 60% of males. On local training schemes, clerical, personal services (mainly hairdressing) and caring took over 60% of female entrants, while engineering (42%) and construction (20%) were much more significant for males.

Overall then, the youth labour market held up in Swindon in the 1980s. As a result, many older assumptions about the relationship between education, training and employment remained intact. Employment structures remained sufficiently open to offer a degree of choice to nearly all young people. In the context of impending demographic change, competition in the Swindon youth labour market is likely to be competition between employers for youth labour rather than between young people for jobs.

Despite its industrial base, Swindon never seems to have been a hotbed of left-wing sentiment. This may partly have been because in a town surrounded by a large agricultural hinterland, many workers were recruited from the countryside. Perhaps also the economic dominance of the single employer exerted a dampening effect on radicalism. The local poet and author Alfred Williams, himself employed at the GWR workshops, writing about the works just before World War I, commented that the smiths were not given to discussing political and social problems, and he also pointed out that

> 'the political views of the men in the shed are known to the overseer and are, in some cases at any rate, communicated by him to the manager; there is no such thing as individual liberty about the works'.

Swindon first became a separate parliamentary constituency in 1918, when it was won by the Coalition Conservative candidate, and it remained Conservative for most of the period until 1945. After 1945 it became a fairly solid Labour seat, with the party winning 60% or more of the votes in 1945, 1964 and 1966. The seat was lost in a by-election in 1969 but reverted to Labour in 1970. Since then, in company with most towns in southern England, Swindon moved steadily towards the Conservative Party, with a Conservative Member of Parliament being elected in 1983 and 1987. However, the Thamesdown Borough Council remained under Labour control.

Paderborn

Paderborn is a town in the east of North Rhine-Westphalia (close to Bielefeld), experiencing a slow but constant increase of population and industry. The town is the administrative, industrial and commercial centre of the Kreis Paderborn district and in 1988 had a population of 123,000. Paderborn played an important role in the Hanse trading confederation and ever since the thirteenth century handicrafts and trade have flourished. From 1858 to 1960 the railway engineering industry was a major employer and, at its height, 2,000 people worked in the two plants. After World War II, however, the

railway line between the Ruhrgebiet and Berlin lost its former importance and likewise the railway junction at Paderborn. At the time of
the study just 1,200 people worked in the railway repair and maintenance shops. The railway is still an important employer in Paderborn but never reached the overall domination that it once possessed
in Swindon.

After 1955, under the *Ostwestfalenplan*, existing companies were
modernised and expanded, and special areas for the establishment
of new industries were designated. The *Bundesraumordnungspla-
nung 1975*, and other plans for the development of the region, gave
Paderborn an important infrastructural role. New roads to Paderborn
were built, a new motorway was put under construction and the
administrative bodies and social services - hospitals, job centre and
so on - for the entire district were relocated in the town.

At the time of the study, trade and industry in Paderborn were
characterised by variety. There were major private companies producing lamps, furniture, food and beverages, steel tubing, automobile accessories, and computers. In 1987 24% of the Paderborn
workforce were employed in the processing industries, 19% in the
steel industry and mechanical engineering, and 13% in the service
industry. The rest was spread across all the industrial sectors. The
wide range of enterprises had created a fairly stable labour market.
Recently the computer and office equipment industries had grown
in importance. Nixdorf AG alone employed about 10,000 persons
(including 2,200 apprentices) in its Paderborn plants. Eleven per cent
of all employees in this field of industry in Germany worked in Paderborn (Arbeitsamt Paderborn, *Der Arbeitsmarkt 1/88*). Other major
private sector employers were Saute (food industry) and Beutler
(mechanical engineering). There were also several major public sector employers in Paderborn as in Swindon: the town and district ad-
mininstrations, the *Arbeitsverwaltung* (employment office) and the
courts of justice. Recent developments in the private sector had created a division in the local labour market: on the one hand there were

slow-growing traditional industries and, on the other hand, fast-growing new-technology businesses.

The numbers employed in the Paderborn region rose by 9% between 1983 and 1988, compared with 5% in Germany as a whole. According to *Arbeitsamt* data, Paderborn's growth rate is unique in Germany. The proportion of adult women in the local labour market in 1987, 36.9%, was below the national level of 40.4%, though since 1987 the participation rate has risen and is now close to the national level.

Despite its flourishing industries, unemployment rates in Paderborn in the 1980s were relatively high by German standards. Unemployment rose sharply in 1981-2 and up to 1988 there were no signs of a decline back to earlier levels (Table 2.3).

Table 2.3: Unemployment rates in Paderborn, 1985-89

| Year | RATE | |
	Paderborn	Germany
1985	12.6	9.3
1986	12.6	9.0
1987	12.4	8.9
1988	11.7	8.7
1989	11.4	7.9

Source: Arbeitsamt Paderborn, 1989.

However, the composition of the unemployed had also changed. The number of long-term unemployed declined, whereas short-term unemployment (less than three months) increased. By the end of the 1980s in Paderborn, persons with vocational training were not generally threatened by long-term unemployment. However, in autumn 1987, 53.4% of the unemployed had formal vocational qualifications. A combination of different factors explain this phenomenon; changes in the local industrial mix in the early 1980s led to a strong demand for new skills. There were still people with the 'wrong' vocational qualifications in Paderborn, and the apprenticeships offered still tended to be in old trades. The recently founded special vocational schools for computer and office equipment experts, and changes in the curricula of technical apprenticeships, had little effect. The latter had been introduced very recently, and after three years' training the apprentices ran little risk of unemployment. But the vocational schools in this field still had very small intakes, and often required previous training for entry.

The age structure of the unemployed in Paderborn was undergoing a visible change. The number of unemployed persons under 30 years of age was declining in the late 1980s, whereas in the older age groups the unemployment rate was still rising. School-leavers' prospects in the labour market were far better than 10 years previously. The population of Paderborn was undergoing a massive demographic change. The number of births had fallen by half since 1964, so the size of school-leaving cohorts had been contracting. Among school-leavers, the percentage aiming at higher education was greater than ever before, following a nationwide trend. There was still competition for the 'best' apprenticeships, but this had declined for two reasons: fewer young people were entering the labour market, and more apprenticeships were being offered by local companies. Three considerations led employers to train more young people: the improved economic situation, the need to recruit in excess of anticipated requirements in order to cope with dropouts, and a desire to hire cheap labour (Table 2.4).

Table 2.4: New training contracts in Paderborn, 1976/77 - 1986/87

Year	Total	Industry/ Commerce	Crafts	Public	Farming	Other Services
1976/77	3347	1450	1347	75	85	390
1977/78	3933	1685	1630	88	133	397
1978/79	4368	1813	1898	99	180	387
1979/80	4418	1846	1930	73	152	417
1980/81	3530	1587	1281	92	148	422
1981/82	4185	1737	1776	93	177	402
1982/83	4703	1949	2029	124	168	433
1983/84	4904	2076	2107	120	197	404
1984/85	4794	2248	1852	114	204	376
1985/86	4589	2159	1702	134	155	439
1986/87	4496	2159	1739	94	104	400

Source: Arbeitsamt Paderborn, *Der Arbeitsmarkt 1/88.*

In 1987 96.8% of applicants registered with the *Arbeitsamt* took up apprenticeships, whereas 10 years previously it had been much more difficult for young people to obtain places. Young adults' labour market problems in Paderborn had now shifted to the early to mid-twenties. Some apprentices encountered difficulties in being taken on by their trainers or other employers. Despite flourishing industries in Paderborn, the problems of youth unemployment had not been entirely solved.

Politically, Paderborn was a conservative town, though it had become less so in recent years. As one might expect in a German town which was predominantly Catholic in religious affiliation, the CDU was the dominant political party. In the mid-1970s the CDU achieved around two-thirds of the vote in Paderborn in provincial, local and national elections, and although its vote declined gradually after that, it was only in the 1989 European and local elections that it fell below 50% for the first time. The decline in the CDU vote had not benefited the SPD or the FDP very substantially, but seems to have been a reflection of the rise of the Greens, who first entered the local electoral scene 10 years earlier.

An interesting feature of Paderborn politics was the survival of the Centre Party (*Zentrum*), which was the major Catholic party in the Weimar Republic and the German Empire. In the 1980s it never achieved even 1% of the vote in Paderborn, but its presence was nevertheless a testimony to the continuing influence of Catholicism in Paderborn's politics.

Bremen

The city-state of Bremen - a former Hanseatic town - is the smallest *Bundesland* of the Federal Republic of Germany and, at the time of the study, had been the one with the highest rate of unemployment for more than a decade. It is formed by the two cities of Bremen (population 522,000) and Bremerhaven (132,000), both located on the Weser river close to the North Sea coast, with some 30 miles of Lower Saxony between them. Many of the economic and labour market data available were for the *Bundesland*.

The effects of recession hit Bremen later, but more intensely, than most other West German regions. Up to 1975, Bremen's economic structure was believed to be less vulnerable to crisis than other regions (Haller, 1975). But in the following years, Bremen's economic development fell behind the general trend. While employment rose in Germany by almost a million between 1976 and 1980, the number of employed people remained the same in Bremen. Then, during the recession in the early 1980s, the gross domestic product in Bremen decreased three years in a row, and in just four years the workforce was reduced by 22,500 (Heseler, 1987). Table 2.5 shows the effect of these changes on unemployment rates in Bremen, together with national rates over the same period.

Table 2.5: Unemployment in Bremen (City)* 1978 to 1988, annual average

| Year | RATE | |
	Bremen	Germany
1985	15.0	9.3
1986	15.2	9.0
1987	15.3	8.9
1988	14.8	8.7
1989	14.1	7.9

Employment office district including some Lower Saxony areas.

Source: KUA/DGB, 1988.

The most important reason for the decline of employment in Bremen was the structural crisis in 'old' industries like shipbuilding, steel, food, tobacco, and radio and TV production. About 80% of job losses between 1975 and 1986 were from these industries. While they employed 52.3% of the industrial labour force in 1975, their share had dropped to one-third only 10 years later. Jobs that were lost could only be partly replaced by 'new' industries like electronics, the air and space industry, and car production. The biggest single shutdown was the closure of the AG Weser shipyard in 1984, when the remaining 1,800 employees (of 5,000-7,000 in the 1970s) were laid off. On the other hand, the outstanding example for new jobs provided by a single firm was the expansion of the Daimler-Benz plant from 4,000 employees in 1975 to 14,000 in 1988, making it the biggest private employer in Bremen.

Traditionally, the service sector had been of major importance in Bremen, with its heavy reliance on trade and transport, especially shipping. The service sector increased in relative importance during the recent economic slowdown, though the absolute number of employees in the tertiary sector did not change greatly (Table 2.6). The relative increase from 56.5% (Germany: 43.7%) of employees in

1974 to 64% (Germany: 50.3%) in 1985 was entirely due to the contraction of the industrial labour force. Bremen's service sector is dominated by distributive services in the ports, retail, wholesale and transport, which themselves had been severely affected by the local economic crisis. A positive feature in the Bremen labour market had been the growth of employment in the public sector, especially science, higher education and health services, and job creation programmes (ABM).

Table 2.6: Three-sector structure: Bremen/German percentages of employees

| | Primary Sector | | Secondary Sector | | Tertiary Sector | |
	Bremen %	Germany %	Bremen %	Germany %	Bremen %	Germany %
1974	0.9	1.0	42.6	55.2	56.5	43.7
1985	0.5	1.1	35.4	48.5	64.0	50.3

Source: Heseler, 1987.

Unemployment among under-20 year-olds rose sharply between 1981 and 1983. While youth unemployment throughout Germany decreased from 1984 onwards, it stayed constantly high in Bremen until 1985. Only since 1987 has this figure dropped below 1,500. This decline was due to demographic trends: the population of 16 year-olds (4,064) was less than half the population of 23 year-olds (8,262) in 1988, and for 12 year-olds it was down to 3,577. In addition, there had been a tendency for young people to stay in education for longer, and a variety of schemes and measures had been introduced to improve their qualifications or just to keep them off the streets.

The absolute number of unemployed between the ages of 20 and 24 was almost three times higher in Bremen than the number of unemployed under-20 year-olds. Because of the slow economic recovery in Bremen, young adults leaving vocational training between 20 and 25 faced increasing risks of unemployment, part-time or temporary employment (Stegmann and Kraft, 1988).

In 1986/1987 there were 27,724 young people in training in Bremen (*Land*). This figure included both trainees on non-firm based schemes who attended part-time vocational schools, and the apprentices in the dual system.

As Table 2.7 shows, male apprentices in Bremen were trained mainly in crafts and technical occupations, while females formed the majority in clerical and service apprenticeships. Generally, higher school qualifications improve individuals' chances of entering training. Many apprenticeships that used to require a certificate from *Hauptschule* are now taken by young people who have finished *Realschule*. More than 20% of all apprentices in Bremen had the *Abitur* or a comparable qualification.

Although girls usually have better educational qualifications than boys, they lose out in the competition for attractive training. Almost 60% of apprentices in Bremen were boys, but 60% of all unsuccessful applicants for firm-based training were girls. Girls who entered training were overrepresented in occupations with poor prospects, such as low-grade clerical jobs, sales assistants, garment makers and hairdressers. Some measures had been designed to improve girls' access to qualified technical employment, but the percentage in these jobs had stayed below 4% of the total trained in these occupations, some 300 girls compared with almost 8,000 boys.

By 1989, the acute shortage of opportunities to gain recognised vocational training in Bremen seemed to be over. However, youngsters with low educational qualifications, those from foreign countries and many girls were still being trained in jobs without prospects. They were likely to end up unemployed after training, or in dead-end jobs.

Table 2.7: Apprentices/trainees in Bremen attending vocational schools (including non-firm-based training) in 1986/87, by occupational fields and sex

Occupation Sector		number of trainees	per cent male	per cent female	all occupations (%)
1. Business and administration	%	8,292	40.6	59.4	29.9
2. Metal work	%	5,637	94.8	5.2	-
3. Electrical engineering	%	2,484	97.8	2.2	9.0
4. Construction	%	936	89.1	10.8	3.4
5. Wood - crafts	%	581	82.6	17.4	2.1
6. Textiles	%	281	3.9	96.1	1.0
7. Laboratory technicians (Chem., Phys., Bio.)	%	123	53.7	46.1	0.4
8. Printing	%	114	45.6	54.4	0.4
9. Painting/decorating	%	1,213	78.2	21.8	4.4
10. Health*	%	1,057	0.1	99.9	3.8
11. Hygiene	%	1,070	7.9	92.1	3.9
12. Food and domestic science	%	2,744	40.1	59.9	9.9
13. Agriculture	%	399	36.1	63.9	1.4
Non-aggregated occupations	%	2,580	43.1	56.9	9.3
Occupations for the handicapped	%	213	34.3	65.7	0.8
		27,724	57.9	42.1	100 %

* nursing not included.
Source: Senator für Bildung, Wissenschaft und Kunst, 1988.

Bremen has a radical political tradition. The *Bremer Linke* group of socialists, active before World War I, was one of the most left-wing groups in the country at that time. The local daily paper, *Die Bürgerzeitung,* was noted for its independent and left-wing views. The City was one of the first to be taken over by a workers' and soldiers' council in the 'Revolution of November 1918' and, in January 1919, the Bremen Communists, including the former *Bremer Linke* group, set up a dictatorship in the City. Following the failure of the Spartacists in Berlin, however, government troops occupied the city after some fighting and communist rule collapsed. In the 1920s and early 1930s, Bremen was again a stronghold of the SPD and the communists, and a centre of resistance to the Nazi Party. Since World War II, the *Land* government was dominated continuously by the SPD, and the Party received the largest share of votes in all *Bundestag* elections. In the 1987 *Bürgerschaft* elections it won 50.5% of the vote as against 23.4% for the CDU, 10% for the FDP and 10.2% for the Greens. Bremen became the first of the *Länder* to have Green Party representatives in its parliament when the Party passed the 5% barrier and gained four seats in October 1979, and since then the City has been one of the Party's strongholds.

An interesting feature of Bremen political life was the role accorded to the *Arbeiterkammer* (workers' chamber) and the *Angestelltenkammer* (white-collar workers' chamber). Saarland is the only other *Land* with similar institutions. Membership was compulsory for every employee in Bremen. The chambers were concerned with the political, cultural and educational interests of workers and white-collar employees. They were, of course, vitally interested in developments in the local labour market, and they sponsored research into the way the market was changing. Another important activity was running vocational education schemes. They were the two most important providers of non-firm-based training in Bremen.

Liverpool

The development, and to a large extent the decline, of Liverpool, are both associated with its function as a port. Liverpool received its Borough charter in 1207, but it was not until the eighteenth century that the City began to grow substantially. The population probably numbered 5,000 or so in 1700 and this had quadrupled to around 20,000 by 1750 (Marriner, 1982). By 1801 Liverpool had reached 77,653 and was the third-largest city in England after London and Manchester (Corfield, 1982). It grew rapidly in the nineteenth century and the early part of this century and recorded its maximum population of 857,247 in the census of 1931.

The eighteenth century port depended on trade in a variety of products, including coal, salt and agricultural goods. As the century progressed, the slave trade became increasingly important. In the nineteenth century the import of cotton fibre and the export of finished textile goods became dominant elements in Liverpool's trade. There were, however, many contributors to the City's prosperity in the nineteenth century. Foodstuffs and agricultural products were imported from all over the world and processed in Liverpool, the sugar and tobacco industries being prominent examples. The export of finished cotton goods was supplemented by products of the locally-based chemical, metal and shipbuilding industries. There was also the passenger trade, especially in emigrants to the United States. Because of Liverpool's role as a maritime and commercial centre, banking and insurance were also prominent activities.

Since World War I the port has declined dramatically. Factors affecting its long-term decline included the increasing importance of the south and Midlands as manufacturing areas, the loss of passenger sea traffic and, perhaps most importantly in recent years, Britain's shifting pattern of trade. Europe has become increasingly more important than the Commonwealth, and east coast ports have taken over from west coast ports.

As compensation for the decline of the port, the economy was considerably diversified after the last war, with much additional manufacturing being introduced. Thus, between 1945 and 1971, 175 firms and 94,000 new manufacturing jobs were drawn to Merseyside under the inducements of regional policies. The peak years of development, 1959-65, saw nearly 6,000 jobs a year brought to the area; approximately 17% of all mobile industry relocated in Britain in those years (Nabarro, 1980). Since the mid-1960s, however, Liverpool, along with other large British conurbations, experienced a massive loss of manufacturing jobs. The combination of the decline of the port and the decline of manufacturing industry left Liverpool with considerable problems of unemployment and poverty. Unlike some other cities, Liverpool was unable to develop service industries sufficiently to compensate for manufacturing losses.

Liverpool had been losing people since the 1930s. Population loss was particularly marked in the years 1966-71, when policies of widespread slum clearance and the transfer of inner-city residents to overspill towns resulted in an average net loss of 18,535 persons per annum (Liverpool City Council, 1989). After this the decline continued, but at a lower rate (Table 2.8). Between 1981 and 1987 the Merseyside conurbation as a whole lost 4.3% of its population. The Metropolitan District of Liverpool is predicted to lose 16.3% of its population between 1985 and 2001. Population loss was a serious problem for the City, because it had resulted primarily from the out-migration of younger, skilled persons, leaving behind a population which was older, less skilled and more deprived.

Table 2.8: Population change in the City of Liverpool

Year	Number	Annual change
1981	516.700	-
1982	510.500	-6.200
1983	502.700	-7.800
1984	497.200	-5.500
1985	491.500	-6.700
1986	483.000	-8.500
1987	476.000	-7.000
1981-87	-40.700	-6.783

Source: Liverpool City Council, 1989.

A severe contraction in employment had taken place in the City since the 1960s (Table 2.9). Only the white-collar service sector had grown, and even there the growth rate in Liverpool had been less than half that in Britain as a whole. In contrast to a modest growth nationally of blue-collar services (transport, communications, distribution and miscellaneous services), Liverpool had experienced a decline of 50%. This reflected the decline of the port, wholesaling and retailing. The latter was due to population loss and the growth of unemployment in other sectors, which had a marked effect on consumer demand.

Table 2.9: Employment changes in Liverpool by sectors, 1961-85

Sectors	Numbers Employed			% Change 1961-85	
	1961	1971	1985	Liverpool %	Britain %
Manufacturing	130.140	110.611	47.455	-64	-37
Other production industries	30.140	20.130	10.662	-65	-39
Blue-collar services	174.820	129.218	87.500	-50	+8
White-collar services	64.750	86.135	85.000	+31	+68
Total employment	400.940	346.094	230.617	-43	-5

Source: Liverpool City Council, 1987.

Unemployment in Liverpool had been consistently higher than the national level (Table 2.10), especially in the 16-19 age group. A further problem was the tendency for Liverpool's unemployed to be out of work for considerable periods of time. The rate for those unemployed for more than five years, for example, was more than twice the national average in 1989. It is difficult to resist the conclusion that labour market prospects in Liverpool for both young and older workers are bleak, and are likely to remain so in the foreseeable future. In some ways the City seems to have entered a vicious circle of decline in which population loss and business contraction continue to reinforce one another.

Table 2.10: Unemployment rate in Liverpool at January of each year

	RATE	
Year	Liverpool %	Britain %
1985	25.4	13.6
1986	26.1	13.9
1987	20.0	11.6
1988	19.1	9.6
1989	16.1	7.1

Source: Liverpool City Planning Office.

Liverpool has a rather unusual political history, dominated by religious sectarianism. The influx of large numbers of Irish Catholics in the nineteenth century created a situation where the political parties sought to win advantages by positive or negative stances towards the immigrants. The Liberal Party allied itself with the Irish and the Irish Nationalist political organisation, while the Conservatives allied themselves with the Protestant reaction. It must be emphasised, however, that this anti-Irish reaction was not based solely or even primarily on religious sentiment so much as on the fear of workers of being undercut in the labour market. It was the Conservatives who were the most successful, and they succeeded in effectively excluding the Liberals and subsequently the Labour Party from political control of the City for over a hundred years. The Labour Party did not succeed in winning control of the City Council until 1955, long after it had become dominant in most of Britain's other major cities. After that, political control of the city swayed back and forth, the situation being complicated by the re-emergence of the Liberal Party in the 1970s as a significant force in the City. But throughout recent times the Conservative Party's support steadily declined, with no member on the City Council in 1989. By 1987, of the seven parliamentary seats, six were in Labour hands and the other was Liberal.

A recent development in Liverpool's political fortunes was the capture of the local Labour Party organisation, and hence the City Council, in 1983 by Militant, a Trotskyist faction. After attempts to defy the national government on the setting of levels of 'rates' (local taxes) and expenditure, the organisation was defeated by fines and injunctions in the law courts, expulsions from the Labour Party, and the withdrawal of local trade union support. Subsequently, the City reverted to mainstream Labour Party control.

CHAPTER III

Education and training

Education and training systems

Figures 1 and 2 show the structure of British and German education systems and give the ages at which transition along the different routes on them occur. We shall examine the main features of each national system and then special characteristics in each town.

The British education system is funded mainly by central government, but is run by local government through Local Education Authorities (LEAs). Over the last 10 years central government initiatives, especially in the training field, have tended to centralise the system more, originally by channelling funds through what was in the early 1980s called the Manpower Services Commission (MSC) and subsequently the Training Agency (TA). School-based education came under further central direction with the establishment in 1988 for the first time in Britain of a national curriculum, accounting for 70% of the subject matter taught in schools. The monitoring of its implementation is in the hands of Her Majesty's Inspectorate (HMI), again an arm of central government responsible for the maintenance of standards in schools throughout the country.

Figure 1: Chart of the educational system in Britain

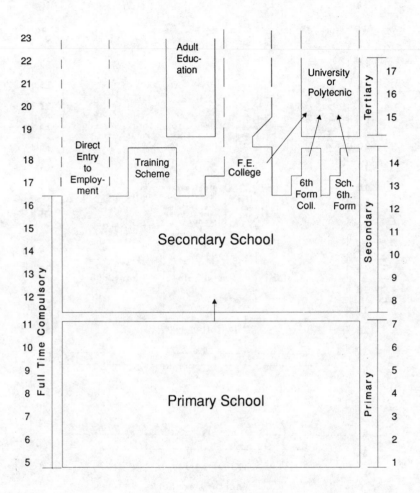

Figure 2: Chart of the educational system in Germany

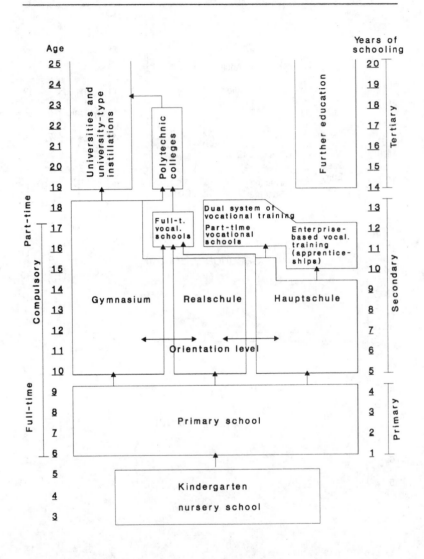

Source: Max Planck Institute for Human Development and Education, *Between elite and mass education,* State University of New York Press, Albany, NY, 1979.

Certification, on the other hand, is still in the hands of relatively autonomous examining boards, though the newly-established National Council for Vocational Qualifications (NCVQ) has the job of standardising and rationalising at least those in the vocational sphere. LEAs retain a strategic role in planning the broad thrust of education locally, and in bidding for and overseeing the implementation of funding obtained from central government initiatives such as the Technical and Vocational Education Initiative (TVEI). In 1989, central government delegated many of its former responsibilities in the training field to bodies operating at a local level, the Training and Enterprise Councils (TECs). These are responsible for vocational training and operate independently of the Local Education Authorities which are responsible for education in schools and further education (technical) colleges.

Most 11-16 education in Britain is run on the comprehensive principle, with no division between different types of secondary schools. However, over 20 LEAs in England and Wales have retained grammar schools for which children are selected at age 11. There is also a substantial private sector which takes around 9% of secondary age pupils. As Figure 1 shows, at age 16, young people can stay on at school in sixth forms to take advanced level examinations (A-levels: the standard prerequisite for entry into higher education); or they can repeat the earlier school-leaving examinations, the Certificate of Secondary Education (CSE) or O-level (for most of our sample), or the General Certificate of Secondary Education (GCSE) which replaced CSE and O-level; or they can study for pre-vocational qualifications such as the Certificate of Pre-Vocational Education (CPVE) which takes a year to complete. Alternatively, they can proceed to further education (technical) colleges, join a training scheme (YTS), get a full-time job, or become unemployed. Because of small numbers in many schools' sixth forms and the consequent non-viability of many courses, in recent years there has been a move by many LEAs to merge post-16 educational provision into single institutions: 'tertiary' colleges.

In Germany there is in one sense more devolution of power in relation to school- and college-based education, and in other senses less (Taylor, 1981). The *Länder* governments have responsibility for all school and college education. However, training policy and standards are the responsibility of the federal government, as advised by the *Bundesinstitut für Berufsbildung* (BIBB) on which professional groupings, the Educational Authorities of the *Länder*, employers and trade unions are all represented. Unlike its British counterparts, the professional bodies responsible for vocational qualifications, the BIBB is more concerned with the content of technical vocational training programmes than the nature of the certificate finally awarded. Below the level of the BIBB, each *Land* has a vocational education committee, again comprising employer, trade union, and *Land* government representatives, and at local level the local chambers of commerce and craft guilds have major responsibility for its operation.

Despite the relative autonomy of the *Länder* in the management of education locally, all operate a tripartite system of secondary education: *Gymnasium*, *Realschule* and *Hauptschule*, and post-16 they operate the 'dual system', as enshrined in federal legislation. As Figure 2 shows, at the age of 11, a child may enter the *Gymnasium*, which is the route to the *Abitur* and higher education, or a senior vocational school (*Fachoberschule*). Alternatively, he or she may enter the intermediate school (*Realschule*), usually en route to an apprenticeship or a *Fachoberschule*, or *Gymnasium* to take the *Abitur*. Thirdly, he or she may enter the general high school or *Hauptschule*, which normally leads to an apprenticeship in a manual craft or retail trade. In both of these latter schools, at age 16 or 17 most young people who have obtained the leaving certificate usually leave with a view to obtaining an employer-sponsored apprenticeship, which normally takes three years. Such an apprenticeship involves three or four days each week in firm-based training, and the rest of the time in a vocational school, the *Berufsschule*.

An alternative route is to continue from *Realschule* into a specialist vocational school (*Berufsfachschule*) full-time, either to get vocationally qualified in certain fields, such as the paramedical services, or to move to an apprenticeship later. For boys, compulsory military service, or its longer community service alternative, extends the transition to employed status or higher education by up to two years. For those unlikely to get an apprenticeship an alternative is to stay on for an extra year to do pre-vocational courses. Those who leave and fail to get apprenticeships have to attend the *Berufsschule* up to the age of 18, usually as part of a remedial training scheme.

British areas

Swindon

Swindon is the main centre in the Thamesdown Educational Area. In 1985 Thamesdown adopted a tertiary system for educational provision for 16-19 year-olds. Ten secondary schools previously catering for young people between the ages of 11 and 18 were converted into institutions providing education up to the end of compulsory schooling, age 16, when the GCSE is taken. Those young people wishing to continue their education on a full-time basis after the age of 16 subsequently fed from these secondary schools into one of two post-16 (tertiary) colleges. One of these colleges concentrated primarily on academic courses, while the other also provided a full range of vocational courses. A 'link' scheme, designed to promote continuity of experience and support for young people moving from the secondary schools into the two colleges, was reported to have been less effective than originally hoped.

The courses available fell into three types:

- **academic:** Advanced level (A-level) courses were available for high academic achievers; a minimum of two A-levels is usually required for higher education;

- **pre-employment (pre-vocational) courses,** such as CPVE, were provided for those wishing to delay labour market entry for a year while skills and general educational levels are improved. Earlier school-leaving examinations, such as GCSE, could also be re-taken;

- **vocational courses** were offered at a number of levels. Technician level courses (for example, the Business and Technical Education Council's BTECs) have a substantial academic component and are now accepted for entry to some higher education courses. Craft and equivalent level courses leading to skilled occupations were also available through part-time study. These and other vocational qualifications bestowed by bodies such as the City and Guilds London Institute (CGLI) and the Royal Society of Arts (RSA) were sometimes taken within YTS.

Both institutions that catered for Swindon's 16-19 year-olds provided academic A-level and pre-vocational courses, whereas full vocational courses were confined to just one of them. Both colleges offered open access to young people, although specific courses had entry requirements. The colleges had recently benefited from additional funding under the Technical and Vocational Education Initiative (TVEI), which supported developments in line with perceived vocational needs and introduced more 'active' learning approaches.

Because youth employment never collapsed in Swindon, neither did traditional patterns of college attendance. 'Day release' vocational courses were still popular (both with employers and employees). Full-time vocational courses remained recognised routes into employment, particularly in clerical occupations, but also in engineering, construction, hairdressing and catering.

In line with national levels, just under one-half of 16 year-olds in Swindon remained in full-time education during the 1980s. In Swindon, many 16 year-olds entered employment directly: 31% of 1985 fifth-formers in the ESRC 16-19 Initiative. Employers' assessments of current and projected labour requirements against the (national) demographic trend towards a decreasing number of young adults appears to have stimulated Swindon firms to engage in 'active recruitment' in the local schools. Active recruitment strategies included offering attractive wages and training to 16 year-olds, with a view to shaping the young people to meet the firms' specific requirements. College and careers staff reported difficulties in convincing young people of the benefits of securing a broader foundation in education and training in the face of the short-term attractions of high earnings and employee status.

In 1985/86, 62 YTS schemes were operating in the Swindon area, but by 1988 the number of schemes had declined because of the demographic trend and the increase in direct entry to employment at age 16 as labour market demand strengthened. A national upgrading of the Youth Training Scheme, which took place in 1986, was intended to establish the scheme as quality foundation training, providing a 'permanent bridge' from school to work (DE, 1986). However, Swindon's experience, as in many other areas of southern England, suggests that for many young people the YTS remained a 'stop-gap' or 'fall-back' in the absence of real jobs. Neither YTS provision nor demand was sustained when immediate entry to work, with or without training, was available, or so it appeared. Most of the exceptions were in schemes recognised as offering high-quality training, such as the Swindon Information Education Technology Centre (ITEC), and schemes offered by companies such as Rover as part of apprenticeship training.

Generally speaking, the intense competition for better-qualified young people in Swindon meant that traditional motivational factors still operated. Good job prospects were a reality for those doing vocational courses, and employers also sought to recruit those taking A-levels. The Careers Office reported few complaints about the quality of YTS but, given that young people could make real choices in the expanding employment situation, providers had to offer credible training or fail to fill their places.

Liverpool

Liverpool is a large education authority controlling, in addition to primary schools, 39 secondary schools, 29 special schools for children with health or learning problems, four colleges of further education and (until 1989) one polytechnic. In several ways it still offered a very traditional pattern of schooling. The secondary schools catered for pupils aged 11 to 18. Liverpool had no plans to convert to a tertiary system. Most higher-attaining pupils and, increasingly, some less successful ones, stayed on into the sixth form. Reflecting Liverpool's status as England's most Catholic city, there was still a religious division in the school system, with 15 state-aided Roman Catholic comprehensives and five other aided voluntary schools (three Church of England, one Bluecoat school, and one Jewish school). In addition, there were 16 community (LEA) comprehensives, and two single-sex (also LEA) comprehensives. Altogether, 16 of the secondary schools, mainly in the Roman Catholic sector, were still single-sex. There was also a secondary residential school at Loggerheads in North Wales.

Most Liverpool 16 year-olds who continued in full-time education remained in their secondary schools, though there were four further education colleges which provided a full range of courses, including GCSE and A-levels, BTEC, CGLI and RSA. The importance of certain local industries was reflected in the range of courses offered; for instance, courses in automobile engineering and maritime studies.

Unsurprisingly, the structure of post-16 education and training programmes, and the take-up of options in this structure, reflected opportunities (or their absence) in the surrounding labour market. The 16-19 Initiative revealed that when post-16 education and training in Liverpool is compared with that in two other English areas (Swindon and Sheffield), Liverpool is characterised by the greatest number of young people entering continuing education and training programmes, but with poorer subsequent employment prospects. Of the three English areas in the 16-19 Initiative, Liverpool emerged with the lowest level of educational attainment, but the highest proportion staying on for full-time post-compulsory education. However, the main difference with Swindon was that throughout the 1980s less than 10% of Liverpool's 16 year-olds were able to leave education and enter jobs. This was in marked contrast with Swindon, where young people could realistically expect to leave school early and find employment easily.

Table 3.1: Percentages of young people entering different types of training schemes in cities in Britain

Roberts et al., 1987 Survey	Firm-based YTS	Non-firm-based YTS	Total
	%	%	%
Liverpool	41	59	100
Walsall	64	36	100
Chelmsford	88	12	100
16-19 Initiative (1987-9)			
Liverpool	59	41	100
Swindon	74	26	100
Sheffield	66	34	100
Kirkcaldy	82	18	100

Source: Roberts et al., 1987, and Roberts and Parsell, 1989c.

Table 3.1 shows that the proportion of young people entering non-firm-based youth training schemes with poor employment prospects was higher in Liverpool than in other parts of Britain (Roberts et al., 1987). It has been argued that employers' uses of the YTS were creating increasingly clear divisions between parts of the scheme. In Liverpool, non-firm-based YTS programmes (college-based courses, training workshops and community projects) might be regarded as 'warehousing' schemes to keep young people off the streets, and more young people entered such schemes there than elsewhere. Despite the fact that non-firm-based schemes might offer just as good, or even better training, than firms themselves (Roberts et al., 1989b), prospects of permanent employment were not as good. It seems clear, therefore, that the growth of non-firm-based schemes in Liverpool was more of a response to the weakness of the local labour market than part of a genuine training strategy.

German areas

Bremen

In 1987, about 10,000 young people reached the statutory school-leaving age in Bremen, that is, ninth or tenth grade of *Hauptschule*, the tenth grade of *Realschule* or *Gymnasium*, or of special education schools.

Approximately 40% of these were preparing for higher education as a result of either continuing at their *Gymnasium* until the *Abitur* examination after grade 13, or by attending academically-orientated vocational colleges (*Fachoberschule*) to take courses in engineering, social work, business, or art and design. The proportion of Bremen youth on these academic tracks rose steadily from the mid-1970s, a trend that occurred in all West German urban areas. Another 40-45% entered the dual system of vocational training, proceeding through a combination of firm-based training and school-based education, on a block or day release basis. Table 3.2 shows the number of young people applying for training in Bremen (City) over the period 1982-88.

Table 3.2: Demand for training in Bremen (City) over the period 1982-88 (30 September each year)

Year	Number of applicants	Numbers not getting any training	Training vacancies
1982	5841	489	27
1983	7483	829	16
1984	8146	1837	33
1985	8452	1036	39
1986	7763	979	83
1987	7129	975	62
1988	6406	426	69
1989	4989	374	155

Source: Senator für Bildung, Wissenschaft und Kunst, p. 47, 1987.

Unfortunately, there were no reliable figures for training places offered, because firms were not obliged to report these to the employment office. The remaining 10-15% of youngsters entered non-firm-based vocational preparation schemes, unemployment or unskilled jobs. Different types of schemes had been established by the employment office and the federal and the state governments, which was often confusing for those for whom they were intended. When describing schemes and measures for those who did not manage to obtain training in the dual system, it is necessary to distinguish between vocational preparation and training, as in Table 3.3.

Table 3.3: Entry into non-firm-based training and vocational preparation in Bremen (*Land*)

	1979/ 1980	1980/ 1981	1981/ 1982	1982/ 1983	1983/ 1984	1984/ 1985	1985/ 1986	1986/ 1987
Vocational preparation	701	929	1147	1159	933	976	873	703
School-based training	911	1087	1180	1497	1471	1574	1717	1467
Non-firm-based training	40	64	64	308	1091	861	1281	675
- II + III	951	1151	1244	1805	2562	2435	2998	2142

Source: Senator für Bildung, Wissenschaft und Kunst, p. 65, 1987.

Vocational preparation schemes

Originally, vocational preparation schemes were aimed at young people who were supposed not to be mature enough for training or employment. Since there is no exact definition of 'occupational maturity', there were a variety of measures with different objectives and organisational structures. The federal employment office (*Bundesanstalt für Arbeit*, BA) offers basic skills courses (*Grundbildungslehrgang*, G) of which the so-called G3 courses were the most common in Bremen, possibly because they had the least specific requirements for entry. Thus, many young people had entered these courses whose only deficiency was that they had been unsuccessful in finding apprenticeships. Quite often, these measures were financed through job creation programmes (*Arbeitsbeschaffungsmaßnahme*, ABM) which makes them 'ABM-G3' schemes. They had the reputation of being set up to keep young people off the streets as well as off the unemployment records, while not supplying them with useful skills or qualifications.

The school-based *Ausbildungsvorbereitungsjahr* ('preparation for training' year, AVJ), aimed at those who had finished *Hauptschule* without gaining a certificate, did not have more than a warehousing function when first introduced, but subsequently offered better opportunities for labour market entry by combining an educational certificate equivalent to *Hauptschule* with a subsequent *Berufsgrundbildungsjahr* (basic vocational education year, BGJ). After successfully completing the two-year AVJ/BGJ course, the young people could continue for two more years learning a trade in school-based vocational training.

There were also several kinds of one- or two-year specialist vocational schools (*Berufsfachschule*, BFS) which offered opportunities to learn vocational skills, achieve educational qualifications (equivalent to *Realschule*) and improve the chance of obtaining an apprenticeship. At the bottom of the hierarchy were the domestic science schools, which were attended almost exclusively by girls and offered practically no prospects. The BFS for child-minding was also attended mainly by girls, and offered hardly any better opportunities because jobs for child-minders were quite rare. The one- or two-year business school (*Handelsschule*) and other BFS in fields like construction, hotel and restaurant service and electrical engineering, offered qualifications that improved young people's chances in the labour market.

Vocational training in schools
In order to meet the dramatically rising demand for training in the 1990s, the Bremen local authority decided in, 1977, to create a school-based scheme called 'BFS/q', providing training for almost 2,000 boys and girls. Unlike the other BFS described above, the BFS/q offered training with a recognised qualification. Examinations taken at the end of the BFS/q followed the guidelines of the different chambers (industrial chamber, crafts chamber) which are responsible for training in their sectors.

Table 3.4: Educational qualifications of BFS/q participants in 1986

No certificate	Hauptschule	Realschule	Abitur or comparable	Total
80	760	438	80	1,358

Source: Stat. Landesamt Bremen.

In 1986, when the peak of the demand was already over, 1,358 young people were trained in BFS/q, many of them with good school qualifications, a considerable number even with the *Abitur* (Table 3.4). As the imbalance between the demand for, and supply of, training opportunities lessened, the BFS/q became marginal, offering training only to those with special problems in the labour market.

Programmes for socially deprived youth

In autumn 1988, almost 30 different institutions in Bremen (City) were providing training following chamber guidelines for 'socially deprived' young people. More than 160 courses were available, with an average capacity of 10-20 places (Sachau, 1988). Most important of all were the educational institutes of the workers' chamber (*Arbeiterkammer*) and its white-collar equivalent (*Angestelltenkammer*). Some of the relevant organisations were founded specifically for the purpose of applying for money from the European Community Social Fund or other sources of finance. These courses, like BFS/q, were usually second-best choices for the trainees. The resistance of employers to hiring graduates from these schemes was partly due to prejudice or ignorance about the quality of training received. But another fact of the situation was that, like their British counterparts, employers valued the 'real work' experience of firm-based apprentices above the broad range of training offered in other schemes. Additionally, the occupations for which young people were trained did not always meet the requirements of the labour market.

The dual system of vocational training had not been able to provide opportunities for all young people in Bremen. Although the situation eased after the mid-1980s, it seemed likely that additional schemes and school-based training would be necessary in the future to meet the demand for skilled workers. They would also be an essential means of giving a fair chance of qualifications to those with social, educational or physical disadvantages.

Paderborn

After 10 years of compulsory full-time education, a young person in Paderborn could choose from a variety of vocational and educational opportunities. However, the level of vocational training that was available for an individual depended on the education received up to school-leaving age. Opportunities available in Paderborn could be divided into 'regular provision' and 'schemes' introduced in response to youth unemployment. Both reflected national trends.

Regular provisions

In 1988, 1,588 students enrolled in the state-run *Gymnasiale Oberstufe* for the three-year full-time academic course provided for high academic achievers. The *Abitur* requires a minimum of two major courses (six lessons per week) and four minor courses (four lessons per week) and final examinations in the two major courses and two of the minor courses. The majority of students who pass the *Abitur* enter higher education.

Under the dual system of work-based training and part-time vocational education, schools' apprentices and instructors sign articles of apprenticeship on the basis of training regulations. In general, the duration of training is two to three years. In Paderborn, the number of training contracts reached a high point of 4,904 in the early 1980s. Since then the number of contracts fell (4,496 in 1988), but so did the figure for applicants.

In 1988 the number of participants in the *Berufsfachschulen* (specialist vocational schools), including *Handelsschulen* (business schools), was 1,410. Paderborn had several schools of this kind. In addition to vocational training under the dual system, full-time training was offered in these schools which prepared young people for subsequent employment and simultaneously improved their general education. Three types of specialised vocational schools existed:

- those which provided training for occupations recognised under the 1969 Vocational Training Act;

- those which provided preparation for training in one of these occupations; the time was usually credited to the subsequent in-plant training;

- those which provided training for other occupations for which an independent vocational certificate was required, as in social work, for example. The majority of these schools' students were girls.

In 1988, 283 young men were enrolled with the *Fachoberschule*. These schools provided two-year full-time courses and built on the education received at the *Realschule*. Instruction in general subjects and in technical theory and practice were given, and led to qualifications for entry to *Fachhochschule* (polytechnic). The *Berufsgrundschuljahr* (BGJ) (basic vocational training) was introduced with the object of offering a one-year full-time course of practical and theoretical instruction in the basic aspects of a particular trade. It thus provided young men and women with the opportunity to obtain a wider view of requirements in the trade, and to make more informed choices at the end of the course.

The aim of *Fachschulen* was to provide advanced technical education and a broad general education. Prior to entry, the completion of relevant vocational training was required. Courses were full-time and normally lasted for at least one year. In Paderborn, the 283 students in *Fachschulen* specialised in the fields of engineering, textiles and clothing, domestic science, social work and agriculture. Since the early 1980s, a combination of fewer school-leavers and more apprenticeships had reduced participation in *Berufsfachschulen,* which were always regarded as an alternative to the dual system. Following the national trend towards an expansion of higher education, more students in Paderborn had enrolled in *Fachoberschulen.* With changes in local industry introducing new skill requirements, the rise in figures in the *Fachschulen,* which qualified students for new professions, seemed likely to continue.

Schemes

The rise of youth unemployment from the late 1970s onwards led to a number of nationwide initiatives, funded or partly funded through the *Bundesanstalt für Arbeit* (federal employment office) on the legal basis of the *Arbeitsförderungsgesetz* legislation. The initiatives were not meant to be permanent fixtures and were often organised on a yearly basis, according to demand. Educational institutions bid for 'courses' and run them for a period of time. Different initiatives were aimed at different clients, but all had to register with the *Arbeitsamt* in order to enter a 'course'.

The following initiatives operated in Paderborn in 1988:

- *Arbeiten und Lernen:* 21 hours per week work in community institutions and 19 hours' school for one year for the young unemployed. These schemes were training young people to work and were providing a general education (if necessary, the secondary school examination would be taken);

- *Lehrgang zum nachträglichen Erwerb des Hauptschulabschlusses:* one-year preparation for the external examination for the *Hauptschulabschluss;*

- *Grundausbildungslehrgang:* this scheme was aimed at those still awaiting an apprenticeship, or who had not decided on a profession. The minimum participation period was two months, the maximum 12 months. During this time basic practical and theoretical skills in different occupations were taught, in order to keep motivation high for vocational training and to broaden the young people's chances on entering the labour market;

- *Förderungs- und Eingliederungsmaßnahmen:* these schemes were aimed at those needing special support after leaving school because of their physical or mental disability;

- *Vermittlung/Erweiterung beruflicher Kenntnisse:* these schemes were aimed at young unemployed people up to age 25. Opportunities to learn daily routines and work discipline were provided and further skills were taught, depending on the individuals' existing qualifications.

In Paderborn, unlike other German towns, there had been no schemes with funding independent of the federal employment office. Following national trends, more girls (331) than boys (247) enrolled on Paderborn's schemes. Table 3.5 shows the 'follow-up steps' of participants from the different schemes.

Table 3.5: Follow-up steps of participants from six different schemes in Paderborn, October 1987 - September 1988

	Scheme No.						
Follow-up step:	1	2	3	4	5	6	Total%
apprenticeship	8	9	18	14	7	21	13.3
vocational school	-	5	-	2	1	11	3.3
job	27	38	6	2	12	42	22.0
continue scheme	-	-	-	2	13	-	2.6
other scheme	22	29	-	-	1	44	16.6
dropout	10	36	1	-	1	41	15.4
other	-	25	3	2	13	21	11.1
still looking	7	3	3	28	26	24	15.7
Total of participants	93	170	31	25	55	204	100%

Source: Arbeitsamt Paderborn, 1988.

As Table 3.5 shows, schemes 1, 2, and 6, which were designed for older unemployed young people who had finished their general education, had the highest dropout rates. Nearly a quarter from all the schemes ended up in jobs without vocational qualifications. Some individuals may have decided not to enter the labour market, but it seems likely that the majority simply would not have found jobs in Paderborn.

CHAPTER IV

Entering the world of work

Introduction

Most previous Anglo-German comparisons of vocational education and training have proceeded by noting the most distinctive features of each country's methods and outcomes, and have then moved swiftly to policy recommendations for one or both countries, but usually for Britain, which has been regarded as having the greater need to learn and benefit from shared experience (Rose, 1990). Our methodology is different. It involves breaking into each country's system, then examining in detail the learning experiences and progress of young people following broadly similar routes into the workforces. One reason for this approach is the likelihood of there being differences between the systems as presented in official statistics and by government and other authoritative pronouncements, and what actually happens on the ground. A related consideration is the possibility of there being significant intra-country variations in the learning experiences offered on ostensibly similar routes, and in the opportunities to which the routes lead, depending on, among other things, local labour market contexts.

The main presentation of our findings in the next four chapters looks in detail at the samples' experiences on each of the four trajectories previously distinguished. However, before examining what happened on each route, it may be useful to give an overview of the respondents' own perceptions of the skills and abilities they had acquired in two areas: work-related competence and use of information technology.

Development of work-related competence

Our questions on this topic inquired about the extent to which the young people felt they had acquired valuable skills, had carried out important tasks or roles, and had generally felt involved in, and challenged by, their post-16 education, training and employment experience. Tables 4.1 and 4.2 compare the average number in the British and German samples reporting the experiences in each trajectory in each town, and the overall average numbers in the two countries reporting each experience.

Table 4.1: Average number who reported experiences in each trajectory in each town in each country

| Trajectory | Britain | | | | Germany | | | |
| | Liverpool | | Bremen | | Swindon | | Paderborn | |
	A	B	A	B	A	B	A	B
I	24	3	16	11	29	4	20	6
II	25	4	18	10	25	5	20	6
III	22	5	12	13	25	6	14	12
IV	16	10	8	16	19	10	12	13

Note: (1) A = Quite often or very often

B = Never or rarely

(2) Numbers are averaged across all the experiences - total for each cell = 40

63

Table 4.2: Average numbers who had each experience in each country

	Britain		Germany	
	A	B	A	B
Been given responsibility	28	3	14	6
Been able to make decisions for oneself	30	2	14	11
Had a chance to use initiative	26	4	13	14
Developed new skills and abilities	24	6	19	10
Set own goals/targets	21	6	14	13
Felt stretched/challenged	17	9	16	11
Felt a sense of achievement	24	4	21	5
Felt all abilities were being used	17	8	17	10
Worked as a member of a team	30	5	14	15
Had to work to a deadline	24	7	17	15
Been asked for advice by others on how to tackle a problem	21	12	11	10

Note: (1) A = Quite often or very often

B = Never or rarely

(2) Numbers for each experience are averaged across trajectories across towns for each country i.e., total for each cell = 40

Striking differences emerge from the young people's answers:

• first, in both countries, the experience varied between trajectories with those in higher trajectories more frequently reporting the experience than those in the lower trajectories (Table 4.1). This was particularly true in the Paderborn sample, where there was a sharp drop in frequencies from trajectories I and II to trajectories III and IV. In the British samples, there was only a small difference in frequencies between trajectories I to III but then a sharp drop to trajectory IV. Clearly, the higher the trajectory the more likely the young person was to have had the experience, though in

Germany trajectories I and II were virtually identical. It is also notable that Paderborn and Swindon were marginally ahead of Bremen and Liverpool respectively in all trajectories, suggesting that the former's more successful economies were enhancing the vocational experience available to young people.

• Secondly, for all but one of the 11 experiences on which the young people were questioned, the frequency was higher for the British sample than the German sample (Table 4.2). Thus, more British respondents reported they had been given responsibility, had been able to make decisions, had had a chance to use their initiative, and so on. For some experiences, the ratio of British to German reporting was about 2 to 1. Only for 'felt stretched/challenged' and 'felt all abilities were being used' were the two counties similar. At least in relation to the vocationally relevant experiences covered here, the British young appeared to be markedly ahead of their German counterparts, including, somewhat surprisingly, those in the 'academic' and 'skilled' 'trajectories', I and II.

Use of information technology

A specialised kind of skill which young people are expected to acquire for the modern work place is using information technology (IT). A central plank of policy in both countries has been the belief that all young people need exposure to information technology prior to entering employment, though the evidence suggests that the requisite skills can usually be learnt subsequently in the job itself with little difficulty, (Linn, 1985; Fitzgerald, 1985; Wellington, 1987). However, it was clearly of interest to discover to what extent the educational and training policies were succeeding. In Britain the 'Microelectronics in the Classroom' initiative, launched in 1985, was an attempt to introduce IT hardware into every school and to equip teachers to use it. In reality, there was a huge gap between what was happening in a few schools and practice in the majority (Linn, 1985; DES, 1987; Fothergill, 1987). Exactly the same process was under way in Germany, although there the federal nature of the education system led to inconsistencies both in policies and practice, with IT in education being described as 'a confusing muddle', due to unco-ordinated developments by different *Länder* (Social Europe, 1986). They were, however, using the same rhetorical justification for their policy as in Britain, and this met a similarly critical response. Criti-cism was directed particularly at the lack of educational underpin-ning for development. As the trade unions concluded:

'industry and politicians.....[have been] urging the introduction of lessons in computing in all schools without the purposes or the qualitative standards of such lessons having been adequately discussed..... An irrational fear was inculcated among the public that children without a 'computer diploma' would in future no longer find a job' [GEW, 1987].

The experience of the two British towns was fairly typical, in that children's experience of IT in schools could vary widely, depending upon school policy, subjects taken and the approaches of their tea-chers. Moreover, resource constraints ensured that most pupils' direct experience of IT in school was likely to have been limited. For example, in Liverpool in 1987, the computer-pupil ratio was 1 to 81 pupils on average across the city. The overall position in Swindon was only marginally better, with a ratio of about 1 to 70. In both places then, it comes as no surprise that less than a third of the sam-ples had what they considered to be only a little experience of IT at school: in Liverpool 46 respondents and 50 in Swindon.

In both German towns, the average number of computers per 'mainstream' school was equally low (Paderborn - eight per school, Bremen slightly fewer). However, within vocational schools those following certain occupational routes, such as clerical, were much more likely to have gained some experience of IT. In Bremen, 59 young people out of the 120 outside the academic trajectory had experienced IT in school, with a further 20 having had some experience in their training; although in practice this was more likely to have been at *Berufsschule* than at work. The equivalent figures for Paderborn were 91 and 15. The higher Paderborn total is because more Paderborn trajectory III respondents were at *Handelsschule*, in which the compulsory curriculum included working with computers. To compare the experiences of IT in formal education in the two countries, it is necessary to include members of the British samples who had gained such experience at a further education college. There were 40 such respondents in Liverpool and 56 in Swindon.

Only a minority of respondents in each area considered that they had a lot of experience of IT, with many more indicating either some experience or a little, or no, experience (Table 4.3). Again, national differences were apparent, with more British young people reporting IT experience than German young people, four times as many in Swindon, for example, reporting 'a lot' as in Bremen.

Table 4.3: Experience of using IT

	A lot	Some	A little or none	Total
Swindon	25	70	64	160
Liverpool	21	67	77	160
Paderborn	13	77	75	160
Bremen	6	50	104	160

There were a number of avenues where youngsters could acquire such experience (Table 4.4). School, formal vocational education and IT courses featured in both countries. Table 4.4 shows that the most common places for learning about IT in both countries were school and college. In the British towns, experience of IT at work was more common than in the German towns, and experience of IT at home was greater in Germany.

Table 4.4: Places where IT experience had been acquired

	Liverpool	Bremen	Swindon	Paderborn	Total
Home	27	55	28	61	171
School	46	59	50	91	246
Work	44	5	69	15	133
Ausbildung	-	20	-	15	35
College	40	-	56	-	96
Training	18	-	15	-	33
Elsewhere	12	23	2	22	59

Some young people with computers at home were spending a substantial amount of time using them. Thus, one Bremen respondent reckoned that he spent 30% of his free time using his computer, playing games and writing programmes. Another, who was unemployed, was word-processing job applications and using a graphics programme to prepare herself for a design apprenticeship. It was their greater experience at work and in college which was responsible for the British samples' overall lead in the use of IT. The particularly low figures for Bremen could be partly due to the fact that this sample contained far fewer clerical workers, trainees or apprentices, than in the other towns.

Despite their limited experience, most young people in both countries showed a strong positive attitude towards IT. The majority felt that training in IT would help them in the future. The main difference was between trajectories, with most of the respondents in trajectory I agreeing with this proposition, and far more in trajectory IV disagreeing.

Origins and significance of the national differences

The figures presented so far appear to indicate that in important respects the British system was proving superior to Germany's in the development of general work-related skills and experiences. However, before drawing such a conclusion, some caveats are needed. First, because the experiences were self-reported, there could have been a cultural bias, exaggerating the differences. For example, we cannot be certain whether the questionnaire items were interpreted in precisely the same way in both countries, with the Germans adopting different and perhaps tougher criteria for giving an endorsement. The British respondents were generally the more positive about their experiences and prospects throughout the questionnaire. Secondly, the samples were not strictly representative of the populations in each town, but were equated for each trajectory. In the German towns the overwhelming majority (over 80%) of young people were actually on trajectories I and II, less than 5% were on trajectory IV, but half the German samples were drawn from trajectories III and IV. In Britain the population was spread more evenly across the four trajectories.

If our competence figures are considered in isolation from the relative sizes of the different trajectories in the two countries, then a misleading picture and conclusions may drawn. The British situation is less satisfactory than it appears, while the German situation is healthier. By their early 20s, only about half of all young adults in Britain have either gained higher education qualifications, or the experience or certificates that are recognised for employment in skilled jobs; a long way behind the numbers in Germany. British young people's apparently superior vocational experience is largely intrinsic to the training they had received; it has less extrinsic value in term of certified competence.

A further caveat comes from considering that at age 17-18 the British samples were much more likely then their German counterparts to have already completed their education and training, and to be experiencing real work. Work-related competences are likely to be acquired at a later stage in German young people's careers. Overall, the German samples were at least two years behind the British samples in relation to entering employment proper. At the time of our fieldwork, 39% of the Liverpool respondents were in employment and 61% in Swindon, whereas in both Paderborn and Bremen only 7% expected to be full-time employees, even in one year's time. The transition to adult employee status was tending to be more rapid in Britain, whichever trajectory the young people were following. This will not account entirely for the British samples' greater (apparent) wealth of learning experiences, because within Britain these experiences had been most frequent in the academic trajectory, where the transition to adult employee status took longest. However, international differences in the pace of the transition alert us to the possibility that the effectiveness of vocational learning may depend not just on the quantity of skills and experience gained by a given age, but also on the contexts in which they have been gained and, in particular, how learning experiences are organised sequentially.

Finally, another contextual difference that is illustrated time and again in the following chapters, concerns how in Germany all four trajectories, but particularly the academic and the routes to skilled employment, were the more structured and bounded. In order to reach their goals, the German young people had to follow prescribed curricula and obtain stipulated qualifications. In Britain there were more varied routes to specific vocational destinations, and there was far more switching between full-time education, training schemes, and employment. This is one reason why the British samples were obtaining the more varied experiences on all the trajectories. In Swindon and Liverpool, individuals' career development often appeared haphazard, whereas the Bremen and Paderborn samples were travelling in relatively straight lines. There was more switching of positions, and also more changing of career goals in the British areas. In Swindon and Liverpool, 45% and 51% respectively had changed their minds about their vocational goals since completing compulsory education, compared with just 26% and 31% in the German areas. A dominant theme of later chapters is the greater flexibility and correspondingly much greater uncertainty in the British system than in the German one.

CHAPTER V

The academic route

Introduction

In both countries, the traditional academic route into higher education is well marked: success in two or more A-levels (Britain), or the *Abitur* (Germany). The numbers obtaining these qualifications are markedly different in the two countries, however, with a much greater proportion achieving them in Germany in any one cohort: over 30%, compared with around 20% in Britain (for more detailed figures, see BMBW, 1988, 1989 and DES, 1988a, 1989). But, achieving entry-level qualifications does not mean that young people will necessarily enter higher education directly, or even will intend to enter at a later date. The local labour market can be a significant factor in influencing perceptions and possibilities of going into a job or apprenticeship at age 16 rather than remaining in full-time education and, likewise, upon completion of A-levels or the *Abitur*.

The relative age participation rates in higher education in Britain and Germany are markedly different. In Britain, after school or further education college, only about 13% of the age group enters higher education. This is marginally increased as some young people retake A-levels and others follow vocational routes which take longer to complete, but even with such additions, the overall participation rate for 18-21 year-olds in higher education is only 14%. (Entry as mature students, over the age of 21, makes the overall participation rate still less than 15%.) Even using a broader definition of higher education, to include what was formerly regarded as advanced further education (those courses which require an entry level of one A-level or equivalent), the participation rate still rises only to 27% (DES, 1988b).

The comparative figures for Germany show that the advantage of having larger numbers on the academic trajectory (over 30% of the total) is translated into substantial numbers actually going into higher education (although often a little later than in Britain). Of all who had qualified for higher education entry in 1987, only 26.8% enrolled that same year. The figures over the last 15 years show a tendency to delay higher education entry because of national service, apprenticeship, or sabbatical years. Between 70% and 80% of *Abiturienten* enter higher education within three years of completion of their schooling, and the numbers have been increasing recently. When mature students are added (and there are more of these in Germany than in Britain), the participation rate is over 30%, over double that in Britain. There is widespread agreement in Britain about the need for higher participation rates in higher education.

In Germany, the complete absence of any employment opportunities, other than very marginal ones at age 16 means that a job is effectively not even an option. Similarly, while theoretically pupils can leave school after 10 years, in order to continue their education in an apprenticeship or special vocational school, it is unlikely that this 'opportunity' will be taken by academically talented young people, as it would leave them with the lowest school-leaving certificate and poor career prospects. Academic youngsters may opt for apprenticeships, but this is more likely to be after completion of the *Abitur*. Indeed, there is only minimal dropout from this academic trajectory before completion of the *Abitur*.

The longer and less specialised 16-19 curricula in Germany are instrumental in carrying much higher numbers into higher education than in Britain. The subsequent pattern of higher education experience is also likely to differ, in that German students tend to enter later and take longer to earn their degrees. The average time spent studying for a degree at a German university in 1987 was 7.5 years. In that year the average age of graduation was 28.4. Students in other higher education institutions were graduating slightly faster.

Educational experiences: British sample

Data from the ESRC 16-19 Initiative show approximately equal percentages of Swindon and Liverpool young people opting for post-16 academic education (20.5% and 19% respectively on samples of 518 and 444 from the older cohort), despite education to work transitions at age 16 being much more likely in Swindon than Liverpool (31% - 11%). The figures for the post A-level progression, however, are sharply different. Twenty-eight per cent of Swindon respondents with A-levels went into higher education, while 51% went into employment, whereas in Liverpool, 38% with A-levels went directly into higher education and only 18% into employment. The buoyant Swindon labour market, and intense competition for 'high-level' school-leavers, offered the A-level group a genuine alternative.

The absence of a local labour market effect on the numbers staying on at 16 to take A-levels in Swindon, may be because youth labour markets are segmented, with employment at 18 providing better prospects for academic young people, while for those less well qualified the key decision point is at age 16. The job prospects for well-qualified young people at age 18 were very good in Swindon, with the major offices of the large financial institutions like Allied Dunbar and Nationwide Anglia exerting a particular pull. Those entering higher education had even better prospects, and upon graduation would effectively enter a national labour market. The hierarchical nature of the education system and strong demand for graduates at the time of this research meant that, virtually without exception, academic track respondents in both cohorts, in Liverpool as well as in Swindon, had good reason to be highly optimistic about their employment prospects. However, their optimism was sometimes tinged with a perception that their educational choices could limit their eventual job prospects. Thus, one Liverpool respondent with arts A-levels had nevertheless opted to do a BSc.:

'in this environment for jobs an arts degree would merely be a qualification rather than an automatic entry to a job'.

Even those with poor A-level grades, or who had passed only one examination, found a number of other educational avenues open: for example, higher national qualifications. Thus, the A-level route looked secure, in that it was not only the major route into higher education, but was also respected by employers, and had national currency and respectability. However, in Britain this route is under pressure, because its curricular frameworks, approaches and assessment fit uneasily with those adopted elsewhere: most notably in GCSE and vocational qualifications and increasingly with those of higher education too. Certainly the lack of 'fit' causes problems with progression both into and out of the A-level programme.

The academic track young people provided both illustrations and illuminative comments on their education. The ambivalent nature of A-levels was recognised by one respondent: she realised that education performed a job-allocation function and 'they [qualifications] make a great deal of difference to future life', but she was not impressed by the relevance of the content: 'from my own experience I found that leaving college with A-levels was no use'. The competing attractions at age 18 of a well-paid job versus higher education produced a tension for one Swindon respondent. She chose one path and then the other:

'I left college at 18 after completing my A-levels. I got a job with a large employer in financial services where I worked for a year. At first I enjoyed the work and the money was very good. However, in the last few months I began to feel very dissatisfied with my work and future prospects. As a result I left my job and returned to full-time education to become a teacher, and I feel I have made one of the best decisions of my life'.

Similarly, a Liverpool respondent saw the switch from one path to another as highly significant:

'leaving the security of a full-time job with the bank was a huge chance that I took. But I wanted to give myself the chance of attaining a higher qualification. If one has the chance for higher education then it should be taken'.

This tension was perhaps expressed even more poignantly by a Swindon student who was doing a full-time college course and working part-time testing electronic devices in a large factory to help finance her studies. She would have liked to go on to higher education, but:

'I have been given the impression that I will not be able to go to university because of financial problems. I would have liked to study a degree in law but my father is retiring next year and my mother is on a very low wage'.

The possibility of doing A-levels in different types of institutions was also reflected by our respondents. Thus, even in Liverpool, with its strong tradition of schooling from 11 through to 18, some had opted to go to a college of further education to continue their academic education. One of the older cohort had gone to college to take four A-levels. Although he passed them all, the grades were disappointing. Nevertheless, he had managed to enter a college of higher education where he was studying for a BSc. In contrast, Swindon operated a tertiary system whereby young people wishing to continue post-compulsory education had to transfer to one of two post-16 colleges. Both offered A-level courses, although the smaller college offered primarily academic or general education, while the other operated a full range of vocational education, combined with some academic and general courses. The images of these colleges expressed by outsiders were respectively of a sixth-form college and a college of further education, although both were intent on blurring such traditional demarcations. However, although these settings may have influenced attitudes towards education in general and to the particular institutions, the close prescription of A-level syllabuses and examinations meant that curricular experiences would be similar in key respects. The strength or weakness of the youth labour market also seemed to be having an effect on the numbers from different social backgrounds choosing the academic route at 16. The almost exclusive domination of this academic trajectory by young people from middle-class backgrounds in Swindon, in a sample where the majority (almost 60%) came from working-class homes, gives food for thought: 34 of the 40, 85% of the academic track sample in Swindon came from middle-class homes.

Genuine and viable alternatives, whether in employment, training or other education, seemed more likely to appeal to working-class 16 year-olds and their parents. This suggests that the strengthening of other routes into higher education and curricular reform of A-levels, making them more attractive to a wider population, will be essential if an expansion of higher education is to be achieved in Britain. The demographic downturn does not greatly affect the numbers from higher social-class backgrounds, from whom the bulk of higher education entrants are still drawn, so the numbers entering are unlikely to be affected by this trend. However, the prospects of widening access may be set back by the increased labour market choices available, which may make other options even more feasible and attractive. The introduction of student loans may act as a further barrier. The experience of Swindon suggests it may be difficult to hold, let alone increase, the number of those on the academic track going directly into higher education, if there is a strong demand for such labour.

Educational experience: German sample

The data from official records show that in both Bremen and Paderborn about 50% of all pupils in secondary education were attending a *Gymnasium*. The *Gymnasium* has developed from an elitist institution into a major part of the school system. Not only is the *Abitur* the essential higher education entry qualification, but it has also become the required qualification for some vocational training. As a result, other school-leaving certificates have been devalued, in the sense that they are worth less in the competition for apprenticeships. Although the labour markets in both German towns were strengthening, the numbers of *Gymnasium* pupils opting out after the tenth year had not grown. The attraction of other routes was very limited because the *Abitur* was still regarded as the necessary key to entry into all attractive segments of the labour market. The *Abitur* examination is usually taken at age 18-19 in the *Gymnasiale Oberstufe*, but it can also be taken in a *Fachoberschule* by those who previously attended *Realschule*. The German samples included respondents who were taking the *Abitur* in both locations. However, the routes to them varied. Thus, in the younger cohort, four respondents did not have straightforward careers in the *Gymnasium,* but had changed from the *Realschule* where they had received an apprenticeship-oriented school-leaving qualification. Two of these respondents expected to enter higher education after finishing high level apprenticeships. Another respondent had chosen to enrol with a *Fachoberschule* after finishing the *Realschule,* in order to take the *Fachabitur* (specialised *Abitur*) and start an apprenticeship. All of the younger cohort expected still to be at school by the end of the year, and most had not formulated any definite career plans. The majority in both cohorts expected to enter higher education straight after leaving school or, in the case of the young men, after they had finished national service. In the older cohort there were examples of young people whose final aim was higher education, but who first wished to gain vocational experience in an apprenticeship. A typical career plan mentioned by the sample was *Abitur,* followed by an apprenticeship in banking, followed by the study of economics or law in higher education.

Although these young people were categorised as on the academic track because of their present status, they did not all expect to stay in the 'academic world'. Those who decided to opt out could not expect to enter the labour market at a higher level than pupils with other school-leaving certificates, but they were more likely to qualify for higher-level apprenticeships. Durrer-Guthof and Kazemzadeh (1984) found that *Abiturienten* were applying for apprenticeships or courses in special vocational schools leading to a very limited range of professions. Our survey showed a preference for apprenticeships in banking, insurance, office work, the civil service, and health profession courses in special vocational schools. The latter was the case for a young woman from Bremen who was starting a course to become a physiotherapist. 'It is very important to me, the connection between working with people and doing something physical.' In 1987 15% of all *Abiturienten* planned to achieve a 'double qualification' (vocational training and degree), while another 15% had no higher education plans at all (BMBW, 1989). However, most *Abiturienten* prefer to enter higher education straight from school. Indeed, in Germany there has been a recent trend towards purely academic education. In former years many *Abiturienten* regarded an apprenticeship followed by study at a university as a more secure way into the labour market, as with an apprenticeship they would have something to fall back on. Although this view is still held by many young people, the improved situation in the academic labour market has led to more applications for higher education without any kind of break between school and entry. This is a return to the more traditional pattern which existed prior to the growing problems in the youth labour market in the 1970s.

Employment experience: British sample

It might be expected that the academic track samples would have had less experience of work. However, this was not the case, especially for the older cohort in Britain. Besides vacation employment and part-time work, either in the evenings or at weekends, they might have either tried for, or obtained, full-time employment. Certainly the healthy state of the labour market in Swindon meant that temporary and part-time opportunities abounded, and most of the sample there had experience in some type of employment. Employers were keen for labour, but not desperate, and it should be remembered that these young people were typically seen as of a high standard. Conversely, those deemed to fall below certain standards in relation to either educational or employment records could find it difficult to obtain jobs. (This issue will be considered more fully in relation to the trajectory IV samples.)

In addition to those who were trying to supplement their grants - 'I try to obtain some temporary work in order to keep myself and pay housekeeping while I'm on vacation' - some students wishing to enter particular careers had sought experience in the relevant fields, whether through paid or voluntary work. Thus, one psychology student, intending to become a social worker, had done voluntary work with the elderly and handicapped and saw that this would 'help me in the future working with the elderly'. She believed that showing such commitment would also increase her chances of being accepted in her chosen employment and training after graduation. Overall then, even respondents continuing into higher education in Britain were likely to have a range of employment experience, certainly more than their German counterparts.

Another type of employment experience for the academic track sample was among those who had obtained permanent employment. As we explained earlier, the state of the youth labour market had a profound influence upon the types of transition possible, with many more Swindon than Liverpool respondents opting for employment upon completion of A-levels. The vast majority of the academic track samples in both Swindon and Liverpool had proceeded to A-levels without looking for jobs, apprenticeships or training places. Just two out of 40 in Swindon had actively investigated other possibilities at the end of the fifth form. One had applied for a job through his family, while the other had made two applications for apprenticeships. However, on completion of A-levels this picture changed. Some of those intending to go into higher education had also looked for employment. For some this was insurance in case their A-level results were poorer than expected, but given the large numbers in Swindon who opted for employment from this track, it is clear that this was regarded as a genuine alternative. However, presenting education and employment as alternatives may be simplistic, for a number of respondents were on paths which explicitly intertwined the two. This was sometimes the result of personal decisions to 'take a break' before entering higher education, or to prepare for a preferred career path. For example, one respondent had done a year's work in amenity horticulture after A-levels before going to agricultural college. (Agricultural colleges typically asked for at least a year's relevant work experience, unless the applicant had been brought up on a farm.)

Thus, choosing to enter full-time employment did not necessarily mean that the avenue of higher education was closed, even in the near future. However, a large number of respondents in Swindon were opting into permanent career employment at this age. The active recruitment campaigns of employers stressed the career opportunities for entrants at this level, and the young people themselves, while describing their current positions in fairly lowly terms, such as bank clerks or 'administrative assistant calculating company pensions and allocating premiums', nevertheless planned to have careers in banking or to become financial advisers. As competition for these young people in Swindon was fierce, and employers had to compete with the attractions of higher education, firms were offering packages of employment and training opportunities. We shall see later that these same employers were adopting very different strategies for recruitment at 16, further evidence of the segmentation of the youth labour market.

Overall then, in both Liverpool and Swindon, high academic attainment was being rewarded with a panoply of education, training and employment opportunities. But the local contexts were having profound effects on the structuring of these opportunities. The buoyant youth labour market in Swindon resulted in such young people being actively courted by employers, who vied with each other to offer career employment rich in opportunities for training and progression. In contrast, in the tighter labour market in Liverpool, it was much more likely that the young people would have to enter higher education and move away from the area before the potential accumulated in education could be realised in employment full of training and other opportunities.

Employment experience: German sample

All the German respondents on the academic trajectory were still in full-time compulsory education and, apart from pocket-money vacation jobs and part-time work at weekends or in the afternoons, they had few opportunities for employment. Some of the young men and women in the older cohort intended to look for apprenticeships. The number of applications already made varied from one to 20, and although they were from the most highly-qualified members of the age group, their applications had not always been successful. Some potential apprentices regarded entry into higher education as a possible alternative if they were unsuccessful in securing the training that they wanted. This was the case in both towns. For example, one young woman in Paderborn originally wanted to become an interpreter and to take up non-academic training, but decided differently when her plans did not materialise; she was studying physics at the time of our inquiry. Other respondents were anticipating that the reverse might happen. Thus, in Bremen, one young man expected to be at university after leaving school, but was also prepared to take an apprenticeship if he was unable to enter higher education.

It seems that respondents on trajectory I were aware of the different tracks that would open for them by the acquisition of the *Abitur*. At the same time, they knew that they had to compete with fellow *Abiturienten* for higher education places and with other school-leavers for apprenticeships. The differing speed of transitions compared with Britain meant that although very few of the German sample had more than minimal employment experience at the time of our survey, they would not necessarily enter higher education with less experience than their British counterparts. Indeed, only some of the German respondents intended to go straight from school into higher education. Other possibilities included military or community service, apprenticeships, or simply taking a break from study. The later starting ages and longer periods of degree study meant that eventually the German student groups would probably include more young people with substantial experience outside education than their British counterparts. Wider experience, including employment, was likely to be in store for many in this group before they entered higher education, but seldom within the time-frame that we were examining. The different patterns, pace and financing of higher education meant that many students would be working at the same time, in order to finance their studies at university and *Fachhochschule*, as Table 5.1 shows.

Table 5.1: Students working in order to finance their studies, 1986

		Completely	Partly	Completely or partly
Undergraduates not living at home				
University	%	6	30	36
Fachhochschule	%	6	27	33
Undergraduates living at home				
University	%	9	39	48
Fachhochschule	%	8	34	41
Postgraduates	%	40	26	65

Source: BMBW, 1986.

Overall then, the stereotype of the naïve graduate who knows little of the world of work outside education looks increasingly unrealistic for both countries.

Vocationally relevant experience compared

Although the British samples were generally more likely to have had some labour market experience than their German counterparts, and many were already in full-time jobs, work experience, if mainly of a casual kind, was not unknown in Germany. Moreover, as the figures in chapter IV showed, work-related skills and experiences were reported relatively more frequently by German respondents on the academic trajectory than those on the routes to semi-skilled and unskilled employment.

Table 5.2 amplifies the picture further by comparing experience and skills between the four towns.

As we might expect, the reporting of work-related skills and experiences was consistently higher among the British than the German young people. Substantially more British than German respondents reported being given responsibility, making decisions for themselves, having a chance to use their initiative and working as a member of a team. There were virtually no differences, however, for developing new skills and abilities, feeling a sense of achievement, feeling able to use their abilities, and being asked for advice. It was also notable that within each country, for most of these skills and experiences, the young people in the expanding labour markets (Swindon and Paderborn) were ahead of the others.

As we noted in chapter IV, drawing conclusions about superiority from these figures is fraught with difficulty. Perhaps the most that can be safely said of them is that, even in the academic track, vocational experience across a wide range is perceived as more widespread among the British young people, and as more available in a context of expansion rather than contraction.

Table 5.2: Work-related skills and experiences

	Liverpool		Bremen		Swindon		Paderborn	
	A	B	A	B	A	B	A	B
Been given responsibility	27	4	13	20	13	1	14	8
Been able to make decisions for oneself	29	2	15	10	34	1	22	7
Had a chance to use initiative	25	4	12	11	29	4	21	1
Developed new skills and abilities	28	4	28	9	24	4	19	5
Set own goals/ targets	24	1	9	16	27	3	20	9
Felt stretched/ challenged	21	5	13	11	30	5	24	4
Felt a sense of achievement	20	2	17	3	30	3	25	2
Felt all abilities were being used	14	6	14	14	23	6	13	10
Worked as a member of a team	28	3	9	18	32	2	14	8
Had to work to a deadline	32	-	23	7	37	-	29	5
Been asked for advice by others on how to tackle a problem	19	3	18	6	24	16	19	4

Note: Total sample size in each town = 40

Conclusions for policy

Those in the academic trajectory in both countries generally had very good prospects compared with their contemporaries on other trajectories. However, the much wider participation in higher education in Germany since the early 1970s meant that the comparative advantage of graduates over non-graduates was much less than in Britain. Another cause for concern in Germany has been that access has been widened without much curricular reform. Suggestions have been made that initial university courses should be broader and shorter (reduced to three years) for the majority of entrants, with smaller numbers going on to take more specialised qualifications. Another area of concern could be that the exclusive right of *Abiturienten* to enter higher education may undermine the apprenticeship system, and some *Länder* have been developing possibilities for direct access from apprenticeships to higher education without the *Abitur.*

The lower participation rates in higher education in Britain, coupled with a buoyant demand for these young people and the current demographic downturn, mean their prospects are extremely favourable. The converse of this, however, is that it may prove difficult to widen access to higher education. By the end of the 1980s, applications for higher education in Britain were at record levels, but the changing youth labour market, with its opportunities for employment at 18, may mean that the numbers making a transition straight from school or college into higher education will not increase as rapidly as it is hoped (by the British government). This reinforces the case for higher education recruiting more mature students, and not only those without formal entry requirements.

For differing reasons, in both countries there is scope for collaboration between educators and employers to offer packages of education and employment with built-in possibilities for access to higher education. At one level, British academic trajectory young people appear to be better equipped vocationally than their German counterparts; but that is may be because of their greater early labour market experience. For those continuing to higher education the differences are unlikely to be sustained, which raises similar questions about curricular reform for both countries. Indeed, the need to tie in technical and vocational qualifications, such that they offer clear progression and at least potential access to higher education, is likely to become a priority for both. This latter point is taken up in the concluding chapter.

Conclusion

Although there is a widespread agreement that higher education participation rates are required in Britain, labour market trends may undermine numbers of youngsters choosing to go into higher education, because of the opportunities for, and attraction of, employment post-A-level.

The possibility of complete exit from the education system at 16 (in practice virtually impossible in Germany), exerts significant attractions, particularly for working-class young people. It is particularly important, therefore, to build other routes into higher education. While there is a smooth curricular progression in Germany into higher education from a wider base (30%), the narrower form and format of A-levels may be a barrier to this in Britain. Higher education curricula may need to be re-examined in Germany, perhaps to make them shorter and less specialised. The issue of the nature of higher education curricula will also have to be addressed in Britain if wider access is to be achieved.

In both countries, the strategy of going for the highest level school-leaving certificate has labour market utility, even if youngsters do not intend to enter higher education directly. This is particularly the case when the labour market is buoyant. The British youngsters had a greater sense of 'skill-ownership' than their German counterparts, although it is difficult to ascertain whether this relates to curricular differences, greater employment experience, or the more advanced stage of transition of the British sample (e.g., older cohort youngsters invariably already in higher education), or other cultural differences. To disentangle some of these factors would require both closer curricular examination and a longitudinal study, which follows some of these youngsters through to the completion of their transitions. In systems where the average ages upon completion of higher education are 22 (Britain) and 28 (Germany), stage in transition is as important as chronological age. The research has shown that the widely differing times taken to complete transitions in the two countries mean that it is foolhardy to look at shorter time periods (say, ages 16-19 or 18-21) and try to make direct comparisons.

In both countries, greater interest is starting to be expressed in the possibility of employers and educators collaborating to offer young people a coherent package of education, training and employment, which has built into it possibilities for access to higher education. More generally, the whole issue of the need to tie in technical and vocational qualifications with academic ones, such that they offer clear progression routes, is becoming increasingly important.

CHAPTER VI

Routes to skilled work

Introduction

Germany's principal route to skilled work is the dual system, which is sometimes presented as all-encompassing and monolithic. However, in practice there are different versions of the system. This diversity relates to patterns of experience in different types of company, occupation, region, labour market and mode of educational provision. This richness and diversity was reflected in the experiences of respondents heading for skilled employment in the two German towns. Diversity was similarly apparent in the experiences of the British respondents, but was immediately evident in their numerous routes to skilled employment. The three major routes were through YTS, full-time further education, and directly into employment at age 16.

One significant difference between the routes in the two countries relates to the time taken before individuals were likely to perform a full set of work duties. In Britain, by age 19, many young adults had already achieved fully-skilled status and, even if still in training, they were performing most aspects of the skilled role. In Germany at the same age, education and training still figured prominently, and work tasks were most likely to be performed under supervision. Indeed, even when German apprenticeships are completed, skilled workers may continue to upgrade their status through further education and training right through to *Meister* level, where they themselves have training responsibilities.

German sample

About two-thirds of all young people in vocational training in Germany are in the dual system. This means they are apprentices and students at the same time.

In both German towns respondents had to apply for training contracts. The strength of labour demand in Paderborn was such that in 1987 96.8% of all applicants registered with the *Arbeitsamt* (employment office) found apprenticeships. Competition still existed for white-collar apprenticeships with good career prospects, whereas in some crafts and service professions (for example, builder, baker, butcher) there was a shortage of applicants.

The situation in some occupations had led to initiatives by the *Kammern* (guilds) and employers. The greatest shortage of apprentices was in the building industry and, in order to make this field of work more attractive to young people, training allowances had been increased significantly. They were the highest allowances paid in Germany at the time of our research (Table 6.1).

Table 6.1: Training allowances in DMs

	Bank	*Kaufmann*	Craft	Mechanic	Industry
1st year	850,-	663,-	385,-	<-->	628,-
2nd year	935,-	747,-	410,-	<-->	674,-
3rd year	1025,-	839,-	477,-	<-->	743,-
4th year	-	-	539,-	<-->	832,-
	Joiner	Hairdresser	Butcher		Builder
1st year	443,-	280,-	585,-	<-->	682,40
2nd year	542,-	350,-	605,-	<-->	1061,60
3rd year	657,-	420,-	655,-	<-->	1339,60

The search for an occupation had usually begun while the applicants were still at school. Not all respondents reported successful applications before they left school, but some described situations where they were awarded training contracts at the end of July (all apprenticeships begin on 1 August). Just one respondent in Paderborn, but 11 in Bremen, had not obtained the particular apprenticeships they wanted. Young people in both towns had typically made multiple applications before they were successful. Comparing those in trajectory II with some cases in trajectory IV, those in II had not given up their searching, despite many disappointments. While looking for apprenticeships, respondents in the two German samples had used a broad infrastructure, including the employment office, reading job advertisements in newspapers, telephoning employers and asking their families and friends (Table 6.2).

Table 6.2: Search strategies

	Number mentioning each strategy	
	Bremen	Paderborn
Employment office	1	21
Newspaper	8	20
'Phoned employer	3	19
Asked family	2	14
Asked friends	5	16
Any other way	9	7

Unsurprisingly, the respondents in both samples had made frequent use of the careers advisory services at the employment offices. Not only did most employers report vacancies to the employment offices, but comprehensive information on the occupations themselves was available for applicants. With regard to the operation of the labour market, employers were having to find new ways of attracting apprentices besides using traditional means, such as newspaper advertising.

Irrespective of local labour market conditions, the respondents reported very different experiences with local employers when they applied for training. A young man in Bremen applied for an apprenticeship as a technician after he had finished a scheme (*BGJ -E- Technik*) and reported 'I got an apprenticeship with the first company I 'phoned'. In contrast, a dental nurse from Paderborn described a situation in which many dentists had not responded at all to her applications but had kept all her papers:

'for example, photographs, copies of school-leaving certificates and so on. They didn't think that they cost a lot of money. One doesn't write one application only...The search for a suitable apprenticeship was not easy. Again and again I was disappointed by being turned down. I got my job at the very last minute'.

A hairdresser from Bremen remembered good and bad experiences with employers in response to her applications. Bad experiences were:

'my school-leaving certificate didn't look like it should (5 in English) and therefore I was turned down. With another employer I worked for a trial period and I haven't heard anything from him'.

Another trial period was more successful for her '... and I was taken on straight away'. An office clerk apprentice in Paderborn stated:

'in 1988 I had great problems finding an apprenticeship. It took 28 applications and 14 interviews before I was successful'.

'The start of vocational training symbolises the first and most decisive step in leaving adolescence and entering adulthood. The transition from school to work is a change from an educational to a work organisation' (Hurrelmann, p. 98, 1988).

However, apprentices in Germany are not given the full status of a member of the labour force. Their situation is characterised by the contradiction that, on the one hand, they perform gainful employment including the adoption of a daily schedule and work discipline, and have partial financial independence whereas, on the other hand, the law regards apprentices as young people who have to be guided through vocational training and assisted in their personal development. All curricula for apprenticeships in different fields have in common that the apprentice is progressively introduced to the skills of her or his job, and gains the required understanding. Nevertheless, some of our respondents had not experienced their work as a process of vocational development, but saw iniquities in the way work and pay were distributed by their companies. A young woman in her first year as an office apprentice with a solicitor, reported that besides her paperwork and the use of a wordprocessor she had to run errands and do the clearing up in the office. She reckoned that all apprentices had to deal with the unskilled work. This did not have any great influence on her relationships with colleagues which she considered to be 'relatively good', but 'the pay leaves a great deal to be desired (not more than DM 400 [£133] per month)'. A young woman from Bremen, a hairdresser in her second year, performed all the skills that were required in her profession.

> 'My relationships with colleagues are good, but the money is not enough (DM 400 [£133]), especially when one has to do overtime. This is a kind of exploitation.'

A technician apprentice in his first year felt that he was working for the satisfaction of his employer's needs to the cost of his own qualification. Although he enjoyed his work, he thought the pay was not good enough (DM 393 [£130]). On the other hand, a management trainee in his first year in a large company was very satisfied with his present situation. During his apprenticeship he went through all relevant departments in the company and earned DM 663 [£221].

These examples reveal a central problem in the dual system: the implementation of training curricula. In large companies the apprentices had usually found training situations which were well-planned and scheduled. The training took place in different departments or training workshops conducted by (mostly) the specially-trained Meister. The vocational training of the young person was to the fore. Smaller and medium-sized companies obviously felt they had a responsibility to train young people, but were weighing up the consequent costs. The training of apprentices sometimes took place in a situation of contradiction, when *Meister* and company owner were one and the same person. On the one hand, necessary training requirements had to be met and, on the other, the employer wanted to use the young person's capacity for work. In many cases this conflict had led to apprentices feeling that their training could have been better.

In some professions, all the skills could be learnt in less than three years. In hairdressing this was often the case. The apprentices worked full-time (except during their time at the *Berufsschule*) and, in some cases, did the same work as skilled employees but were paid training allowances. Nevertheless, in Bremen 34 (85%) and in Paderborn 36 (90%) of the apprentices were satisfied with their work, and all respondents reckoned that they would bring their apprenticeships to successful conclusions. In Bremen 29 (72.5% of sample) and in Paderborn 32 (80%) were satisfied with their standards of living and only two in each town were dissatisfied. Although, in most cases, the young people's training allowances were too low to gain full independence from their homes, they gave the apprentices more independence than they had known at school. Not all the apprentices could expect to be able to stay with their companies after their final examinations. A respondent from Paderborn represented others in expressing insecurity about her future. 'I would like to stay and maybe this will be possible.' Other respondents experienced this insecurity as well, but coped with it in a more positive way, at least mentally, by anticipating the possibility that they might have to leave the companies even though they would have preferred to stay.

'Now, this is difficult to say [if she can stay on]. If offered the chance I would stay with the firm, but to improve my position I may have to change companies.'

British sample

Unlike in Germany, where the apprenticeship is still pivotal for vocational education and training as a whole, routes into skilled employment are much more varied in Britain.

Firm-based YTS

The high level of youth and adult unemployment in Liverpool meant that YTS was still the most likely alternative to education. In Swindon, in contrast, the labour market opportunities were such that a much fuller range of avenues (including jobs) was open, and YTS had not fully established itself as a popular alternative, except where it was part of, or could at least open up the possibility of, a full apprentice-ship, similar training, or employment with prospects. In such cases, particularly if the young person's status was 'employed YTS', and the scheme was based upon a single employer, they may have been aware that administratively they were on YTS, but they saw them-selves primarily as 'employed'.

Some large employers used YTS to supplement their recruitment, whereby they took on young people who did not necessarily meet their 'normal' entry requirements, but who they would be prepared to keep on if they made satisfactory progress. Examples of this prac-tice could be seen in several occupational areas: for example, with insurance accounts clerks, as well as engineering technicians. The success of some young people, who previously would not have been deemed 'suitable', had made some of the companies review and open up their recruitment policies. One major local employer ac-knowledged that those recruited onto YTS, with few if any educa-tional qualifications, sometimes compensated with keenness and enthusiasm. This had taught the company that to take one isolated marker of ability (educational attainment) could be misleading:

'there is now a preference to select upon a range of qualities: that is, to weigh up other factors and all categories of information'.

In some occupational areas, such as hairdressing, firm-based training had been so thoroughly incorporated into the structure of YTS that this was now the major route into the occupation. In other areas, such as secretarial, firm-based YTS was one possibility, but honing occu-pational skills initially through further education remained very popular in both Liverpool and Swindon.

Few of those ending up in skilled employment in Swindon had even applied for YTS upon completing the fifth form (only 10 of the 40 in trajectory II). In practice, some of the apprenticeships incorporated YTS, but this was seen almost purely as a funding and administrative technicality for those seeking apprenticeships. Certainly it is important to differentiate, in practice, between schemes, according to how much emphasis was given to further education and training in firm-based YTS. Some schemes had very extensive training, including substantial time in further education, and trainees were studying for fairly high-level vocational qualifications. In such schemes, training sometimes continued beyond the end of YTS. For example, a truck mechanic had continued his studies to take technician qualifications. There were, however, some schemes, which while fulfilling the minimum criteria, gave only limited education and training, the rest of the time being spent in not very demanding work experience. This rarely occurred in Swindon, although there were some schemes between the two extremes, particularly in the retail or clerical placements of 'umbrella' managing agents. But these schemes were being 'squeezed', particularly by the attractions of permanent employment, and also by other routes which offered more substantial education and training.

Firm-based YTS, however, was a highly significant route into skilled employment in Liverpool. In the absence of employment opportunities, competition for YTS training with prospects was fierce. Consequently, in line with national trends, entrants had become better qualified over time (Raffe, 1988). As with German apprenticeships, however, the chances of being kept on varied considerably. Thus, all the older cohort respondents who had been on firm-based YTS, had successfully managed two-step transitions.

The range of firm-based YTS covered in the younger cohort was wide (trainee court clerk, picture-framer, engineer, florist, hairdresser, office clerk, electrician, and so on). As other research has shown, the young people had mixed views about YTS (Raffe and Smith, 1987; Clough et al., 1988; Banks and Evans, 1989). Many valued the training and were thankful that they had the opportunity for it, especially if the scheme was of high quality, but might still resent other aspects, for example, the level of the training allowance. This view was expressed by an apprentice installation electrician:

'I took a full-time course in college and then a YTS, which was a good scheme [technician engineer], but I hated the money because all my friends had proper apprenticeships. I then got a full-time job and now my prospects look great, and I am starting to enjoy life again'.

This experience contrasted sharply with some of the bitter comments on YTS from trajectory III and IV respondents (chapters VII and VIII).

Full-time education

Gaining vocational qualifications through full-time education was another route into skilled employment in the British areas. The high demand (and intense competition among employers) for young skilled workers in Swindon meant that young people who completed such courses could be reasonably confident that they would be able to enter employment in their chosen spheres. The existence of a tertiary system, and unhindered access to careers advice in schools, served to increase awareness of the possible options before 16 year-olds. Some of those staying in full-time education to take vocational qualifications had made a firm commitment to this route, and did not make any job applications at the end of the fifth form. Others did, but the number of applications was usually small (less than five), which strongly suggests that these individuals were being fairly choosy. Indeed, their aim was finding skilled employment, as they were more likely to have sought apprenticeships than ordinary jobs.

Once embarked upon their vocational courses, they had become increasingly attractive to employers, and a number had not completed their studies because they obtained skilled employment. Thus, one Swindon respondent left a two-year computing course partway through the second year to become a junior computing technician.

It should be emphasised that such individuals were not 'failures', dropping out of courses which they were finding too difficult, but rather were making positive decisions to go into employment.

In some occupational areas, notably secretarial, colleges had become wary about sending young people on work placements because the employers were so likely to persuade them to stay. The advent of National Vocational Qualifications (NVQs), and the increasing modularisation of courses and qualifications, meant that the young people would be able to continue their education part-time, at a later date, or through a work-based route. Even so, with some initial qualifications and experience in employment, these young people might find it unnecessary to study for formal qualifications to the same level as if they had stayed in full-time education. This reflected not only the decisions of individuals, but also the value placed upon qualifications traditionally in different areas. Thus, a number of our respondents switching from education to employment in engineering continued their education, usually through day release, while those in the clerical field were much less likely to do so.

The subsequent success of those going into full-time vocational education in securing skilled employment which was rich in education, training and career opportunities, and which was highly paid, shows the coherence of this career route. It was also available as a traditional way into service occupations: hairdressing, catering and caring. Labour market conditions, and the need to make such courses more work-related, had wrought change here, with the experience of the young people being much less exclusively education-based than it might first appear. Thus, in all three areas just mentioned, young people were likely to obtain substantial work experience, either through formal placements at college (in offering services to customers), or through part-time employment. In catering, the case of one Swindon respondent who did two part-time jobs (£40 for 18 hours' work) in addition to attending college full-time, was fairly typical, with some other students doing substantially more. Coupled with employment opportunities during vacations, it meant that these young people could offer both educational and employment experience upon completion of their courses and, as such, the education to work transition was far from abrupt for them.

There was another group taking full-time vocational qualifications: those doing general business studies courses. Again, these were proving very popular, with one Swindon respondent taking such a course with the intention of becoming an advertising or marketing consultant.

The final group in full-time vocational education were those who wished to enter higher education, but had chosen a vocational rather than an academic route. Some of the preceding groups had the option of building up their vocational qualifications and subsequently deciding to enter higher education, but the distinguishing characteristic of this group was their initial intention to enter higher education. Two older cohort respondents had already gained entry to higher education through this route (taking Ordinary National Diplomas (ONDs) in Electrical and Electronic Engineering, and Building Studies). The feasibility of making such transitions in Britain is likely to increase if government policy prevails (DE, 1988) and particularly if higher education institutions waive their traditional entrance requirement of two or more A-levels in an attempt to increase recruitment at a time when the numbers of 18-21 year-olds are declining.

A further possibility for 16 year-olds was to stay in full-time education to improve their academic qualifications, without aiming for higher education entrance. They might then move into full-time vocational education or employment. Some took mixed combinations of different types of course. Examples included resitting or taking additional GCSEs, so that required entry standards for the courses or jobs of their choice could be reached, and non-advanced further education (vocational) courses, such as CPVE, CGLI, RSA and BTEC.

Local contexts made a difference here. In Swindon, some young people had spent an extra year improving O-level or GCSE performances and had then moved into technician or other posts offering career training. Many more stayed for longer in non-advanced further education in Liverpool, but this was much more likely to improve their likelihood of getting semi-skilled employment than skilled jobs. In Swindon there were cogent reasons, in terms of employment opportunities, to stay in full-time education beyond 16. Certainly, the existence of a full range of other opportunities meant that it was likely to be a positive decision rather than an attempt to 'postpone a decision'. Unless entry into skilled employment was secured directly at 16 (for example, through an apprenticeship or other substantial training scheme), then the eventual employment opportunities were much richer, in terms of level and range of work, for those who stayed in education. Individual decisions to stay on were also likely to be influenced by educational attainment and perceptions of how to cope with the further education on offer.

The employment opportunities in Swindon also meant there was usually a close correspondence between vocational subjects studied and subsequent employment. As a result, the local further education college was 'bulging at the seams' with students taking vocational courses. They had even needed to press unconventional areas such as 'rest rooms' into sites for teaching, to cope with the level of demand. These were not all full-time students, and some intended to go into higher education, but the vocational link between education and employment was very clear.

In contrast, the lack of local employment opportunities had frustrated one Liverpool respondent who, after leaving school in 1987, 'wrote after many jobs and was refused'. He then went on to a full-time college course, followed by a spell on a YTS, 'which was a good scheme', training to be an engineering technician. Lack of money while on YTS, however, meant that the individual sought alternative employment and was successful in obtaining a full-time job, 'and now my prospects look great'. Overall then, the 18 months leading from school into skilled employment had involved three changes, considerable uncertainty and persistence with job applications, before the transition was successfully completed.

Directly into employment

Those entering clerical employment had sometimes already picked up vocational qualifications at school. For trajectory II employment, however, additional education and training (including day release) were usually necessary, or there had to be the possibility of career training (for example, in the civil service, banking, or insurance). In Swindon, some respondents who were in non-skilled employment experienced this as a route into progressively more skilled jobs. Initially they had entered employment, for example, doing junior clerical work, and then from this base they were intending to secure, or had already obtained, jobs with career opportunities, which they were unlikely to have attained direct from school.

Employers sometimes offered traineeships (not including YTS) to try to secure their share of talented school-leavers, and apprenticeships were also available. Medium and large employers in engineering and transport in Swindon considered it necessary to offer full apprenticeships, and even with these they struggled to fill vacancies. Thus the 15 (of the 40) trajectory II respondents in Swindon who had applied for apprenticeships had made only a few applications (three or fewer). This reflected the scarcity of formal apprenticeships, the buoyancy of the local labour market, and the possibility of other routes to skilled jobs. Whether the label 'apprentice' is applied in Britain nowadays relates more to tradition than length or type of training (Raffe, 1988). Thus, the administrative, business and clerical sectors talk of 'trainees', not 'apprentices', whereas in engineering, construction and hairdressing, 'apprentice' is more likely to be used.

It was not too difficult for Swindon school-leavers to obtain apprenticeships, and the quality of training delivered was usually high. Their long-term prospects were also excellent as, once again, labour market competition bolstered both the general quality of training and the possibilities of progression. Thus, the Swindon apprentice toolmakers, maintenance fitters, truck mechanics and pattern-makers would be given encouragement and opportunities to progress to technician jobs and possibly beyond.

This route into skilled employment was important in Swindon, but much less so in Liverpool, where there was not only a more limited range of opportunities but, given the much greater supply of school-leavers, employers were more likely to use the YTS as an 'extended probation'. There were, however, still some examples of Liverpool 16 year-olds going directly into employment which opened avenues into progressively skilled jobs. One such respondent, with a strong individualist orientation ('I think most people deserve what they get'), and believing in the value of enterprise, had gone into catering:

> 'in 10 years' time I see myself as a restaurant manager. At the moment I'm only 17 years old and I haven't stopped working since I left school. My employer sees me as an ambitious young lad who will do well for himself. By the time I'm 40, I hope to own my own restaurant or hotel'.

Comparisons

Curriculum

In both systems the emphasis in this trajectory was upon work-related learning, which raises questions about the content and integration of the theoretical component. The system in Germany intends theoretical and practical training to be integrated and indivisible parts; although in practice many employers question the relevance and up-to-dateness of the *Berufsschule* provision. Some large employers have opted to provide both parts themselves. Some *Berufsschulen* are similarly trying to bring about curricular reform. The situation in Britain is even more fluid with the advent of YTS, in which the off-site component can be privately run, and a host of curricular initiatives, both within and outside mainstream education, and training seeking greater integration of on- and off-the-job learning. This has culminated in the *Review of Vocational Qualifications* and the introduction of NVQs, with the intention of effecting a complete reformation of vocational qualifications driven by employment-led standards. The way in which the reform is being implemented brings dangers that the new qualification system will look backwards at the tasks, functions and jobs of the past, rather than towards what will be required in the future. The German system, although formally built on integration, has, in practice, atrophied to an extent that it is due for a more widespread process of renewal and reinvigoration along the lines already developed in its engineering industry.

In both countries, a debate has been fermenting around issues of integration, work-based learning and transferable skills.

Finance

British 16 year-olds entering the labour market directly have, from the outset, certain responsibilities and can quickly consider themselves full members of the labour force. In contrast, German apprentices have the status of young people who have to be guided through training. This situation is reflected in the different remuneration for much the same work in the two countries: a heating and ventilation technician in Swindon earned £450 (DM 1,350), while an apprentice from Paderborn in the same job received a training allowance of £150 (DM 450). As financial independence is a major step towards adult status, many British teenagers had an advantage over their German contemporaries, in that they were likely to be earning normal adult wages a few years earlier. This is perhaps the main incentive for leaving education.

Comparing the costs of training apprentices in the two countries, Jones (1985) investigated the relationship between the costs that have to be paid by employers, and the financial benefits created by the working input of the apprentices themselves. His analysis shows higher costs for training in Britain, because of the higher pay that apprentices receive (Table 6.3).

Table 6.3: Cost of training (% of full adult salary)

	Britain	Germany
1st year	50%	20-30% of full salary
final year	90%	30-45% of full salary

Jones considers these costs a crucial factor in the downward trend of the apprenticeship system in Britain. However, apprentices in Britain are likely to carry out a much fuller range of normal work duties than in Germany. The much lower training allowance in Germany means that apprentices are, in many cases, treated as cheap labour, so even during economic depression the total number of apprentices has increased. With regard to the costs of trainees, it can be argued that in Britain YTS has performed a similar role in many instances. This has been the case in depressed labour markets, where the scheme has often been used as an alternative to either the apprenticeship system or employment, because employers have had the freedom to offer trainee allowances rather than wages.

Comparing the uses employers make of the YTS and the dual system, some similarities are apparent. Both systems can be divided into two categories: high-level training to produce skilled labour and to give the individual good career prospects and training, or as a period in which the trainee provides an employer with cheap labour and cannot expect good career prospects. The former is much more likely in buoyant labour markets. In Germany, the 'training culture' and the greater commitment of most employers to training, tends to overshadow the significant minority who see young people primarily as cheap labour. Jones argues that German employers spend double the amount of British firms on youth training (Jones, 1986). In Britain, employers pay higher youth wage rates and recoup this by spending less on training and getting more production from young workers. As Rose (1989) points out, demographic trends may push youth wages up, which may make it even harder to resist 'the traditional practice of recouping high youth wage costs by investing little in training'.

A recent report exhorted Britain's young people to show

'a greater willingness to invest in their own development, at least in terms of foregoing alternative earning opportunities while in training' (Training Agency, 1989).

However, higher youth wages may increase the resentment of those on much lower training rates.

Feelings of exploitation while on training rates were much more likely in Britain, because although the rates were similar to Germany's, the British respondents could make unfavourable comparisons with their contemporaries who were in employment. In Germany, virtually all young people were being paid training rates. The financial advantage for those British respondents entering employment directly or within a year of leaving school, compared with their German counterparts, was marked. Thus, while those in our samples who were on the YTS received about the same money as German apprentices, those who had made speedy transitions into employment earned considerably more.

The existence of so many youth jobs meant that Swindon respondents on routes to skilled status were more likely to be dissatisfied with their standards of living than the samples in the other three areas (Table 6.4). That some in the younger cohort who were still at college or on YTS were 'chafing at the bit' to be earning like many of their contemporaries was, perhaps, understandable. However, these accounted for only five of the 13 who expressed dissatisfaction, and it is instructive to give the occupations, weekly earnings and ages of the others (Table 6.5).

Table 6.4: Satisfaction with standard of living

A = Satisfied
B = Dissatisfied

	Liverpool		Bremen		Swindon		Paderborn	
	A	B	A	B	A	B	A	B
Trajectory II	29	7	29	2	26	13	32	2

Table 6.5: Average earnings in different occupations in Swindon

	Age	Weekly wage (£s)
Telephonist/receptionist	17	69
Apprentice tool-maker	17	66
Design room assistant	19	80
Legal secretary	19	108
Civil engineering technician	19	132
Junior computer technician	19	127
Panel beater	19	125
Electrician	19	80

The key point is that, although such complaints would presumably get very short shrift in the other three towns, in the context of the Swindon local market, the dissatisfaction was realistic. The young people's reference groups were local and they had comparatively good reason to consider themselves to be getting raw deals.

In contrast, despite lower rates of pay and more young people on training schemes, only seven Liverpool respondents expressed dissatisfaction with their standard of living. They presumably recognised that they had at least reasonably good prospects in a context where, despite job prospects improving during the years leading up to 1989, this was only to a level which left 18-19 year-olds in the local labour market facing near-evens chances of being unemployed (Roberts, et al., 1989a). The German respondents, generally on even lower training rates, rarely expressed dissatisfaction with their standards of living.

Work-related skills and experiences

Table 6.6: Numbers reporting work-related skills and experiences in trajectory II

Skills and experiences	Liverpool		Bremen		Swindon		Paderborn	
	A	B	A	B	A	B	A	B
Been given responsibility	29	1	17	15	28	1	22	5
Been able to make decisions for oneself	27	1	14	9	28	2	15	11
Had a chance to use initiative	26	3	16	13	29	2	19	8
Developed skills and abilities	33	3	23	9	21	2	26	5
Set own goals/targets	23	3	17	13	20	6	18	10
Felt stretched/challenged	12	7	21	7	23	3	21	3
Felt a sense of achievement	28	2	25	4	27	-	23	2
Felt all abilities were being used	19	8	21	5	19	5	21	5
Worked as a member of a team	28	5	16	11	35	-	18	14
Had to work to a deadline	26	6	13	16	24	6	20	9
Been asked for advice by others on how to tackle a problem	19	5	11	11	21	19	12	9

Note: (1) A = Often
       B = Seldom/never
   (2) Total number in each cell = 40

The use of skills and experience of challenge were expected to be high on this trajectory, and this proved to be the general case in all four towns. The Bremen and Liverpool samples reported fewer skills and experiences than the Swindon and Paderborn samples; a product, perhaps, of their stronger labour markets and wider range of opportunities; the types of occupation concentrated in each town might also be a factor.

Because of the differences in the status given to the young people in the two countries at this stage of their careers, the samples reported rather different work experiences. In Britain, they were much more likely to have been given a full range of duties, including making decisions, being given responsibility and developing initiative.

The higher numbers of German respondents who seldom, or never, had these experiences, underlines the point that the German samples were still in transition, whereas the British samples were more likely to have fully entered employment. Taking these findings into account, it is not surprising that more British respondents (28 in Liverpool and 35 in Swindon, compared with 16 in Bremen and 18 in Paderborn) had the feeling of having 'worked as a member of a team'. However, the wider range of experiences and skills for which the British respondents claimed ownership, is more difficult to explain exclusively in these terms. Whether it was greater exposure to work, better training, lower standards, or a generally more positive view of their capabilities among the British, remains to be discovered.

Conclusion

Britain offers young people a variety of routes to vocational training and formal qualifications, whereas opportunities in Germany are dominated by the dual system. Britain has a plethora of routes to skilled employment, involving varying mixtures of employment, education and training. Local labour markets and employment structures have a profound influence, whereby local labour market contexts structure opportunities, but once on firmly-established skilled routes, young people's prospects are generally good. In Germany, the apprenticeship system is always the dominant local influence, and this does not necessarily map on to longer-term local labour market opportunities in a straightforward manner. In occupations where long-term prospects are good, performance during an apprenticeship will be more significant than prior educational attainment. However, there are occupations where the chances of being kept on as a skilled worker upon completion of an apprenticeship are remote.

All the German apprentices in this study had a clearly-defined and institutionalised junior status, and they were rarely given a full range of tasks appropriate to a skilled worker. If they were given them, it was more likely to be in small companies and occupations like retail, where all aspects of the role could be learnt easily within three years. In contrast, whichever route was taken in Britain, it was highly likely that by the age of 19 the young people would either already be 'full employees' or, even if still 'in training', this would contain a significant amount of real work. While there may be a debate about the desirability of employee status, and whether the formal education base needs extending and deepening, one effect of earlier exposure to the responsibilities associated with 'real' work was that work-related competences were probably being developed earlier among our British respondents. The British emphasis on work-related learning may have some advantages. However, one crucial difference between the two systems is quantitative rather than qualitative. In Britain, fewer young people are trained for skilled employment, despite the fact that in a number of areas, both occupational and regional, there are shortages of skilled labour. Thus, while the German system may produce a surplus of skilled labour, at best the British system tends to be tailored to immediate requirements, which creates periodic skills shortages. The two systems also differ sharply in pay and training rates. In Germany, there is general acceptance that teenagers are still in training and should be paid accordingly. In Britain, the existence of youth jobs, and the earlier and more explicit work component while in training, contribute to pressure to pay higher rates. Indeed, in buoyant labour markets like Swindon, such pressures are virtually unstoppable.

A great advantage of the German system is that it produces a high general level of skills, part of which is gained through continued contact up to the age of 18 with the educational system. However, when one looks at particular individuals and occupations, then problems surface. The motor of the whole system is supposed to be the occupational identity forged by the apprenticeship system (Heinz,1990). Yet for a number of occupations, such as baker, there are very many more training places than opportunities for skilled employment. The changing pattern of work has undermined the need for a full three-year apprenticeship to become a fully-competent worker in fields like retailing.

Other occupations, including construction, have largely neglected their systems of training in recent years. Critics point to the inflexibility of the dual system (Schmid and Baissert, 1988). It should be remembered that many of its systemic problems end up as problems for individuals, and increasing numbers (over 20%) do not complete their apprenticeships. Currently, there is concern about the operation of both systems of training. In Britain, there is concern about inadequate generic skill levels in the workforce, while in Germany the concern is how to reform and reinvigorate the dual system. In addition, both countries face the challenge of how to educate and train young people so that they can adapt to changes in role, organisation and working environment.

CHAPTER VII

Uncertain routes, diverse destinations

Introduction

So far our consideration of the education, employment and training of young people in both countries has given a relatively rosy picture. It is beneath the academic and skilled routes that there have traditionally been problems.

The composition of the samples from the German towns for this chapter's trajectory is shown in Table 7.1.

Table 7.1: Numbers in each type of German vocational school in trajectory III

	Paderborn	Bremen
Handelsschule	26	5
Voc. training institution	8	18
Special vocational schools	3	6
Hauptschule/Realschule	2	-
BGJ/voc. prep. courses	-	7

Note: The remaining individuals had either a mixed background or did not fit these dominant categories in other ways.

The majority in the Paderborn sample were in the *Handelsschule*, preparing for apprenticeships, whereas most respondents in the Bremen sample were in non-firm-based training. The samples from the British towns are roughly classified in Table 7.2

Table 7.2: Numbers in each type of training situation in trajectory III

	Swindon	Liverpool
Firm-based YTS (with few or no vocational qualifications)	7	7
Non-firm-based YTS	8	19
Job	18	12
Other education (school/college)	7	2

Those in Germany attending the specialised vocational schools might appear to match the British trajectory II respondents, who were also attending colleges full-time, most closely. The reason that the Germans were placed in trajectory III is that most of the specialised vocational schools were set up only because the dual system could not absorb all those who wished to enter it. They therefore existed as a lower status route and as a means of later entry into the dual system. Those following this route - predominantly girls - had often failed to win places in the dual system at age 16. For similar reasons, it was appropriate to place the BGJ alongside non-firm-based YTS. Both are often seen as a last resort after failure to gain access to the more attractive alternative of an apprenticeship in Germany and a job in Britain.

The labour markets of the towns from each country were very different, with the contrasts between Liverpool and Swindon being particularly marked. This was noticeable for young people on trajectories I and II, and was even clearer for those on III and IV. Where the labour market was as buoyant as in Swindon, it was sweeping up nearly all the available labour, including young people with low educational attainment. The impact of the local labour markets in Germany was less visible because the young people were still temporally quite a distance from full entry to them. Educational attainments at the age of 16 were facilitating easier access to different types of apprenticeship. However, those who were unsuccessful at this age could undertake further study and effect a later entry.

Other educational routes in Britain

Besides the routes available for those seeking higher education or qualifications associated with skilled employment, there were other opportunities for full-time education for 16 year-olds in Liverpool and Swindon. One option was to retake, or build upon, initial school-leaving qualifications (GCSEs, CSEs or O-levels). Sometimes this was to meet specific job-entry requirements, or to improve general employment prospects. In Swindon, the job situation meant that a decision to continue in education was likely to be beneficial. The paths of two respondents who stayed on to retake O-levels exemplified this. One had applied for an apprenticeship, had declined the YTS place offered instead, but did not apply for any other jobs. The other did not apply for an apprenticeship, job or YTS. Both were successful in gaining additional O-levels, but in the meantime their subsequent career aspirations to become a policeman and nurse respectively were modified, and the former went to work for an estate agent and the latter for a large building society. Both had then progressed in the first two years of their employment to estate agent negotiator in charge of a small office, and senior finance clerk. This again illustrates the willingness of Swindon employers to offer attractive employment to anyone demonstrating educational achievement.

In contrast, the weak job market in Liverpool meant that the choice at 16 was often between YTS or staying at school. For some, continuing education was passing time, but for others it had enhanced their employment prospects. Thus, one of the younger cohort who had passed one O-level at 16, had stayed on to retake some O-levels and CSEs without any clear idea of what she wanted to do. However, this strategy had been successful for another Liverpool respondent whose one additional O-level had helped him to secure employment with the Department of Health and Social Security, calculating other people's benefits.

An alternative to strengthening initial school qualifications was to undertake a programme of pre-vocational education (typically CPVE). This was very much a minority option in Swindon; those with decent academic attainments went straight into higher-level academic or vocational routes. Trying to recruit those with lower educational attainments onto pre-vocational programmes was often proving an unequal struggle in Swindon, against the attractions of employment at 16. Even among those recruited onto CPVE, some regarded it as a 'stop-gap'. Thus, one Swindon respondent left school with medium-grade CSEs, and applied for over 20 jobs (was offered two but declined them) before going to college to do CPVE. He left after two terms and, in rapid succession, did part-time work, YTS and then became an office junior. Whilst many young people in Liverpool could, and did, obtain additional qualifications, this strategy was less likely to be effective in terms of eventual labour market rewards than in Swindon (Roberts et al., 1989a). The young people themselves often recognised this and had applied for many jobs, but the depressed youth labour market had left them with few alternatives, probably none of which they had found very satisfactory. Overall, young people with moderate or low educational attainments at 16 in the depressed Liverpool labour market were faced with a long and uncertain road before staying on would pay any dividends in terms of enhanced job prospects.

This was also dependent upon them being successful on their courses; just staying in the education system was unlikely to improve their prospects. This was illustrated by another career from the Liverpool older cohort. The young woman had stayed at school to retake 16-plus qualifications and additional CSEs, then did a further year at college, gaining clerical vocational qualifications, before going into employment, but only on a temporary basis as a receptionist. In the more buoyant Swindon labour market, some case histories of trajectory II respondents showed that 'other' educational routes could be used as bridges to further and higher education, or skilled employment.

Experiences of German samples

In the German samples, educational and vocational training on this trajectory were part of the regular provisions for the age group. So, in both towns, there were a number of *Berufsfachschulen* (specialised vocational schools), *Fachoberschulen* and the *Berufsgrundbildungsjahr* (BGJ). In both samples, two general tendencies were revealed concerning the motivation of respondents in the *Fachschulen*. There were those with a genuine and long-standing interest, and those who regarded further full-time education as a temporary expedient before starting apprenticeships or entering higher education.

In the *Berufsfachschulen* (including *Handelsschulen*) in both towns, the students were more likely to display a deep interest in the occupations they were learning about. The course providers had to be contacted before the young people left school and, in some cases, the individuals had needed to make several applications, for example, for courses in nursing and kindergarten teaching. The practical training on such courses could vary. Nurses, for example, spent a substantial part of their time on wards, whereas physiotherapists were taught for two years and then worked for a probationary year in which they applied their knowledge. The numbers of *Berufsfachschulen* students in Bremen and Paderborn had remained stable in the late 1980s. The numbers had not been greatly influenced by the economic climate, and the *Berufsfachschulen* had continued to give students fairly good career prospects. This educational route could therefore be regarded as different, but in no way inferior, to the dual system. Both the education, training and the general prospects were often better than for apprentices.

The *Handelsschule* was divided into two standards: *Handelsschule* (one year with the possibility that this year could be credited towards an apprenticeship) and *Höhere Handelsschule* (two years).

The latter enabled pupils from the *Realschule* to gain higher education entry qualifications for special subjects, and theoretical commercial knowledge. Young people attending the *Höhere Handelsschule* were following the same strategy (to gain the highest possible school-leaving certificate) as those in trajectory I who wished to enter apprenticeships after completion of the *Abitur*. However, in comparison with their trajectory I counterparts, they hoped to broaden their chances in the labour market by early specialisation. As with the *Berufsfachschulen*, so the *Höhere Handelsschule* could not be regarded as below the apprenticeship route. However, some young people on this trajectory would have preferred to have entered apprenticeships directly.

The *Handelsschule* was preparing school-leavers for apprenticeships in particular trades. Attending such a school was not compulsory, but could help in the competition for apprenticeships. Others understood it as a time for vocational orientation or another chance to brush up on school-leaving certificates. In both towns, pupils had typically applied for apprenticeships first, and decided to attend the *Handelsschule* only when their applications were unsuccessful. Altogether nine respondents (out of 31) in the *Handelsschulen* had applied for apprenticeships before enrolling full time.

Access to higher education

The above commentary on both countries has focused upon other educational routes being used to gain access to further vocational education, training or employment. It is also worthwhile looking at a possible continuum through further education into higher education, even though few respondents were interested in such a follow-through.

In Germany, to enter higher education, a person would nearly always require the *Abitur*. If this was not obtained at the *Gymnasium*, then it needed to be acquired, for example, through the *Höhere Handelsschule* or in a modular form, by studying in the evenings. Up to now in Germany, there have been few access courses for mature students, though interest is increasing in the possibility of direct entry after completion of an apprenticeship, and preferably after at least two years' subsequent vocational experience. Both avenues, however, were being explored by only a few *Länder* and universities at the time of our research, and overall there was no perceived national shortage of entrants to higher education in Germany.

In contrast, there had been an expansion in the possible routes into higher education in Britain; by 1989 there were over 600 access courses. There was also rising interest in using vocational qualifications as a means of entry into higher education. The 1988 white paper (DE, 1988) explicitly urged higher education institutions to adopt more flexible entrance requirements.

Comparison of special schemes

The BGJ in Germany and non-firm-based YTS were broadly matched, because both types of schemes tended to attract those who had been unsuccessful elsewhere. Indeed, whatever the official views about the places of these schemes in education and training, in the eyes of most young people in both countries they were on 'schemes', and residual ones at that. However, in both countries, there were exceptions in fields such as electronics or IT, where some young people with quite high aspirations were happy to be on schemes, even though these were seldom their first preferences. This means, however, that it is advisable to treat the more technically-advanced schemes separately from the others.

Non-technical schemes: experiences of the German samples

The non-technical schemes were of greater significance in the depressed labour markets. The BGJ provided a one-year full-time course of practical and theoretical instruction in basic skills in an occupational area. The BGJ was originally introduced for young people who failed to obtain a school-leaving certificate and wished to obtain one, or for young women and men who wished

> 'to obtain a wider view of trade requirements in the field, allowing a more informed choice of a particular trade to be made at the end of the course' (Taylor, p. 340, 1981).

Indeed, part of the motivation for its introduction was an attempt to 'crack' the dual system and offer the possibility of a broader foundation.

BGJ took place in the *Berufsschule*, but unlike young people in the dual system, those on this scheme were in full-time education. The attempt to break at least partly the mould of the dual system had not worked in practice either in Paderborn or Bremen, for the vast majority of BGJ entrants had sought apprenticeships at 16 or 17, and only a few were using it as a genuine orientation phase. The declining numbers of participants in both towns, as more apprenticeships had become available, reinforces this point (Table 7.3). A young man in Bremen reported that he had planned to take the '*Fachabitur* examination' but this did not work out, because he had no vocational qualifications and as a way out had enrolled on the BGJ.

Table 7.3: Numbers enrolled in the BGJ

BGJ	1985	1986	1987	1988	
Bremen	761	594	531	378	50% decline
Paderborn	338	271	219	182	46% decline

Although the general education and training received in this kind of public education may have helped the students to cope with their unsatisfactory situations for the time being, the further qualification did not necessarily mean easier entrance to the labour market. As more people gained higher school-leaving certificates, employers correspondingly raised their entry requirements. BGJ provision could be expanded or contracted, depending on the state of the local labour market. There was neither direct pressure nor financial incentive to go on BGJ: young people had to choose it, even if reluctantly. However, there was indirect pressure, in that not to go on a BGJ, if a person was unable to get an apprenticeship immediately, meant that effectively he or she would be giving up all chance of one later. The careers of some respondents in trajectories II and IV show that some had used BGJ as a route into apprenticeships, while others had still failed to make this transition, even after completion of the BGJ.

The BGJ provision itself was invariably workshop-based, comprising a broad orientation to practical work in fields such as woodwork, metalwork, carpet-laying and catering. The education was much more practical than in the dual system, with perhaps two-thirds of the time being spent on practical activities, and just one-third on theoretical instruction. Indeed, unlike the dual system, with its often almost complete separation of theory and practice, the instructors and teachers in the BGJ worked closely together as teams. In both cities, BGJ was accepted as a means of keeping young people's hopes for apprenticeships alive, and improving their education if there were insufficient other opportunities. While the Paderborn youth labour market was healthier than in Bremen and Liverpool, it was not as buoyant as in Swindon. So 219 young people attended the BGJ in Paderborn in 1987, and the local unemployment figures showed that at the end of the year 42 people with BGJ were unemployed. Hence such schemes had some continuing relevance. In both Paderborn and Bremen, however, their real function was always as a 'holding pool', which was expanded in the mid-1980s, then contracted:

'the BGJ in school form is diminished in function to being an expanding holding pool for surplus, but aspirant, potential apprentices' (Russell, 1985).

Non-technical schemes: experiences of the British samples

Even some firm-based YTS schemes were difficult to fill in Swindon, and the non-firm-based YTS schemes, with the exception of the Information Technology Centre (ITEC), were not even considered by the vast majority of young people. Although quantitatively not very important, the two non-firm-based schemes did fulfil an important role, in that they took school-leavers requiring special support. The schemes also trained young people in occupational fields not covered by firm-based schemes. Thus, one Swindon respondent had chosen a non-firm-based scheme because it enabled her to work with horses. She was taking horse-management qualifications and wanted to become a qualified groom and point-to-point jockey.

The work with young people with learning difficulties was more significant. Such young people might have had difficulties when trying to get jobs, even in Swindon, and yet had been reluctant to stay in an educational system in which they had been conspicuously unsuccessful. Attention to basic literacy and numeracy, coupled with real or simulated work experience and help with job searching, could then assist the individuals to enter the labour market. Even then, the jobs themselves might be typical of trajectory IV. One young woman, after a short spell of unemployment, had become a nanny. Another, still on a scheme, wanted to become a sales assistant. Once again, as with other educational routes, the schemes operated quite successfully in Swindon, because they could offer trainees genuine expectations of jobs upon completion. In the depressed labour market of Liverpool, while valuable help might be given in improving basic skills, there was often little chance of the young people gaining employment at the end of such training, which severely compromised the value of the vocational preparation.

It has been argued (Roberts et al., 1989b) that despite the quality of some of the training on the schemes, the lack of subsequent employment and the likely return to unemployment means that most non-firm-based YTS must realistically be regarded as 'warehousing'. In Liverpool, it was probably the case that the majority of non-firm-based schemes were, in effect, warehousing measures. This can be inferred from official statistics, but what these do not reveal is the vehemence of the opposition and the feelings of exploitation of those on such schemes.

The Training Agency conducts a 100% follow-up on all YTS trainees in the year after they have left their schemes. In Liverpool, the cumulative figures for 1988 revealed that of the 5,107 respondents 2,268 (44%) were employed and 1,283 (25%) were unemployed. The employed figure, of course, would look less impressive if it did not include those who were already employed at the start of their YTS. When school-leavers had gone onto YTS in Liverpool without employee status, their schemes were unlikely to lead to employment. That 3,667 (71.8%) of the respondents said that they were satisfied with their training might be some compensation, but the hostility of those for whom YTS resulted in neither quality training nor enhanced job prospects was understandable. Let some trajectory III respondents themselves comment:

'I feel that young people today are being victimised by the government. They provide cheap labour for unscrupulous employers who have no intention of offering a job to the trainee. The government should set a limit on the number of YTS trainees they are allowed to take. Also, the schemes should be looked at and checked properly. Some of them are not providing proper training and the people employed on them are not really interested in the trainees. They are well paid while the trainee is on a pittance'.

'Since leaving school I have been on a couple of YTS schemes. On the most recent one I gained an RSA certificate in retail, but because there was not enough time during the year, I could not do the full course from which I would have obtained a diploma, even though I was top of my class and capable of completing the course. This made me feel that I had wasted my time putting in the effort to try to achieve something which I had no choice but to start in the first place, due to unemployment.'

Hostility was also expressed by some trajectory IV respondents who were particularly upset by YTS effectively having been made compulsory by recent (1988) changes in social security regulations. Even those who praised some aspects of the training were often resentful at the size of the training allowance.

'At the moment I feel very disillusioned with the electronics scheme I am on. It was not what I expected, as I thought a lot of audio and television repair would be involved. Also, some of my friends on the scheme have been disappointed with their placements, saying they were treated unfairly. On the whole, I believe schemes are good for experience, but I personally do not like them, money being a problem. I am losing some of my apathy which I had earlier on and am trying to think positively.'

We do not claim that YTS was uniformly poor, but rather that YTS in Liverpool in the period 1985-88 generated some fierce criticism among our respondents because, even where the training was of reasonable quality, this did not necessarily prevent a return to unemployment. Non-firm-based YTS in Liverpool was regarded by many young people as an inadequate substitute for employment, not as a pathway into it.

In both countries, firm-based training took precedence over other routes for young people who were not pursuing higher-level qualifications through education. In Britain, even firm-based training on YTS was often seen as an inadequate substitute for a job. There was a clear difference in the training cultures of the two countries, which became particularly manifest at the trajectory III level. In Germany, both employers and young people expected everyone to be involved in education or training at this age, whereas in Britain, neither group appeared fully convinced of the value of formal routes. Getting a job, then learning on-the-job, seemed to be regarded as the best option by many in both groups.

Technical schemes

In three of the towns it was possible to obtain non-firm-based training in electronics/IT, which was markedly more popular than the schemes discussed above. In Paderborn, rather than non-firm-based provision, Nixdorf ran a private vocational school, but only those who had already completed an apprenticeship were eligible for such training.

A place at the Swindon ITEC seemed well regarded by those who chose this option. Three of the Swindon sample had been to the ITEC. One was subsequently employed by the ITEC itself as a desk-top publisher, while another was working as an electronic assembler with the Ministry of Defence, testing and repairing avionics equipment, and hoped eventually to become an electronics technician. Both had achieved vocational qualifications and expected to continue working in electronics and IT. The former had originally wanted to be a computer operator and the ITEC had been a positive choice, while the latter had initially wanted to become a postman. The third ITEC trainee was less successful, in that after completing his course he was employed part-time on computer contract work for six months, saw few prospects and sought full-time employment. After one short spell in work and another unemployed, he was working in another temporary job at the time of our survey.

Places at the Liverpool ITECs seemed to be held in similar esteem, although the immediate job prospects were not as bright. One of the Liverpool sample was at an ITEC and had already obtained City and Guilds qualifications in electronics. He was ambitious, believing that the most important thing at work was to get ahead, and he ranked good career prospects, along with security and a friendly atmosphere at work, as the most important factors when choosing a job. He expected to be in an apprenticeship in a year's time. Before the ITEC course he had applied for five jobs. In Swindon, he would probably have entered the labour market directly from school. In Liverpool, however, the ITEC course was offering an opportunity to obtain additional qualifications which would, perhaps, ultimately result in him finding a more skilled occupation than he had originally aimed for.

This respondent was matched with one from Bremen who was currently on a BGJ scheme in electronics. The latter claimed to have a lot of experience of IT obtained at home, at school and on his course, and believed that this would be useful in the future. He expected to be in an apprenticeship in a year's time, and eventually wanted to attend university or *Fachhochschule*. He did not believe that it was very difficult for young people to get jobs in the area, and considered it very unlikely that he would move away, although he expressed dissatisfaction with the city. His main criteria for a good job were the chance to apply his own ideas, good prospects and a friendly atmosphere. He had very high self-esteem and was confident about the future.

Unsurprisingly, high-cost technical training in occupational areas where there are acknowledged skill shortages can sharply improve young people's prospects, even in depressed areas. However, it must be remembered that this tends to be very much a minority provision. For example, in Liverpool's non-firm-based YTS sector, over 95% of trainees were on non-technical schemes.

Training offering little progression or prospects

Among the criteria for inclusion in trajectory II was whether the young person was in firm-based training. In Germany, the operation of the dual system meant that individuals undergoing firm-based training could be confident of reaching skilled status. For some, however, training was playing 'second fiddle' to work, and for others it could be difficult to obtain jobs in the trades after completion, though just finishing an apprenticeship had some labour market utility, even if work was sought in a completely different sector. Employers often specified that applicants should have completed skilled training.

In Britain, firm-based training (under the YTS) was a less secure route, especially in Liverpool. Some schemes gave little genuine training and offered limited chances to obtain vocational qualifications. Many Liverpool respondents had found that firm-based training not only failed to lead to skilled status, but did not help them to secure any type of employment. Low-level vocational qualifications were likely to prove perishable if not quickly supplemented by further qualifications and/or a stable employment record. Overall then, completion of YTS itself did not necessarily confer any continuing value, as would completion of an apprenticeship in Germany. It is true that in certain occupational fields, and in a buoyant labour market, even modest training could launch a career, but in a depressed labour market, training that did not lead to substantial vocational qualifications had a very limited shelf-life. In contrast, all respondents in trajectory III in the German towns remained in the mainstream training system.

Table 7.4 shows that, as on other trajectories, the British respondents appeared to have been given greater responsibilities, more freedom to make decisions and to use their initiative. Also, they were much more likely to have worked as members of teams and to have met deadlines. This is hardly surprising, given that all but one of the British sample had experience of work either as employees or on YTS. This suggests that existing patterns of British vocational preparation were succeeding in developing the very types of skills which school-leavers have been criticised for lacking. It also suggests that the workplace can be a highly effective site for learning (Evans, Brown and Oates, 1987). Indeed, the only generally negative response to our questions on skill acquisition on trajectory III was in Liverpool, where a slight majority felt they had not been stretched or challenged. This time there were no clear general labour market differences within each country. For most experiences, each pair of towns was evenly matched.

Table 7.4: Numbers reporting work-related skills and experiences in trajectory III

Skills and experience	Liverpool		Bremen		Swindon		Pader-born	
	A	B	A	B	A	B	A	B
Been given responsibility	29	2	8	9	33	3	13	12
Been able to make decisions for oneself	27	3	11	11	36	1	15	13
Had a chance to use initiative	29	1	10	18	28	3	9	16
Developed new skills and abilities	26	5	20	7	27	4	17	11
Set own goals/targets	23	6	8	16	17	5	17	12
Felt stretched/challenged	17	8	13	14	15	7	17	14
Felt a sense of achievement	23	5	20	2	25	3	18	6
Felt all abilities were being used	20	4	15	11	20	8	17	9
Worked as a member of a team	29	4	11	22	32	3	8	18
Had to work to a deadline	19	12	13	19	22	9	14	15
Been asked by others on how to tackle a problem	24	5	7	10	21	19	11	6

Note: (1) A = Often

B = Seldom or never

(2) Total number in each cell = 40

Clearly, the British young people themselves felt adequately equipped for the jobs they were performing. Whether those performing skilled work would have benefited from fuller and more thorough training raises wider issues about accreditation, quality and job content. Nevertheless, their training was perceived by them as adequate for their current jobs, whereas there appeared to be some serious problems in Germany. There young people were having specific skills developed which generated a sense of achievement, but in sheltered situations which did not require responsibility, initiative, being challenged or operating as a member of a team. This did not apply only on trajectory III: the Anglo-German comparisons among respondents on trajectories I and II were also adverse, though less markedly so (for Germany), along these dimensions. The time horizons of trajectory III respondents in both countries appeared very short: success was seen as getting a job in Britain, and getting into firm-based training in Germany.

Acceptability of on-the-job acquisition of skills

The different approaches to vocational preparation in Britain and Germany are, perhaps, best illustrated by respondents who were either performing, or in the process of completing transitions to, skilled employment, but who were placed in different trajectories because they were achieving significant vocational qualifications in Germany but not in Britain. Thus, in Paderborn, a fitter on a building site was expecting to complete his apprenticeship and become qualified after finishing his time in the dual system, but he needed to pass the appropriate examination before he could claim skilled status. In contrast, a Swindon respondent had been employed as a carpenter by a building contractor. He worked in the carpentry shop but did not attend college, nor had he any vocational qualifications. Instead, his learning was entirely on-the-job, with his tasks and responsibilities gradually being extended as he worked on first and second fixes. He earned £100 per week at the time of our survey and described himself as a carpenter, without any indication of having a junior designation, such as trainee. His employer recognised him as a carpenter and presumably with just a little more experience he would be acceptable to many other employers.

Some British respondents who had pursued vocational qualifications had achieved only fairly basic ones, which stopped well short of the fully-skilled level. For a large number of manual and non-manual jobs, the expectations were unclear, with established practitioners holding a wide range of qualifications, from none to full craft or technician certificates. Thus, a young Liverpudlian with a basic City and Guilds qualification in painting and decorating who had learnt his trade with a previous employer, regarded himself as a skilled painter and decorator: given that many painters and decorators do not have any qualifications, he was formally better qualified than many. Another example was a Swindon respondent who was working as an estate agent in charge of a small office, although he had no vocational qualifications. The idea of so many people being allowed to trade in such circumstances, and there being no bar upon anyone setting up as a plumber, estate agent or carpenter, would be an anathema in the more formal and regulated German system.

The German system prescribes a much fuller off-the-job educational component, and workplace training is likely to be formalised, with apprentices working under the supervision of a *Meister* who is qualified in both the technical and training spheres. There is little possibility of the ad hoc acquisition of skills on-the-job or elsewhere being recognised, unless the individual subsequently obtains the requisite vocational qualifications. There is normally no possibility of acquiring de facto skilled status as in Britain.

Changes of career direction

Descriptions of national systems often assume a degree of rationality and a clear sense of vocational direction on the parts of individuals, which sometimes does not accord with the experiences of the young people themselves. Both the British and German systems were trying to cater for uncertainty although, in practice, relatively few young people were using the opportunities for the explicit orientation or sampling that was supposed to be available in programmes such as CPVE or BGJ, because these provisions were generally seen as less preferable to other routes. Neither system seemed to make much allowance for young people changing their minds after they had started down particular paths. However, the biographies of individuals in all four towns showed that some had changed their minds after experience of the work itself, or the associated education and training.

Entry into semi-skilled employment

In Germany, the effective absence of youth jobs means that entry to semi-skilled employment is normally in adulthood. Large employers offering permanent and well-paid semi-skilled employment may insist that such vacancies are filled only by those who have completed apprenticeships. For example, Daimler-Benz in Bremen had adopted this policy in recruiting production-line workers. The apprenticeship did not have to be in a relevant trade. The line of argument of such employers is that they can give the specific training required, but are looking for people who have demonstrated perseverance and a 'willingness to learn'. The employer is then confident that the workers will have the flexibility and adaptability not only to retrain as required, but also to respond constructively if unexpected problems arise. The hiring of only 'quality' labour also helps to guarantee that other internal labour requirements can be met: for example, by those who want to go on to become supervisors or to specialise in other ways. Such jobs with large employers are likely to be filled by individuals who have completed apprenticeships in other trades, most likely in those trades and with those firms where the trainees have few prospects of being kept on. Individuals who drop out of apprenticeships may also seek such work, but they are likely to have to settle for less well-paid and secure employment, often with smaller companies. Large employers, therefore, support the dual system, not only by offering high-quality and much-prized apprenticeships as a means of entry to skilled employment, but also through their recruitment policies for semi-skilled workers. This clearly adds to the labour market value of successfully completing an apprenticeship, and rein-forces the commitment of employers and young people to training.

The situation in Britain is radically different. For a start, the line between semi-skilled and skilled work can be hazy, with the possi-bility of people just gradually working their way through the barrier. Employment with some recognised skill content, but not requiring qualifications, and with few prospects of access to further education and training, as in low-level manual and clerical work, made up the majority of youth jobs in Britain prior to the mid-1970s. The changing pattern of demand for labour following the economic recession, meant that the market for such youth jobs never fully recovered. This was allied to an increase in the numbers of young people in the 1980s and the widespread introduction of YTS. The net result was that, in depressed areas like Liverpool, the chances of young people getting non-skilled employment were greatly reduced. Where they still man-aged to obtain such jobs at the time of our research, the major means of entry seemed to be through YTS. In contrast, the Swindon labour market was so buoyant that a return to the pre-1970s' model of youth jobs, with limited opportunities for further training, seemed possible.

Let us examine some actual transitions to semi-skilled employ-ment in Liverpool and Swindon. In the latter town one young woman had wanted to become a supervisor in a large office. She obtained five O-levels, then stayed on to study for one A-level (which she did not pass), plus Stage 1 typing. She then started a low-level clerical job, but had since switched employers to become a debt recovery assistant with a large fuel card company. The money was quite good (£87 per week), and it was for this reason that she had switched jobs. She still wanted to be an office supervisor, and claimed a lot of IT experience at work. This case exemplifies some of the difficulties Britain will face in trying to establish a training culture. The employer was willing to pay a good wage to recruit the labour needed, and the individual, although ambitious, did not see any need for further train-ing. She believed that her initial education and, more importantly, her experience at work, would enable her to move into a supervisory position. In exactly the same vein, another young person had started work in a building suppliers. Without any formal training or further education, he had since progressed to become warehouse and contracts assistant manager, earning £113 per week. His lack of formal qualifications seemed unlikely to bar further progress. Such success stories constantly reinforce the view that opportunities for a smart young person do not need to include further education and training: keenness and a willingness to learn on-the-job will suffice. Not all the British respondents in semi-skilled jobs had career opportunities with their existing employers. However, the current rewards (£83 per week for a pharmacy dispensing assistant; £93 per week for a data-control clerk inputting data on VDUs for a large bookseller; £115 per week for an industrial cleaner on contract work) meant that there was no pressure or apparent need to undertake further education or training. Another young Swindon woman had initially started a firm-based YTS hairdressing apprenticeship, but had left to become sales co-ordinator with a small manufacturing company. She had worked there for two years, earned £115 per week, and was actively seeking other work at the time of our research. She wanted to become a sales representative, and was confident that her employment experience would get her such a job.

Conclusion

Those in trajectories I and II have generally quite high educational attainment, which has been used as a platform for launching skilled or professional careers. Those in trajectories III and IV generally have lower educational attainment, and this is where labour market differences become most marked. There are a number of exceptions, however: in Germany the dual system discriminates in favour of boys, even though they have, on the whole, not reached the attainment level of girls. Also, some specialist training in Germany takes place outside the dual system, even though this requires high educational attainment. Overall, however, with the exception of Swindon, where jobs were easily obtained, most youngsters in this trajectory were seeking to enter the formal employment and training structures. For those on non-technical schemes, this was often a vain hope.

The systemic weaknesses and relative lack of commitment to education and training in Britain, are well illustrated by the experience of both Liverpool and Swindon youngsters. Liverpool youngsters were often well equipped to carry out jobs for which they had some experience, but for which permanent vacancies did not exist or were very scarce. By contrast, the Swindon experience showed the dangers of a resurgence of jobs without training. Such an analysis applied both to purely educational routes, or to those based on YTS. In Liverpool, both could be seen as 'warehousing', rather than greatly increasing youngsters' employment chances, whereas in Swindon they were more likely to be temporary bridges into employment, with little prospect of further education and training.

The prospects of German youngsters in this trajectory, excepting those seeking specialist qualifications, were dominated by the dual system. Whether on educational routes in the *Handelsschule,* or on non-technical schemes such as BGJ, the intention was invariably to get an apprenticeship. Indeed, many had already tried, and the scheme was a less-preferred alternative. Such schemes were innovative and had entertained great hopes for effecting a reformation of the dual system but, in practice, they had become effectively 'holding pools', the size of which were directly related to the state of the labour market. Youngsters' hopes of an apprenticeship were kept alive, and while seldom being employers' first choice, they did still have a realistic chance of entering the dual system (unlike their trajectory IV contemporaries on remedial schemes and measures). The opportunities, however, were likely to come in occupational areas where the long-term prospects were not very bright.

The experiences of German youngsters in this trajectory seemed relatively impoverished, in contrast either with those in trajectories I and II, or with their British counterparts, who had much more experience of 'real' work. Doubts are raised about the adequacy of both systems of vocational preparation for this group of young people. Both are, perhaps, too narrow, and the very emphasis on specific vocational preparation makes their experiences 'perishable' if the transition to employment is not speedily accomplished. The two systems are probably at their most divergent in their treatment of on-the-job acquisition of skills. Indeed, the formality of one system, and the lack of regulation in the other, sometimes lead to almost mutual disbelief from those looking at each other's systems.

Both systems need then to breathe new life into firm-based training, such that it facilitates the development of youngsters' flexibility and adaptability. They need to avoid locking youngsters into firm-specific labour markets and give more attention to the development of generic, as opposed to job-specific, skills.

CHAPTER VIII

Routes to nowhere?

Introduction

Youth unemployment was a major problem in the 1980s for both Britain and Germany. Despite the introduction of training schemes, profound imbalances between supply and demand for labour in parts of both countries meant that many young people had great difficulty in gaining any place in their workforces. Those trying to survive outside formal education and employment, however, had a number of alternatives. These included peripheral employment (seasonal or other temporary or casual work), and part-time work. Some who succeeded in gaining regular employment were trapped in unskilled work with little access to training opportunities. Our trajectory IV samples comprised seven distinguishable groups whose common problem was that their situations seemed to amount to 'routes to nowhere'. These situations were:

- permanent unskilled employment, with little or no access to training;
- peripheral work, usually with periods of unemployment and/or on remedial schemes;
- remedial schemes;
- domestic careers;
- part-time employment;
- the armed forces;
- long-term unemployment.

The members of these groups did not match one another in the two countries because of fundamental structural differences. Thus, certain groups were almost exclusively German and others exclusively

British. In both German samples, most respondents on this trajectory were on some kind of scheme. They had either gone straight into the schemes after leaving school, or had gained some experience of work and unemployment before they were sent onto schemes by the *Arbeitsamt* (employment office), or had asked to be enrolled. The British samples on this trajectory were on a wider variety of routes to nowhere.

Permanent unskilled employment with little or no access to training

There were only a few examples of German respondents in full-time jobs that did not require any vocational qualifications, and all were from the older cohort. It was practically impossible to opt out of education and training completely in Germany before age 19. The unskilled jobs were mainly in small firms, because larger companies usually provided opportunities for training even if, in practice, these were not always taken up. One German example was a female from the older cohort in Paderborn, who had started work in her mother's cigarette shop. Hence, this particular sub-group was almost entirely British. And the lack of job opportunities for 16 year-olds in Liverpool meant that only in Swindon was unskilled work a significant option. A small number in the Liverpool sample had, however, managed to obtain unskilled jobs at 16. Many of these jobs had poor prospects, and the pay, conditions and general duties were often not considered very desirable. These young people were hanging on, in some cases rather grimly, because at least they had jobs. One worked as a machinist in a cushion cover factory 'overlocking cushion covers and making tea', while another had worked as a pub kitchen worker for two years, although she hated almost everything about it.

'I don't like my job because my bosses have their daughters there working. It is too far to travel...the atmosphere is horrible. The money is very low. I work nights and days...If I did leave, I would have to wait 13 weeks for the dole. When I was at school I was going to go

139

on a YTS in the summer, then go back to sixth form. But I was offered a full-time job in the summer, so I took this job, and I never stayed on at school. Now I am sorry that I never stayed on.'

Others, working as junior labourers on building sites and sales assistants in shops, were more sanguine. One of the younger cohort had started work in a fireplace manufacturing firm and, although initially given the most routine tasks in the building and painting of fire surrounds, he hoped eventually to become a joiner. He was one of the very few who looked as though they might make the transition to trajectory III-type employment. Only a minority in Liverpool on trajectory IV looked as though they would have opportunities even for regular unskilled employment.

There were, in contrast, many such jobs in Swindon. One large company always seemed to have vacancies for labour to perform routine short-time cycle tasks on assembly and packing. The work was not only seen as boring, but also poorly paid. 'This is the lowest-paid company (wages-wise) in Swindon. They have so many workers come and go, men included, for better-paid jobs.' The same worker was thinking 'of applying for a different job ... packing, masking and spraying bumpers and car body panels'. Three of the young mothers in the sample had found employment: it was easy to get such a job there even without qualifications. Such work, in practice, was mainly done by women and, despite the high wages paid in a number of Swindon factories, one respondent was unequivocal: 'factory work in Swindon for women is poorly paid'. Another person at the same factory was equally disconsolate: 'I think the government should select a few people to pose as employees to assess whether the wages are fair or not'. There were similar examples of young women in Liverpool in factory jobs and supermarkets. The jobs were modestly paid, lacking in prospects and security as well, in many cases. Thus, one older cohort respondent had lost her job as a checkout operator after having held it for three years since leaving school.

Some young workers seemed quite content to have found what they hoped would be permanent unskilled employment. The lack of training and prospects was not considered a problem. Many of the unemployed regarded such jobs as enviable. One Swindon respondent worked as an extrusion operator making rolls of polythene for plastic bags and, although he had little prospect of progression, he felt some of the skills he had learnt outside work could have vocational value. 'Experience of fixing electrical gadgets around the home like radios, irons and razors could be useful in an electrical trade.' However, one Swindon respondent in such a position gave a cri de coeur about his lack of training opportunities.

> 'I would like to see more companies offer training for those without O- and A-levels. As long as you have the determination and confidence and are willing to learn I don't see where the A- and O-levels come into it. Also, there is training for the unemployed but it seems to be just for them. Why can't employed people go for it as well?'

This individual was a solitary, but classic, example of a young person trapped in a job without training. He had left school without qualifications in 1985, worked during the summer and then had a spell of unemployment before starting work at the beginning of 1986 as a guillotine operator cutting paper for a medium-size local firm which made pocket files. He had applied for about a dozen jobs after leaving school, but did not apply for YTS, although he did seek an apprenticeship as a painter and decorator. He was dissatisfied with his present position and had applied for some seven jobs in the last six months. He felt that his present job did not stretch him in any way, did not use all his abilities nor gave him any chance to employ initiative. At the same time he felt that 'it is important to hang onto a job even if you don't really like it'. He believed that good career prospects were one of the most important criteria in a job, was very dissatisfied with the education he had received and felt that his lack of qualifications was hindering his prospects of training for a more interesting job. He doubted whether he would have the kind of job he wanted in 10 years' time, but was confident that he would avoid unemployment and would never be dismissed from a job because of unsatisfactory work.

Peripheral workers

Some respondents had obtained peripheral employment on a seasonal, temporary or casual basis. Examples included window-cleaning and working on a market stall. Attempts to draw precise boundaries around these jobs were unnecessary, because the young people's careers clearly signalled the attributes of such employment. A peripheral employment career was, perhaps, of greatest significance as a means of economic survival in the depressed labour markets of Liverpool and Bremen.

The young people on trajectory IV in the Bremen sample were drawn primarily from an ABM scheme seeking to integrate vocational and basic skills. Although some respondents had entered the scheme straight from school or unemployment, with no work experience, others had initially been successful in finding apprenticeships. Thus, six of the Bremen sample had dropped out of apprenticeships and ended up on the scheme. One young man had managed to find several occasional jobs after leaving school, but all were short-lived. Although the young people on the scheme often hoped to obtain further apprenticeships, their initial experiences in training or employment had made them less optimistic than those entering the scheme straight from school. Those who did not remain in training or education were likely to end up on the scheme at some stage. Their pessimism appeared realistic, in that their prospects looked fairly bleak, even upon completing the scheme. The combination of initial instability and time spent on the scheme meant that they were unlikely to obtain apprenticeships and, without such training, many other employment avenues would remain closed. In the depressed labour market of Bremen they looked as though they would always struggle to obtain more than peripheral work.

Young people in Swindon had more opportunity to obtain peripheral work, and the availability of such jobs meant that few had been
unemployed continuously for long spells. The existence of temporary
or seasonal work usually offered some respite. But, although this
could break up long-term unemployment, it rarely offered a route
into more stable jobs. Thus, when a trainee paint-sprayer was made
redundant during his first year at work, this was followed in the next
three years by four spells of unemployment, interspersed with three
periods in full-time employment. None of these were core jobs, and
while the spells of unemployment might not have constituted a major
problem in themselves, they represented a 'drift' where the young
person, once out of regular employment, was finding it difficult to
effect a return. Indeed, the development of a poor employment record could itself operate as a powerful barrier to gaining permanent
employment. This was poignantly expressed by another Swindon respondent, who had applied for numerous jobs and held moderate
job hopes of becoming a warehouse worker, but had found that 'once
employers know my unemployment record they don't want to know
any more about me'. However, the Swindon labour market was open
and strong enough to allow speedy recovery for some who lost their
jobs or were made redundant. After initial instability, being sacked,
then made redundant, and following a short spell of unemployment,
one Swindon respondent had become a central records administrator
with a large car fleet management company. The decisive factors here
were probably the individual's educational attainment (O-levels) and
that the spell of unemployment was brief. Two other Swindon cases
had each spent two years in post-compulsory education, one retaking
O-levels, the other a low-level commercial qualification. The former
then became unemployed for a spell, found a job, but was made
redundant, then found another job as an office junior in a firm of
solicitors. The second also had a spell of unemployment before settling in a job as a garage forecourt cashier.

As time spent unemployed lengthened, so a shift seemed to occur
from being regarded as the victim of misfortune such as redundancy,

to being seen as defective, which then acted as a bar to core employment. This attitude was sometimes expressed by young people in jobs. For example, an apprentice toolmaker was notably unsympathetic:

'there is absolutely no excuse for anyone in Swindon who is unemployed. If they say they cannot get a job they are either not trying or are unemployable, due to health or a criminal record'.

There were opportunities in Swindon to recover from set-backs, but individuals with few, if any, qualifications needed to do so quickly if they were not to be marginalised. As unemployment records lengthened, such young people were deemed unsuitable for core employment, although they could be taken on for short-term jobs, such as seasonal work at a local cake and pie factory. Employers seemed to prefer other methods (employment of part-timers, especially on evening mini-shifts, or temporary workers) to going below their 'bottom line' in the search for core workers.

A similar picture was apparent in Paderborn, where unemployed young people, including those dropping out of apprenticeships, were likely to be placed on a scheme (*Arbeiten und Lernen*; LVE; BVJ;). The schemes seldom did much to enhance the trainees' attractiveness to employers, although they could improve the young people's basic education. A number of older cohort respondents on such schemes had no long-term plans, just seeing the schemes as temporary while waiting for jobs. Others maintained hopes of obtaining apprenticeships, although being on low status schemes, especially if coupled with a previously unstable employment record or spells of unemployment, greatly reduced their chances of being offered such opportunities. The schemes themselves were identified with those having problems with their education or employment. Subsequent hiring judgements were often made on the basis of generalisations about the 'quality' of the young people entering, not what particular individuals were achieving on the schemes.

In the Paderborn sample, many respondents were on the *Arbeiten und Lernen* scheme, which was set up to provide young people with some general education (in mathematics and German for example) and work experience. They worked for the local Council, repairing property, gardening, restoring footpaths, and so on. During workshop hours, the participants were instructed by *Meister*, and by teachers and social workers during schooling periods. Most entrants had unstable careers at school and had left without any school-leaving certificate. Despite this disadvantage, they had managed to find apprenticeships or jobs. Indeed, all participants from the scheme in our sample had some work experience, but most had dropped out and all had been unemployed for at least three months. Strikingly, the occupational fields in which they had started apprenticeships were limited to areas with shortages of applicants, such as cook, baker, builder. A young woman from Paderborn recalled that

'it was difficult to find something. I wrote applications, made visits, yes, some contacted me and turned me down, others did not even respond. At school they advised me to go to the bakery. There I worked for a trial period and then started the apprenticeship'.

A young man on the scheme reported similar experiences. After he had been to the employment office, which gave him the address of a bakery in his neighbourhood, he worked for a trial period and was taken on afterwards. Both gave up their apprenticeships after short periods because they were 'fed up' with the early starts in the mornings and with the work itself. The young man left the bakery after two weeks because

'I had to do all the work nobody else wanted to do. One Saturday, for example, I had to clean the bakery all on my own although the *Meister* was there. That was enough'.

Another respondent reported that, after leaving the *Hauptschule*, he worked for some 15 months and during that time gave up two apprenticeships (joiner and painter), because of health problems.

On the whole, the respondents on the scheme had problems sticking to a daily routine. Additionally, their inability to cope with domestic issues involving parents and friends sometimes led to them staying off work without permission. Employers did not show the kind of understanding and support that these young people needed. Although the scheme rules were rigid and the participants had to stick to a daily routine, the scheme offered a counselling service. On this scheme the young people earned roughly DM 834, plus social security contributions. Compared with the apprenticeship allowances they had received previously (joiner DM 443 in the first year), this usually represented financial progress. But this progress was short-term, as their long-term prospects were poor. The scheme's connections with local employers enabled the young people to learn about available jobs and apprenticeships, and increased the chances that they would be recruited, albeit nearly always into unskilled jobs.

In 1989 the *Arbeiten und Lernen* scheme had 62 participants, of whom 12 left during that year or were sacked, while 35 entered the labour market. Three months later, 26 were still in work and three out of the nine who had left their first employers had already found new jobs. When these young people left the scheme, they had reached an age when schooling or vocational training were no longer compulsory. Most took unskilled jobs; we identified only two who had started apprenticeships. Few had further training aspirations. Some follow-up interviews of respondents after they had left this scheme showed that the reasons why they failed in the jobs had not changed from the time before the scheme. Assessing the reasons for failure, the social workers had concluded that in addition to domestic problems, the young people missed the counselling and understanding available on the scheme. A young woman did not become unemployed immediately after the scheme because the social workers helped her to obtain a job as a 'washing-up lady' in a large supermarket. After two days she handed in her notice because of severe back pain but, on talking to the social workers, she explained that her real reason for leaving was that she felt lonely in the supermarket. Another young woman became employed in a shoe shop as a storehand. She enjoyed the job and the employer was satisfied with her work, but when she heard over the 'phone that her forthcoming engagement would not take place, she left the shop without permission and was sacked. A young man who had acquired many skills and displayed great reliability during the scheme found a job in the metal industry, but could not cope with the stress of shift and piecework, and frequently had days off because he did not feel well. He was sacked, and for three months was not entitled to social benefits.

This scheme was helping young people to learn about job vacancies and was giving them time for personal development and to mature. Overall, there appeared to be three sets of typical 'careers' for those joining the *Arbeiten und Lernen* scheme. One set involved those who left or were sacked by the scheme. Failure here, coupled with previous unemployment or employment failures, virtually guaranteed that the young people would find it difficult to obtain any regular employment. The second type of career was for young people to whom the scheme represented time for personal development and who returned successfully to the labour market, only to struggle again without the counselling and extra social support that they received while on the scheme.

These were, perhaps, peripheral workers in a literal sense; they needed sheltered niches in the labour market. The third set comprised those who managed to go on to secure and retain employment, but this was overwhelmingly unskilled work. Thus, even the successes of the scheme in employment terms were likely to be left on the margins of the employment structure, and this was in a town with a fairly buoyant labour market. Table 8.1 shows how difficult it was to get back onto a skilled track (about 16% overall) from schemes in Paderborn (remember that the jobs invariably refer to unskilled jobs).

Table 8.1: Participation and follow-ups from schemes, October 1987 - September 1988

	1	2	3	4	5	6	Total	%
Apprenticeship	8	9	18	14	7	21	77 =	13.3
Voc. schools	-	5	-	2	1	11	19 =	3.3
Job	27	38	6	2	12	42	127 =	22.0
Continue scheme	-	-	-	2	13	-	15 =	2.6
Other scheme	22	29	-	-	1	44	96 =	16.6
Dropout	10	36	1	-	1	41	89 =	15.4
Other	-	25	3	2	13	21	64 =	11.1
Still looking	7	3	3	28	26	24	91 =	15.7
Total of participants	**93**	**170**	**31**	**25**	**55**	**204**	**578 =**	**100**

Key to Table 8.1

1. *Arbeiten und Lernen;*
2. *Lehrgang zum nachträglichen Erwerb des Hauptschulabschlusses;*
3. *Grundausbildungslehrgang;*
4. *Förderungs-*
5. *und Eingliederungsmassnahmen;*
6. *Vermittlung/Erweiterung beruflicher Kenntnisse.*

Source: Arbeitsamt Paderborn, 1988.

The supremacy of firm-based training itself was creating barriers for those following other routes in Germany. The difficulties that some trades were experiencing in recruiting apprentices meant that there was at least the possibility in Paderborn of recovery onto the more prestigious route, though entry into the labour market proper could remain difficult for those trained in trades with few long-term opportunities. For those who had accepted that they would not become skilled, and who were simply looking forward to having some kind of job, time spent on the schemes reinforced their exclusion from the mainstream. The comprehensiveness of education and training in Germany meant that those who remained outside were relatively more disadvantaged than their British counterparts. While relatively few remained outside the formal system after leaving school, the numbers dropping out of apprenticeships could be as high as 20% in unpopular trades. Although many dropouts entertained hopes of a return via further apprenticeships, they were more likely to end up on trajectory IV. They were peripheral workers in the making.

In both countries, even in buoyant labour markets, young people with poor educational achievements or unstable initial employment records were often struggling to gain reasonably secure employment. Many seemed destined to be continually vulnerable: unskilled, unqualified, subject to periodic unemployment and with employment opportunities which were likely to be limited in both type (very routine work) and duration (contract, temporary, part-time). The problems in Bremen and Liverpool were obviously much more acute, but the existence of young peripheral or marginal workers in Swindon and Paderborn is significant. This clearly signals that demographic change and economic growth will not resolve all the problems associated with youth unemployment.

Remedial schemes

In Britain, the schemes which were most likely to undertake basic skills education were non-technical non-firm-based YTS. However, the prime emphasis on these schemes was training. In some cases, this was little more than a convenient fiction, but Swindon and Liverpool did not possess a clear remedial educational route. This sub-category, therefore, is exclusively German.

In Bremen and Paderborn, young people who failed to reach the school-leaving certificate standard had to remain in full-time education. An additional year could then be spent at the *Hauptschule* or on a remedial scheme. Thus, two Paderborn respondents had left *Hauptschule* without the school-leaving certificate, and had enrolled on a vocational preparation scheme where they could earn the required certificate. In addition, they hoped that this would increase their chances of apprenticeships. However, even some who left secondary education with leaving certificates had chosen to enter the vocational preparation scheme, which was largely remedial in character. These choices were usually made after failure to get apprenticeships. Also, as we saw in the preceding section, some young people could end up on schemes after dropping out of apprenticeships.

The schemes were attempting to provide a grounding in specific vocational skills as well as teaching literacy, numeracy and job-finding, including filling in application forms. The essentially remedial character of all of them arose from the fact that the skills were being developed to increase the young people's chances of entering the dual system. Occasionally, in some occupational areas such as clerical, young people with higher school-leaving certificates enrolled on such schemes. Thus, in Bremen, three individuals joined an ABM scheme with certificates from *Realschule* or *Handelsschule*. Once again, however, this was after failing to gain apprenticeships. Another young person had started, but had not completed, *Handelsschule* and she too ended up on the scheme. Both towns had ABM schemes. These sought to integrate the teaching of basic and vocational skills. Young people could obtain experience of work in practical trades, such as metalwork, woodwork, painting and upholstery. In contrast to those who entered the ABM schemes after unemployment, and who were mostly realistic about their slim chances of gaining apprenticeships, the majority of the school-leaver entrants expected to proceed to apprenticeships after the schemes finished. Such ideas were perhaps not very realistic, but the young people were still hoping. Those who already had some work experience were generally looking for full-time employment. Overall, young people were likely to end up on remedial schemes only if they could not obtain apprenticeships. To British eyes, it may seem harsh to label these schemes as remedial, because some of the trainees had performed quite well at school and certainly had no major gaps in their basic skills. They had simply failed to obtain apprenticeships. However, the centrality of the dual system meant that being unable to enter was seen as a failing which required a remedy.

Domestic careers

All the towns' samples included individuals either following, or soon intending to embark on, domestic careers comprising childcare and housework, sometimes in combination with paid employment. One domestic avenue was looking after other people's children. This seemed to exert some appeal in all towns. In Bremen, one of the younger cohort females was in a G3 clerical branch and expected to be in non-firm-based training in a year's time, but subsequently wanted to be a childminder. In both British towns, some young mothers who were not working would have liked to be childminders as a means of combining their own domestic responsibilities with earning money. In Swindon, one of the younger cohort had been unemployed for nine months, but was working three days a week as a childminder at the time of our survey, though longer term she wanted to be a photographer. Another Swindon respondent was working full-time as a nanny.

Significant domestic responsibilities, even parenthood at a very young age, did not automatically put a respondent into trajectory IV. In practice, however, if having a baby took a young woman out of the labour market for any significant length of time, it could become difficult to get any job in Liverpool, or anything other than trajectory IV-type employment in Swindon. In the latter town, a couple of younger cohort mothers were looking after their children without any immediate intention of seeking work. Both had been unemployed for months before the birth of their children. Similarly, in the older cohort, two young mothers had spent most of the last two years looking after their children. One had previously been unemployed, but hoped within a year to have taken up some part-time work. The other had been on the YTS prior to the birth of her daughter, and had occasionally undertaken some part-time work, even though domestic responsibilities had subsequently predominated. She expected to be in full-time work within the next year, probably as a warehouse worker. The opportunities for factory and retail employment, both full- and part-time, guaranteed that in Swindon return to employment following a domestic career would be easy to effect. Mini-shifts, including twilight ones, were run with the explicit intention of recruiting women with domestic responsibilities. However, as one Swindon female indicated, choice could be nominal, because of financial constraints. She had a young baby and did some part-time work in a shop, although ideally she would have liked a full-time job. Jobs in Swindon were not all that hard to find but

> 'I have a baby, and if I get a job it is normally very low pay, so it is not worth me working after I have paid for a childminder. I would also lose my social benefits. Or the job would be on shifts or hours that wouldn't suit me. I think there should be more to help young mothers [jobwise]'.

None of the young mothers in any of the samples had stable skilled employment. Those with employment experience had, without exception, been doing either temporary or unskilled work. There was no evidence of domestic responsibilities interrupting progress to higher trajectories, but rather of young motherhood's association with already being on a lower trajectory.

Part-time employment

In Britain, part-time employment has been mainly the preserve of married women (Ashton and Maguire, 1983). We saw in the previous section that some young mothers undertook, or were looking for, part-time work. The explosion of part-time employment in the 1980s led to some school-leavers taking such jobs after failing to obtain full-time employment. However, the take-up was less than might have been expected, partly because employers refused even to consider 16-17 year-olds for many part-time jobs (Roberts et al., 1987). In our study, just four respondents in the British samples held part-time jobs: cleaning hospital wards, working as a barmaid, sales assistant in a do-it-yourself store, and in a kitchen making pub lunches. Such part-time work was mostly a matter of expediency in the absence of full-time ei..ployment in Liverpool, whereas in Swindon it was more likely to have been from choice. The cases of part-time employment in Swindon consisted of one female who worked three days per week as a childminder, and three others who coupled part-time work with bringing up their own children. Dale (1989) has argued that one reason why employers prefer to employ part-time those who have another source of income, such as women with working husbands, is in tacit recognition that the work is usually unskilled, poorly paid and with few or no prospects.

In Germany, no-one in either town was engaged in part-time work as their most significant activity. The usual expectation about being in education or training acted to bar the young people from part-time jobs, except alongside study.

The armed forces

Britain abandoned conscription at the end of the 1950s, but in Germany, at the time of our research, all adult males still had to perform national service in the armed forces, or alternative service in the community. It was also possible for young people in both countries to join the regular armed services, but only a handful in our samples were choosing this without first achieving vocational or higher education qualifications. As with those engaged in domestic careers, in Britain there was no prima facie reason why joining the armed forces could not be part of a higher trajectory career. Indeed, one trajectory I respondent in Swindon wanted to join the Royal Navy, while one from Liverpool, currently studying at university, aimed to become an army officer. Interestingly, two Liverpool trajectory III respondents advocated the value of military life for young people. One apprentice joiner said:

'I think they should bring back national service. Straight out of school and into the army for 12 months would teach them discipline and respect'.

The other saw the army as an escape route:

'I joined the army when I left school knowing that otherwise there weren't many job prospects...Now I feel totally secure and know that I've got a job for the rest of my life. I think that any young person who can't get a job should at least give the army a chance'.

However, a number of trajectory IV young people wanted to join, or had already entered, the armed forces in both British areas. One in Swindon had held a full-time job for a short spell, then became unemployed, and worked on a Community Programme (YTS) before joining the army. The other had worked as a sales assistant in a car accessory shop after leaving school, but had no qualifications and was looking for other work and, in particular, wanted to join the army. Three Liverpool respondents who had been unemployed for over a year also hoped to join the armed forces. One made it clear that this decision was taken with great reluctance and reflected the lack of opportunities in Liverpool:

'It's a pity that the present government don't seem to value the opinions of young people... If only I could be given a bit of help from them, I wouldn't need to go to the army for a job. I would be able to stay at home in Liverpool with my family and friends'.

The long-term unemployed

There was no-one in this sub-group in either German sample. This does not, of course, mean that long-term unemployment was not a problem in Paderborn and Bremen, but that the problem could not become manifest so early in a career. However, British samples included individuals who had already been unemployed for lengthy periods. In Swindon, they had all at some stage held jobs and, as such, were really peripheral workers. In contrast, 17 of the trajectory

IV sample in Liverpool could measure their time unemployed in years rather than months.

The corrosive effects of long-term unemployment are well documented (Warr, 1983; Spruit, 1983; Stokes and Cochrane, 1984; Laurance, 1986), and the particular problems faced by young people have been highlighted elsewhere (Warr et al., 1982). In a severely depressed labour market like Liverpool, it was difficult for anyone to fail to notice the widespread impact of unemployment. The effects on their families, friends and others in the community were often acknowledged by young people on other trajectories.

'Most of my family are unemployed. Only myself and one of my brothers have jobs. There are five of us. I, and all the rest of my family, are sick of having no money to spend. Sometimes I can go out with my mates, but we can't go out often. We're all in the same boat...'

Another Liverpool respondent considered urgent action was required to stop 'a hard-set limbo generation from going down the road to oblivion'. Others thought that 'people aged 16-17 are going through depression and are having a hard time now', and that 'having experienced work down south I have no doubt in my mind that we are living worlds apart in terms of wealth and employment'.

A couple of Liverpool young people in trajectory IV highlighted the extent to which they felt neglected or abused by others, especially government and employers.

'They may one day realise that we are real people and not just, in some cases, voters. I wonder if the German government takes much notice of their young people.'

'I believe that nowadays employers are not prepared to give young people a chance. Every time you apply for a job all they ever ask is, 'have you had experience?' But how can young people like myself gain the experience if they are not willing to teach us? With this government, young people are automatically expected to take a YTS whether or not they want to. They get bad pay and gain nothing at the end, only the idea of getting used to a low wage because, unless

155

they are among the lucky ones, that is all there is for them under this government.'

These two articulate older cohort respondents were both engaged in strategies which could eventually lift them out of long-term unemployment. One was reluctantly thinking of joining the army, while the other was attending evening classes and adding to her stock of GCSEs and O-levels: she already had five, hoped to become a nurse and, given the shortfall projected for nurses in the 1990s, presumably stood a realistic chance. The 1988 change in benefit regulations, which led to the exclusion of young people under 18 from eligibility for social security and subsequently compelled them to join the YTS, may mean that it will be difficult in future for so many young people to build such unrelievedly dismal records as in our two Liverpool cohorts. However, whether time spent in warehousing schemes would have led to any improvement in their prospects is debatable. Any reference to YTS seemed to touch a raw nerve with a number of Liverpool respondents from trajectories III and IV. Their experience or understanding of the scheme in the period 1985-88 did not accord with the optimistic view of YTS as a period of training and opportunity.

'I strongly disagree with the present training programmes. I also disagree with this present government making it compulsory for anyone under the age of 18 not in education, to join such training programmes. I think it should be up to the individual to decide what he or she wishes to do.'

'You can't go on the dole now. Everyone has to go on a YTS scheme, so my advice is either stay on at school or have a full-time job... My brother is on a YTS scheme. He is always borrowing money off my dad. The money is very low rate. It is disgusting.'

Coupled with the criticisms of YTS cited in the last chapter, it becomes difficult to maintain that the scheme was always providing quality training. That it sometimes did so was demonstrated by certain trajectory II careers. However, in circumstances where it did not, and young people perceived themselves as simply being used as 'cheap labour', they could become extremely bitter about warehousing measures if there was no apparent alternative. The best hope for such young people in the future may be that, if the Liverpool labour market picks up, they can exercise some choice, as the prospect of employment seems to drive up the quality of training schemes. Certainly, warehousing schemes could not survive such competition.

Experience and skills

Table 8.2: Numbers with work-related skills and experience in trajectory IV

	Liverpool		Bremen		Swindon		Paderborn	
	A	B	A	B	A	B	A	B
Been given responsibility	22	4	6	15	24	5	15	13
Been able to make decisions for oneself	27	-	7	11	29	3	8	14
Had a chance to use own initiative	18	9	4	20	18	7	12	14
Developed new skills and abilities	26	5	20	7	27	4	17	11
Set own goals/targets	19	11	6	16	13	9	9	13
Felt stretched/challenged	6	16	6	16	9	15	9	13
Felt a sense of achievement	15	7	13	10	19	7	20	7
Felt all abilities were being asked	12	15	11	17	8	13	21	66
Worked as a member of a team	16	11	15	19	24	7	19	10
Had to work to a deadline	7	19	10	20	19	14	8	28
Been asked for advice by others on how to tackle a problem	15	6	5	17	22	18	6	16

Note: (1) A = Quite or very often

B = Never or rarely

(2) Total in any cell = 40

Table 8.2 shows the numbers in each town in this trajectory who said they had acquired different work-related experiences. Despite being outside mainstream employment, education and training routes, a majority of the young people felt that they had developed skills and abilities; an indication that, despite all the limitations, they were still making some personal progress. That this was constrained is equally evident in the 60 indicating they never or rarely felt stretched or challenged, against 30 for whom this was (quite) often the case. They were certainly disadvantaged in the range of opportunities experienced after leaving school compared with young people on other trajectories.

The trajectory IV respondents usually had the lower educational attainments at school; then, notwithstanding remedial and other special schemes and measures, they appeared to fall even further behind their contemporaries. This was the case particularly in Bremen, where the schemes from which the trajectory IV sample was drawn seemed to provide few opportunities for trainees to be given responsibility, to take decisions, to use their initiative, or to set their own goals. The new skills and abilities they were developing were often in woodwork, cookery and similar practical areas. Some of the schemes in Paderborn appeared more imaginative and were pursuing a realistic aim: getting the young people through the scheme and into (mainly unskilled) employment. The result was that, overall, the Paderborn sample felt they had more opportunities than in Bremen, although these were still short of the two British towns. The Liverpool young people had a generally positive view of the skills they had developed, even though they often had very chequered careers, including lengthy spells of unemployment. Their skills could have been developed during employment, when on YTS, or possibly during unemployment. A big contrast between the two countries, as noted previously, was that the German respondents on this trajectory were on remedial schemes, some distance from experience of real work. In Britain, the practice of giving responsibility to teenagers in employment, even when they were officially on training schemes, was widespread. The tragedy is, of course, that such development was not necessarily built on in any systematic way. Thus, in many respects, while their experience of 'work' was seen as significant and beneficial by the individuals concerned, this was largely negated if their transition ended up going nowhere. The young people were confident that they had the skills to do the types of jobs for which they had experience, for example on YTS, but for many the jobs were just not there. Thus, many of the older cohort had already been unemployed for a considerable time, and for them the opportunity to go on another scheme was perhaps more likely than a job to break up their unemployment careers. Indeed, in the absence of any marked improvement in the Liverpool labour market, as Roberts and Parsell (1988) comment, the prospects for many could deteriorate:

'risks of unemployment now increase as each cohort moves beyond the YTS, and outgrows juvenile jobs and wages'.

The Liverpool sample's ratings of their own skills and abilities almost exactly matched those in Swindon. The Swindon respondents had, in the main, much more direct experience of work and saw themselves as well-equipped, even though they had no vocational qualifications, might have changed jobs several times, or drifted in and out of employment. The Swindon labour market, however, was very forgiving, and its harshest sentence seemed to be placing young people on the periphery of the employment structure rather than outside it altogether. Those struggling to come to terms with the labour market were clearly identifiable in both countries, the major difference being that, by age 19 in Britain, these individuals were the more likely to have already established peripheral careers with periods in and out of employment. This was not evident in terms of outcomes in Germany but, if the samples were followed for a further year or two, it seemed likely that such careers would be established. The different schemes may have been masking such problems, but it should not be doubted that, for some young adults, even peripheral employment would amount to a success, since unemployment was the likely alternative.

Conclusions

In Germany, it is very unlikely that those under 19 will be officially performing unskilled work. Indeed, it is still more likely that those carrying out a wide range of unskilled tasks do so under the guise of 'skilled training', so that they are actually designated unskilled workers. Even in such cases, however, youngsters would still be attending *Berufsschule* and hence have some access to education and training. Permanent unskilled employment is then, both in law and in practice, an adult career. Indeed, follow-up of older cohort youngsters on schemes in Paderborn showed that some had subsequently settled into unskilled jobs.

In Britain, the state of the labour market determines whether there are unskilled jobs for young people to get. There were very few such opportunities in Liverpool but, in a buoyant labour market such as Swindon, there were not only opportunities, but also plenty of youngsters willing to take them. The continued existence (or resurgence) of such jobs raises the spectre of the classic pre-1970s' problems of young people being recruited into 'jobs without training' or prospects, when the demographic changes mean labour, especially youth labour, is relatively scarce. Another significant factor about unskilled work is the way it reflects a labour market segmentation by gender. Many unskilled jobs in Swindon were widely perceived as 'women's work'.

Where young people did not get, or could not keep, a permanent job, what were the possibilities that they could build a career as a peripheral worker, changing between jobs, picking up temporary or seasonal work if necessary? Alternatively, could they break up unemployment with spells of such work? In depressed labour markets there were few such opportunities, and when schemes ended, in either country, prospects were often bleak. By contrast, the more buoyant labour markets were much more forgiving. Thus youngsters were frequently able to recover speedily from being made redundant or getting the sack and, if necessary, they could 'fill in' with temporary or seasonal work. Indeed, virtually the only barrier to a return to permanent employment in a boom economy like Swindon was if a young person was unemployed for a lengthly period; employers tended to shy away from those with 'poor' employment records, even if they were short of labour.

In Germany, the dominance of the dual system is such that, in practice, time spent on 'remedial schemes' will be much more likely to lead to unskilled jobs on the periphery of the employment structure. There is very little chance of making a full recovery into skilled employment. In both countries, the traditional gendered responses to labour market difficulties were taken by some of our respondents: domestic careers and joining the armed forces. In neither case was this the the exclusive province of youngsters in this trajectory, but they were more likely to view it as a 'way out' of an otherwise bleak future. In Britain, jobs such as childminding are examples of peripheral employment, being open to those with or without formal qualifications. In Germany, formal training for such work is much more likely (for example, there were a number of apprentice housekeepers in the sample), but there are few job opportunities and those that do exist are often low paid and lacking in long-term prospects. Another aspect of 'domestic careers' was trying to combine domestic responsibilities with some paid work. Once again, the buoyant Swindon labour market made such options realistic, although the type of mainly part-time opportunities was again firmly characterised as 'women's work', with labour market segmentation in the form of a secondary labour market clearly in evidence.

The armed services route had different meanings in the two countries. The existence of national service in the armed forces, or alternative service in the community, for all young men in Germany, coupled with a policy of education and training for everyone until 18, meant that it was unlikely that labour market difficulties would become fully manifest before the early twenties. The higher recruitment of young men into the dual system, even though they were outperformed in terms of educational attainment by young women, acted as a further shield. In Britain, push-and-pull factors influenced youngsters' decisions to join the armed forces: the opportunities in the forces contrasted favourably with the lack of opportunities in Liverpool. The final sub-group of this trajectory: those who had already established an 'unemployment career', belonged almost exclusively to Liverpool. There, despite some easing, the labour market was still difficult to enter. By contrast, the buoyancy of the labour market in Swindon meant very few youngsters were likely to experience prolonged unemployment.

The labour markets in the two German towns were between these two extremes, but the extended transitions in Germany meant that the problems facing young people there were yet to come. For less-qualified young people, the state of the labour market was likely to be a more significant influence than the quality of remedial or other special schemes and measures. Indeed, the gains in personal development on schemes were often not built upon subsequently. In all four towns there were already signs that a number of youngsters would struggle to effect a permanent transition into work; it was more likely that they would remain on, or outside, the margins of the employment structure.

Overall, there was evidence that groups of peripheral workers were either established or else 'in the making'. Whether and how many would remain peripheral workers, recover into the primary labour market or start to form a semi-permanent underclass, was difficult to tell at this stage of their careers.

CHAPTER IX

Work attitudes and future expectations

Introduction

Young people's attitudes towards work and its place in their lives have been topics for research and debate for some time (for a detailed discussion of different approaches see Baethge et al., 1988, pp. 15-26). Some research suggests a secular decline of work dedication and a shift towards 'post-materialist' values, such as self-realisation (see Inglehart, 1987). This view has penetrated political debates in Germany, where the Federal Ministry of Youth, Family and Health stated in 1981:

'the meaning of labour declines in society's value hierarchy in favour of the wish for self-realisation and the development of one's own personality' (quoted in Baethge et al., 1985, p. 1).

Other researchers, however, have concluded that it is not so much the actual role of work in people's lives that has changed, so much as young people's expectations. They argue that today's young people wish to develop their personalities at work as well as in their free time, and therefore expect work to be interesting and to provide social contacts as well as a solid material base for independent life-styles (Baethge et al., 1985).

We cannot reduce this issue to '*leben, um zu arbeiten*' vs. '*arbeiten, um zu leben*', ('live to work' versus 'work to live'). This would pose a false dichotomy. Rather, we shall examine our respondents' attitudes towards work to see how their material and social aspirations were related to their career tracks, the local labour markets and national influences.

Aspects of job search

The questionaires listed seven work characteristics: job security, good pay, opportunity to use one's initiative, responsibility, good career prospects, the possibility of becoming better qualified, and a friendly atmosphere. Respondents were asked to pick the three items which they felt to be most important. The most frequently ticked item, 'friendly atmosphere at work', was chosen by around two-thirds of all respondents in both countries, but almost as many chose job security. Atmosphere at work seemed more important for female respondents, whereas job security seemed to be more important for the young men. Career prospects and good pay were next on the list of important job characteristics mentioned by approximately a half of both sexes. Opportunities to gain better qualifications and to use initiative were mentioned by a quarter, and responsibility by one in six. This overall rank order suggests that, apart from friendly atmosphere, most respondents saw their jobs mainly in terms of material benefits outside work. However, the overall rank order suggests, apart from wanting a friendly atmosphere, most respondents saw jobs mainly in terms of material benefits. Evidence that the samples were seeking self-fulfilment at work is rather weak; the social atmosphere at work was of major importance to most respondents. An apprentice hairdresser in Bremen found it most important about her job 'to get on with my colleagues and the boss' as well as the 'contact with the customers'. A Liverpool youngster working as a telephonist and typist was dissatisfied with her present job, not only because of having to do much work for low wages, but also because 'some of my 'workmates' are very hard to get along with. I am very unhappy in my present job'.

Looking at the rank order in the four cities, 'atmosphere at work' was first everywhere except in Liverpool, where 'career prospects' were in the first place. 'Job security' ranked second in all towns except Swindon (fourth). Because of the extremely good opportunities and prospects in the Swindon labour market, the low ranking of this item is perhaps unsurprising. 'Career prospects' seemed to be more important in Liverpool (first) and Swindon (second) than in Paderborn or Bremen (both fourth). Possibly labour market pressures in Liverpool were compelling young people to value prospects and security in jobs rather than their more social aspects.

Table 9.1: Ranking of job characteristics in terms of importance

	Liverpool	Bremen	Swindon	Paderborn
1.	career (110)	atmosphere (108)	atmosphere (107)	atmosphere (112)
2.	security (89)	security (104)	career (103)	security (110)
3.	atmosphere (87)	wages (69)	wages (103)	wages (110)
4.	wages (85)	career (57)	security (83)	career (63)
5.	qualification (44)	initiative (46)	initiative (36)	qualification (59)
6.	initiative (36)	qualification (45)	qualification (28)	initiative (50)
7.	responsibility (26)	responsibility (17)	responsibility (28)	responsibility (28)

The relatively high ranking of career prospects in Liverpool and Swindon, compared to the German towns, could have been due to the higher numbers in employment in Britain. Once a person is working, career prospects are likely to become more salient than they are for students or apprentices, who are more likely to give examinations and vocational qualifications priority. It is useful to examine more closely the young people who were already employed in Britain and who were apprenticed in Germany. In both cases, we find interesting labour market differences within each country. While, in Liverpool, two-thirds of the sample considered career prospects very important, this rose to three-quarters of those who were in jobs. In Swindon, on the other hand, there was little difference in the ranking of this work value between the whole sample and those in jobs. This finding supports the conclusion that those who already had good prospects in a prosperous local labour market tended to rate other aspects of work as just as important. Members of the British samples who were already in employment seemed the most sensitive to the difference between a prosperous and a declining labour market, at least in terms of their work values.

Looking at the German apprentices in trajectory II, we find the reverse pattern. In the relatively strong labour market of Paderborn, the apprentices seemed to be more career minded than the sample as a whole: about a half ranked career prospects as important. In Bremen, however, the figure dropped to a third of the total sample, and declined further to a quarter for apprentices. While the overall lower figures in the German samples may be explained by the apprentices' concentration on learning new skills and taking examinations, the labour market differences add another dimension. Although Paderborn respondents were not in such a strong labour market position as their Swindon contemporaries, they did have a fair chance of entering jobs after finishing training. On the other hand, the Bremen respondents were likely to have experienced greater difficulty in obtaining apprenticeships. So maybe they were accepting their situation ('Hauptsache, eine Lehrstelle', Heinz et al., 1985) instead of thinking too much about the future and all its uncertainties.

Trajectories did not seem to bear much relation to work values, except in trajectory I, where 'using one's initiative' was much more highly ranked (third) than in the other trajectories (sixth), while job security, ranked first or second elsewhere, was only in fifth place. Both findings point to the relatively privileged situations of trajectory I respondents. Especially in Britain, many could take job security for granted, so other aspects of work were considered more important. These young people were looking forward to jobs that would allow them to use their initiative. Thus, using their initiative was important to them, but must have seemed a luxury to other young people. In Germany, for most respondents in trajectory I, the 'real' working environment was still some way off, and this may have influenced their ranking of items.

The samples were presented with several opinions about work (see Tables 9.2 and 9.3). Half of the respondents across all trajectories disagreed that 'a person must have a job to feel a full member of society'. More than half, however, shared the belief that 'the most important thing at work is to get ahead'. Only trajectory I respondents showed less support for this opinion. It could be inferred that for those who were still at school, or who had just entered higher education, the question of a career was still not salient, but they frequently mentioned career opportunities as a vital aspect when choosing a job. It is quite likely that these young people were career conscious, though not to the extent of putting 'getting ahead' in first place. Other job characteristics, like 'using one's initiative' appeared just as attractive to them.

Almost two-thirds of the samples did not think that it was important to 'hang onto a job even if one did not really like it'. The young women and men in the sample assessed this item similarly. Readiness to keep even a disliked job was obviously influenced by labour market options, as the contrast between trajectories I and IV shows. While little more than one-tenth of those bound for higher education agreed with the statement, almost one-third in trajectory IV did so. In all four towns, majorities disagreed with the statement that one should 'hang onto a job', but there were national and labour market differences. More of the German samples rejected the statement, and within each country those in the more prosperous labour markets were the more likely to disagree (Liverpool 52%, Bremen 70%, Swindon 60%, Paderborn 77%). These figures probably reflect the fact that those with good labour market prospects can allow themselves to be choosy about the work they are doing. The national differences have probably more to do with distance from the labour market: the German respondents were further away from having to face the issue.

A majority of all respondents disagreed with the statement that 'earning high wages' was the most important aspect of a job. However, opinions about the importance of high wages differed across the trajectories. The less successful respondents on trajectories III and IV were the most likely to consider the financial aspect important, although more than half of them did not agree with the statement. On the other hand, more than two-thirds in trajectory II, and three-quarters in trajectory I, rejected the opinion. Again, earning decent wages might not have appeared a problem to most of the latter group, and they could expect other rewards in their work besides the money.

Once more, different tendencies in the two countries were apparent. Twice as many German as British young people agreed that 'earning high wages' was the most important thing about a job. In all four towns, the young people from middle-class backgrounds rejected this statement more frequently than others, but especially in Germany. Fewer females than young males considered it important to earn high wages, maybe because they were not expecting to become breadwinners for their families, or because they knew that women did not earn as much as men. The average pay in typical female occupations, such as hairdresser, sales assistant or office clerk, hardly provided enough money for an independent lifestyle, and training allowances in these occupations were extremely low.

'Work is a big part of anyone's life, so one should be able to enjoy it too', said a young woman from Bremen who was about to start college-based training as a physiotherapist after gaining the *Abitur*. Nevertheless, about three-fifths of all respondents said that they would prefer jobs that did not interfere with their private lives and leisure activities. Trajectory IV respondents showed even higher agreement, a reflection of the fact, perhaps, that the working conditions they could expect were the worst of all, so it seemed necessary to draw a line between work and free time. On this particular item, there were no major differences between the prosperous and declining areas.

As Table 9.2 shows, half of all respondents agreed that 'having a career' was an important feature of a job. Given that in both countries those on trajectory I were relatively inexperienced as regards working life, yet had good career prospects, it is not surprising that only a quarter agreed. In contrast, about three-fifths of respondents in each of the other trajectories considered having a career to be a very important aspect of work.

Table 9.2: Important features of a job (numbers agreeing, by trajectory)

	I	II	III	IV	Total
having a career	44	96	90	100	330
hang onto job	19	24	27	47	117
high wages	17	20	39	52	128
work-free time	88	94	87	110	379

The German respondents judged having a career to be more important than their British contemporaries (Table 9.3).

Table 9.3: Important features of a job (numbers agreeing and disagreeing, by country)

	Britain		Germany	
	A	B	A	B
having a career	132	117	198	67
hang onto job	85	179	32	232
high wages	38	224	90	166

Note: A = Agree B = Disagree

Three job factors seemed important to young people in all four towns, independently of labour market conditions: career prospects, security and high wages. These items indicate the priority attached to employment conditions that would allow a desired standard of living, probably at least at the same level as the young people's parents, and preferably better. The young people had not adopted exclusively 'post-materialist' values. Engel and Hurrelmann (1989, p. 38) similarly concluded in their study of youth in Germany that it is wrong to talk about a general post-materialist orientation of youth in the 1970s.

'Materialistic values among the pupils were too important: deprivations with regard to materialistic and status orientations turned out to impede social integration of young people [and] to affect their self-esteem ...'

However, two-thirds of our respondents rated a 'friendly atmosphere at work' among the three most important features of a job. The number choosing this item shows the importance of non-material considerations. The young men seemed to have a slightly greater interest in pay and careers, whereas the young women found the social aspects of work more important, but this difference was small.

Compared with the other three trajectories, the route IV samples were the most likely to endorse the importance of 'having a career', 'hanging onto a job', and 'high wages': features of work that the majority could not expect and were rarely experiencing in their present jobs, when they had them. Trajectory I young people displayed greater readiness to invest part of their creativity in work, but most of them also agreed that work should not interfere with their spare time. We can thus add to the evidence of Baethge et al. (1988, pp. 166-180) that attitudes towards work become more dominated by material aspects (and less by the social situation and the quality of work itself) the more individuals experience the consequences of labour market crisis. It was in our trajectory IV that such a crisis was being felt most keenly.

Expectations about positions in one year

We knew that most respondents would be in a state of transition. A lot were about to finish school, others were on schemes that would not last more than another six months or a year; still others had just started, while others had almost finished, vocational training. Thus, 'what do you expect to be doing in one year's time?' seemed an appropriate question. Would the samples' expectations reflect the trajectories they were on, or would the young people anticipate significant changes? What differences would be due to the national systems of education and training? What kind of impact would age or sex differences have? And how would the local labour markets affect the individuals' expectations?

Bremen - Liverpool comparison

There were large differences between Bremen and Liverpool in the proportions expecting to be in employment and training. Eighty-eight of the Liverpool sample expected to be in full-time jobs in a year, while only 13 in Bremen had this expectation. Sixty-nine in Bremen expected to be in firm-based training, compared with only three in the Liverpool sample. Thirty-one of the Liverpool respondents expected to be at university or polytechnic, compared with eight in Bremen, while 30 in the Bremen sample expected still to be in schools leading towards higher education (*Gymnasium* or *Fachoberschule*) (Table 9.4).

Table 9.4: Expected position in one year, by area

	Liver-pool	Bremen	Swindon	Pader-born	Total
Gymnasium/ Fachoberschule	0	30	0	31	61
Firm-based training	3	69	6	63	141
Non-firm-based training	4	15	0	15	34
University/polytechnic	31	8	35	17	91
Full-time job	88	13	102	13	216
Part-time job	4	3	2	1	10
Government scheme	0	4	0	4	8
Unemployed	3	1	1	3	8
Something else	16	16	14	8	54

Age hardly made any difference in the Liverpool sample, but in Bremen much more. Members of the Bremen younger cohort expected to be still in school or in training, while the older respondents expected to be at university or polytechnic or in full-time jobs.

Swindon - Paderborn comparison

The comparison between Swindon and Paderborn revealed similar differences (Table 9.4). But even more Swindon respondents expected to be in full-time work than in Liverpool, while the numbers in Paderborn and Bremen were the same. However, twice as many Paderborn respondents as in Bremen expected to be at university or polytechnic. None of the Swindon respondents expected to be in non-firm-based training or YTS, whereas 15 in Paderborn had this expectation.

There was little difference between age groups in the Swindon sample, whereas age played a more important role in Paderborn. One-third of the younger cohort in Paderborn expected to be in school in a year's time, compared with less than one-tenth of the older cohort; one-fifth of the older cohort expected to be at university or polytechnic. More respondents from the older cohort thought that they would have full-time jobs, while the younger ones expected to be still in training. It is clear that most of the differences between the German and British cities were due to the different systems of education and training. We shall return to this point later.

Trajectories

The young people's expectations about where they would be in a year reflected the career trajectories they were on. In Liverpool and Swindon, more than four-fifths from trajectory I expected to be at university, whereas very few expected to be in full-time work. In Paderborn, half from trajectory I expected to be still at school, while two-fifths thought they would be at university or polytechnic. In Bremen, two-thirds from trajectory I thought that they would still be at school, while only one-tenth expected to be in firm-based training. Despite their stated expectations, in practice, large numbers of the German respondents in trajectory I would probably start firm-based training. Obtaining the *Abitur* in Germany is more common than taking A-levels in Britain, and is considered advantageous for entry into qualified apprenticeships by many employers: banks and insurance companies, for example. On the other hand, at the time of the study, the labour market prospects for university graduates were not at all good in certain subjects, such as social sciences and humanities. Thus, despite a growing number of young people with the *Abitur* going straight into higher education, for many of them a qualified apprenticeship was still an attractive option. They still had the opportunity of going to university after completion, and a sizeable number were doing just this. An apprentice *Industriekaufmann* (business clerk) in Paderborn was keeping his options open in this way:

'if my firm keeps me after the apprenticeship, I will stay in this occupation. If not, I plan to go into higher education'.

While most of the Liverpool and Swindon respondents in trajectory II expected to be in full-time work, hardly any in Bremen and Paderborn had that expectation. Most of the Germans expected still to be in firm-based training, compared to hardly any in Liverpool or Swindon. Most British respondents expected to have full-time jobs. Most German respondents allocated to trajectory III were, of course, on some kind of scheme. Although most of them would not have finished their schemes within a year's time, just under a half in Bremen and Paderborn stated that they expected to be in firm-based training. We believe that this was more a reflection of what they wanted to happen rather than a realistic assessment. In trajectory IV, there was almost the same pattern of expectations: two-thirds in Liverpool and over four-fifths in Swindon expected to be in full-time work, while around half in Paderborn said they expected to be in firm-based training. In the two German cities, this could be considered wishful thinking in most cases; it reflected the fact that firm-based training was the most highly-valued path into occupational life.

National differences

Most of the differences in the expected positions of the young people in a year did not relate to local labour market conditions but rather to differences in the national education and training systems. The differences between each country's cities were very small. More than four-fifths of the British respondents expected to be in a full-time job or at university, whereas three-quarters of the Germans expected still to be at school. This highlights the point that the British respondents on each career path were about two years ahead of their German counterparts in terms of career development. And this is without regard to the fact that the young men in Germany were liable for conscription and would lose another 15 months (military service) or 20 months (alternative service for conscientious objectors) on their way into an occupation. Almost a sixth of the older German males expected to be in one of these types of service in a year. However, most of the extra transition time in Germany was being used to gain qualifications. The Germans were normally entering the adult labour market later and were generally better qualified by this stage than their British counterparts.

Future plans

To assess their longer-term plans and expectations, the young people were asked whether they thought themselves likely to become self-employed, gain additional qualifications, train for different jobs, move to different areas or countries, or learn a foreign language. The possible answers ranged from 1 (very likely) to 5 (no chance).

Expecting to become self-employed was associated with being on trajectory I, which reflects the fact that many traditionally self-employed professions require academic training. Differences between the towns were slight, but there was a very obvious sex difference: in all four cities males were almost twice as likely as females to expect to become self-employed.

Trajectory was also the best predictor of whether individuals expected to obtain additional qualifications. There was an almost linear decline from trajectory I to trajectory IV. Those with positive experiences in education, who could expect that additional efforts would pay off, were the most motivated to qualify further. Here the Swindon sample displayed the most extreme contrast between trajectories, possibly because the career prospects for those willing to qualify were excellent in Swindon, but those without academic achievements could also be confident that they would be able to earn their livings without gaining further qualifications. In both countries, men were more likely than women to intend to gain further qualifications.

The British respondents were more likely to expect to train for different jobs than the Germans. This was probably because it was·

taking longer in Germany to qualify initially, and the significance of having a *Beruf* (trade, profession) in Germany is stronger than in Britain. It is also possible that the discontinuous or disappointing job experiences of the British samples had strengthened their desire to do something different.

Expecting to move to another area or to another country was almost entirely a question of being on trajectory I in both countries. University-bound young people probably knew that regional mobility would be necessary for good career prospects and, given their educational advantages, were probably more willing than other young people to expose themselves to new experiences.

Expecting to learn a foreign language was also strongly related to being on trajectory I. Here there was also a clear national difference: the German respondents were twice as likely as the British respondents to expect to learn a foreign language.

Confidence

A further set of questions assessed respondents' confidence in their occupational futures. The samples were presented with the following statements, and asked whether they agreed or disagreed with them.

- in 10 years' time I will have the kind of job that I really want;

- I will be able to impress an employer in a job interview;

- I will be able to get on with the people I work with;

- I will avoid unemployment;

- I will never be dismissed from a job for unsatisfactory work.

We expected that trajectory would be related to the respondents' self-confidence, and this proved to be the case. When asked whether they were sure about having the jobs they really wanted in 10 years, four-fifths in trajectory I answered positively, but only two-thirds in trajectory IV. Confidence that they would not become unemployed was shared by nearly three-quarters in trajectories I and II, two-thirds in trajectory III, and half in trajectory IV. Four-fifths of trajectory I respondents were convinced that they would not lose their jobs because of poor performance, though more than two-thirds in trajectory IV also shared this belief.

The influence of trajectory was less evident for the other opinions. Confidence in being able to impress an employer in an interview was slightly more common in trajectory I, while the feeling of being able to get along with colleagues was also almost equally prevalent across all four trajectories. Towns and national contexts turned out to be more important. Surprisingly, the Liverpool respondents were the most strongly convinced that they would have the kinds of jobs they wanted in the future, followed by Swindon, Bremen and Paderborn. Belief in being able to impress an employer followed this pattern.

Swindon held the lead concerning the respondents' belief in being able to avoid unemployment (Table 9.5), which is not surprising, given the city's economic situation. More unexpected was the four-fifths of the Liverpool sample who felt certain that they would not become unemployed. In contrast more than half of the Bremen sample, and two-thirds of Paderborn respondents, felt unsure or doubtful about their future employment chances.

Table 9.5: Whether would be able to avoid unemployment, by area

	Liver-pool	Bremen	Swindon	Pader-born	Total
confident	134	74	151	50	409
doubtful	25	81	9	107	222

Nearly all the Liverpool and Swindon respondents were also certain that they would not lose their jobs because of personal inadequacies, compared with three-quarters in Bremen, and two-thirds in Paderborn.

The five items discussed above were combined to form a scale of 'occupational self-confidence'. To display the influence of regions and trajectories, Table 9.6 gives an overview of the mean scores (maximum possible value = 5).

Table 9.6: Mean values of occupational self-confidence, by areas and trajectories

| | Trajectory | | | | |
	I	II	III	IV	Total
Liverpool	4.63	4.70	4.60	4.28	4.55
Bremen	3.83	3.50	3.03	2.80	3.29
Swindon	4.83	4.70	4.48	3.90	4.48
Paderborn	3.33	3.23	2.80	2.70	3.01
Total	**4.15**	**4.03**	**3.73**	**3.42**	**3.83**

This table shows clearly that the British respondents on average possessed more overall confidence in their futures than the German respondents and that, in both countries, the real local labour market situations were not reflected in the respondents' optimism or pessimism. The young people in both of the declining labour markets were slightly more optimistic than those in the expanding economic areas. Doubts and uncertainty characterised the German view of the future; optimism characterised British expectations.

What is the explanation for the (probably) unrealistic optimism of the Liverpudlians and the (relative) pessimism of the Paderborn respondents? Was earlier work experience providing the British samples with some adult self-confidence that the Germans lacked? Were regional characteristics overcoming local labour market influences (the 'Merseyside spirit'; the crisis of the Nixdorf computer company in Paderborn in 1988, for example)? Were the young people in

Bremen and Paderborn less optimistic because their labour market entry was being delayed by longer periods in training, a situation which did not force them to display the *Zweckoptimismus* ('compensatory optimism') which might be presumed in Liverpool? It is notable that, in all the cities, 'occupational self-confidence' was lowest in trajectories III and IV, reflecting the more precarious employment prospects of the young people there, but these differences were smaller than the cross-national ones.

Conclusions

Attitudes to work and plans for the future add another slant to the Anglo-German differences we found in vocational preparation and experience. The belief the British young people had in their work skills carried over into optimision about future prospects. More Germans, on their longer training routes, were uncertain about them.

'Enterprise' values, such as 'using initiative' and taking responsibility, came at the bottom of the rankings of desirable job attributes in both countries; friendly atmosphere, career security and high wages came top. The British young people were more likely than the Germans to believe that it was important to hang onto a job even if you did not like it. More young people subscribed to these beliefs in the bottom than the top trajectories.

Another indication of the extended transition to employment in Germany was that most of the young people there expected to be still training in a year's time, whereas most of the British expected to be in a job. More British young people expected to train for new jobs in the future and to leave their home town at some time in the future. More of the Germans expected to learn a foreign language and more of them were satisfied with the education and training they had received.

The picture that emerges is of most young Germans on well-established and extended training routes, leading to well-defined occupational identities, but uncertainty whether the economy would enable them to practise what they had been trained to do. In contrast, the British, with their less clearly-defined vocational preparation and more opportunistic approach to employment, had more confidence in their futures even though, in the economically most depressed areas, prospects, especially for those on the lowest trajectories, were least assured.

CHAPTER X

Life patterns in the making

Introduction

Preparation for employment needs to be viewed in the wider context of entry to adulthood. Leaving the family home, becoming a parent, moving to seek opportunities elsewhere, and political participation, make up the range of roles and responsibilities identified with adult citizenship. In recent years, the routes to it have increasingly overlapped with extended education and training, affecting decisions about marriage and parenthood, while at the same time increasing interest and participation in politics. In this chapter we examine the young people's expectations in these other areas of their lives.

Family relations, life satisfaction and mobility

Most of the young people in our survey were still living at home, and were presumably receiving financial and other forms of support from their parents, as well as accommodation. The family is, of course, one of the prime agents of socialisation, and home is the place where most people spend a good deal of free time. For this reason, it seemed useful to investigate respondents' satisfaction with family life, and this topic inevitably raises the issue of attitude to mobility, which has economic significance. It can be argued that, in economies which are changing rapidly, regional mobility will be of considerable importance for the efficient use of labour resources. The structure and operation of housing markets may be of key importance here (see Minford et al., 1987).

The Swindon sample had the highest proportion of fathers in full-time employment (over nine-tenths), the German towns were on about the same level (four-fifths), while Liverpool fell behind, with three-quarters. Over one in three of the mothers were in full-time jobs in Swindon and one in four in Liverpool, compared with just one in

10 in Bremen and Paderborn. In the German cities the most common role of mothers was housewife: two-fifths in Bremen and half in Paderborn. Part-time work was equally common in all four towns. These findings are in line with national figures on female labour market participation, which was higher in Britain than in Germany (59.8% compared with 50.4% in 1985; Maier, 1987). Local labour market differences may have accounted for the highest female employment rate in Swindon.

Cultural factors, such as a more traditional view of the family induced by Catholic influence, may have been exerting a negative influence on women's employment in Paderborn. The largest difference between Liverpool and the other cities was in the level of unemployment: almost a quarter of all Liverpool parents were unemployed.

Table 10.1: Number of unemployed parents, by town

	Liverpool	Bremen	Swindon	Paderborn
Fathers	33	6	6	9
Mothers	36	4	7	3
Totals	160	160	160	160

The Bremen sample had the highest number of 'professional' fathers (20), Swindon had the most 'intermediates' (23). Liverpool (12) and Swindon (23) had more partly-skilled fathers than Paderborn (6) and Bremen (7). The German cities had more fathers in the skilled categories (manual and non-manual) than the British cities (204, compared with 156) (Appendix 3). These differences, which are likely to have been reduced by our sample matching, originate in the different systems of vocational training: the German system provides more formal qualifications and produces more skilled workers than the British system. There is little recognition of the existence of 'partly-skilled' work. Similar tendencies were found among the mothers:

there were four to five times as many partly skilled women in the British samples and more intermediates than in the German samples. Conversely, there were more skilled manual women in Bremen and Paderborn than in Liverpool and Swindon.

A high degree of satisfaction with family life was expressed by our respondents: more than four-fifths were satisfied or very satisfied, with the British marginally more satisfied than the Germans. Trajectories seemed to have very little impact, which is surprising in view of the parental unemployment in the Liverpool sample: unemployment is known to place severe strains on family relationships, with financial deprivation being just one aspect of this problem (Walper, 1988). Parental unemployment can negatively influence the aspirations and educational plans of adolescents (Flanagan, 1988). Children of unemployed parents may become 'victims by proxy' (Kieselbach, 1988; Kieselbach, Lödige-Röhrs and Lünser, 1989; McLoyd, 1989).

Adolescence is reputed to be a time when the desire to display maturity and independence often leads to arguments within the family. Our findings, however, suggest a rather harmonious situation in our respondents' homes. Issues likely to cause arguments did not seem to be a source of family trouble: neither friends, nor hairstyles, nor dress, nor performance at school or at work. All of these 'never' or 'seldom' caused arguments for four-fifths of respondents. The issue that was most likely to cause trouble was not helping with domestic work (Table 10.2).

Table 10.2: Arguments because he/she would not help with domestic work, by town

	Liverpool 1	Bremen 2	Swindon 3	Paderborn 4	Total
never	29	48	38	29	144
seldom	36	48	43	59	186
sometimes	56)	37)	46)	52)	191
	)	)	)	)	
often	29)	22)	22)	15)	88
	) 59%	) 40%	) 49%	) 43%	
very often	7)	4)	11)	1)	23

With almost 60% in the 'sometimes' or 'often' categories, Liverpool was clearly top of the list on this item, Swindon was close to the average, while Paderborn and Bremen, at around 40%, had either more willing young people or less demanding parents! Quite unexpectedly, respondents in trajectory IV reported the fewest arguments about housework. This may have been because those in this group who were unemployed had more time on their hands and were devoting some of it to domestic work. In Liverpool, boys were the less likely to report having arguments with their parents; in the other towns girls were the more likely to be having arguments. As the Liverpool sample was by far the most working class, in terms of social background, this may have been a reflection of the more traditional, male-dominated, culture there.

Occupational plans had led to arguments more frequently in Liverpool and Swindon: one in five families there had arguments over this, compared with one in eight in Bremen and Paderborn. As expected, the trajectory IV respondents were the most likely to report arguments, followed by trajectory III, while trajectory II had the fewest. This is perhaps because the occupational plans of those on skilled routes were stable for the foreseeable future, while the uncertainties of semi-skilled and unskilled situations were a source of friction. Apprentices had, or appeared to have, clear occupational futures.

Friends and peers caused arguments in about a fifth of all families, with a tendency for the frequency of arguments to increase going down the trajectories. It is difficult, however, to see why trajectories should have had any influence here. The operative factor seemed to be social class, with arguments being reported as slightly more frequent in working-class than in middle-class families. We expected to find similar differences between trajectories and social classes when considering arguments over dress and hairstyle, but could not find any evidence of this. Such arguments were marginally more frequent in Bremen and Liverpool than in Paderborn and Swindon, which might have been because in bigger cities like Liverpool and Bremen, non-conformist or oppositional styles were more prominent in the local youth cultures.

Getting married seemed to be still pretty far away for most of the 16-19 year-olds. Even so, many had very definite ideas about when they wanted to marry. Three-quarters of Swindon respondents wanted to marry before the age of 25, but less than a half in Paderborn. If we look at trajectories, we find that about three-fifths of respondents in II, III and IV wanted to be married by the age 25, but only two-fifths in trajectory I. Many of those in trajectory I were obviously delaying their plans to start families until they had completed their education. More German than British respondents did not want to marry at all: 35 in Bremen and 20 in Paderborn, compared with nine in Liverpool and four in Swindon. Two-fifths of those who did not wish to marry were on trajectory IV. Bremen respondents were not only the most reluctant to embrace matrimony, they also wanted to have the fewest children. Almost one-third did not want any children or wanted only one child. In Liverpool, Paderborn and Swindon, the figure was much lower. More than two-thirds in Swindon wanted two children, while in the other towns the proportion was around a half. There were no systematic differences between the sexes on these family questions. None of the German respondents already had

188

children, whereas we found 13 parents in the British samples: 10 in Swindon and three in Liverpool.

Life satisfaction

The German respondents seemed slightly more satisfied with the things they could do and buy than their British counterparts.

One-fifth of the British respondents were dissatisfied with their financial circumstances, but only a tenth in Bremen, and even fewer in Paderborn. As the British respondents had the wider range of incomes, with some being on training allowances and others earning good wages, it could be concluded that there was a greater feeling of relative deprivation among those on allowances or unemployment benefit.

Bremen respondents were the most satisfied with their leisure activities (four-fifths) followed by Paderborn, Swindon and Liverpool. Less than one-tenth of the German samples expressed dissatisfaction with the ways they spent their free time, compared with about one-fifth in Swindon and Liverpool. It was possible that leisure facilities were important contributors to the young people's satisfaction with their home areas. The Liverpool and Swindon respondents were less satisfied than the German respondents with their home areas (Table 10.3). Young people in Swindon were polarised about the quality of life in the town, with some going out of their way to express negative comments about it.

'Swindon is not a very good place for people of our age to live. The social life is limited, despite the town's size. There isn't a good nightclub, amenities (e.g., swimming) are expensive, and no student can afford these prices. There is nothing in Swindon for those without money. Swindon has no character as a town. Because it is expanding, there are lots of modern office blocks, which make Swindon dismal. I wouldn't live here by choice. In fact I'd probably do anything to get away from it if I wasn't still in education!'

A Swindon girl studying at Liverpool University commented:

189

'although the job opportunities are better in Swindon, there is a real lack of facilities, especially for young people, as compared to Liverpool'.

Despite this accolade, Liverpool attracted more 'dissatisfied' responses than any other town.

Table 10.3: Satisfaction with home area, by town

	Liverpool	Bremen	Swindon	Paderborn
very satisfied	9	22	15	31
(very) dissatisfied	24	9	10	11

Almost everybody seemed to be satisfied with their relationships with friends and peers: over four-fifths of respondents in each of the cities and across the trajectories said that they were satisfied or very satisfied.

More dissatisfaction with their education was expressed by the British respondents than by their German counterparts. As Table 10.4 shows, many trajectory I respondents stated they were very satisfied with their education, but trajectory II provided the majority of those who were merely satisfied. Satisfaction dropped from trajectory I to trajectory IV, but just over half of the trajectory IV respondents still said that they were satisfied with their education.

Table 10.4: Satisfaction with education, by trajectory

| | Trajectory | | | | |
	I	II	III	IV	Total
very satisfied	49)	18)	17)	12)	96
	) 80%	) 70%	) 63%	) 54%	
satisfied	79)	93)	83)	73)	328
not sure	16	25	36	33	110
dissatisfied	11	17	16	29	73
very dissatisfied	4	5	6	11	26
Total	**159**	**158**	**158**	**158**	**633**

Everywhere, except in Paderborn, the middle-class respondents were more satisfied with their education than those from working-class backgrounds.

Satisfaction with future prospects was widespread in Swindon, with three-quarters being satisfied or very satisfied. In line with earlier signs of Liverpool optimism, almost three-fifths of the young people there were satisfied, which was some way ahead of the German cities, Bremen and Paderborn (one-half). About 40% in Bremen and Paderborn felt uncertain about what the future held for them, whereas just a third of the Liverpool respondents, and less than a quarter in Swindon, felt that way.

Table 10.5: Satisfaction with future prospects, by trajectory

	|	||	|||	IV	Total
			Trajectory		
very satisfied	32)	20)	22)	17)	91
	) 61%	) 70%	) 48%	) 48%	
satisfied	65)	90)	55)	58)	268
not sure	49	41	64	63	217
dissatisfied	8	5	13	15	41
very dissatisfied	5	2	5	5	17
Total	**159**	**158**	**159**	**158**	**634**

There was a clear trajectory difference concerning satisfaction with future prospects (Table 10.5). More respondents on trajectory I were 'very satisfied' than on the other trajectories. The overall level of satisfaction was highest in trajectory II, with 70% being satisfied or very satisfied, whereas in trajectory III and IV the proportion dropped to below a half.

We expected self-esteem to be related to achievements, and anticipated clear differences between trajectories. Self-esteem was measured using six items from the 'Rosenberg scale' (Rosenberg, 1965). Quite obviously, the scale was 'too easy' as it did not differentiate the respondents very well. More than 70% achieved a 'high' score, that is, five or six positive responses. Trajectory II respondents had the highest percentage of high scores (78%), followed by trajectory I (73%), III (69%), and IV (67%). Thus, in line with expectation, the scale did differentiate between trajectories to some extent. There were no differences between towns or between the sexes.

Family and mobility

Moving out of the parental home at some point is a normal part of adolescent development. The event may be associated with the young adults' occupational status, earnings achieved, or may simply be a desire to 'stand on one's own feet'. In our sample, Swindon had the highest number of respondents already living away from their parents' homes (about a sixth). Possibly the Swindon labour market was offering the best opportunities to earn the money required to pay rent, mortgages and cover the expenses of running a household.

In terms of trajectories, more respondents in I and IV had moved out than those in III and II. In trajectory I this occurred mainly in Paderborn and Swindon; in trajectory IV it was most common in Liverpool and Bremen. Swindon and Paderborn respondents needed to move away if they wished to go on to higher education (despite the *Fachoberschule* in Paderborn), while the Liverpool and Bremen samples were able to study most subjects in their home towns. In trajectory IV, the more likely explanations were family pressures or bad housing conditions, which were most likely to be a problem for disadvantaged young people, coupled with the opportunity to move out to relatively more buoyant local labour markets. Also, of course, moving to look for a job would be highly relevant for young people in this trajectory. One Liverpool respondent certainly believed that moving elsewhere was the key to finding a job:

> 'one thing I would like to point out is that you cannot say there is no work in this country, because there is. I have worked around the London area and have had four jobs in four months ... If they cannot be bothered to try to get work, either at home or away from home, I wish them no luck at all'.

Girls had a stronger tendency to move out, which showed up in all towns except Liverpool, the greatest difference being in Paderborn, where almost twice as many girls as boys (8% males, 15% females) had already moved out. A likely reason is the girls' greater social maturity, but another reason could be that girls were more often required to participate in domestic labour, while it was quite comfortable for boys to have their food cooked and their laundry done. Respondents in trajectories III and IV were the most likely to want to move out before they were 18, while trajectory I had the highest number (57) who planned to leave home by age 20.

Perhaps the most interesting of our questions on mobility was moving elsewhere for a job. There was a big contrast here between Britain and Germany, with far more British respondents expecting to move. Two-fifths of Liverpool respondents and one-third in Swindon said they were 'very likely' or 'quite likely' to move to a different part of the country, compared with just over a quarter in Bremen and Paderborn. Surprisingly, slightly more British respondents expected to move to another country (just over a sixth), compared with the German respondents (about a tenth). Perceived labour market problems cut across these national differences. Two-thirds of Liverpool respondents and just under half of those in Bremen saw great difficulty in getting a job locally, compared with one-third of Paderborn respondents and one-tenth in Swindon. Of course, a desire to move can be prompted by many other factors besides labour market problems. Good qualifications and high 'occupational self confidence' may lead young people to seek opportunities in their national or international labour markets.

Table 10.6: Numbers very/quite likely to move for a job, by trajectory and town

	Bremen	Pader-born	Total FRG	Liver-pool	Swindon	Total UK
Trajectory						
I	23	19	42	23	34	57
II	13	10	23	27	32	59
III	17	19	36	24	28	52
IV	13	11	24	24	26	50
Total	66	59	125	88	120	218

Table 10.6 compares the expressed likelihood of moving to get a job in each trajectory in the four towns. The German totals are lower on all four trajectories, but particularly on trajectory II, possibly reflecting the fact that we were questioning mainly apprentices in this trajectory in Germany. Despite the marketability of German vocational qualifications, this did not appear to be encouraging the expectation of moving. The hope presumably was to stay on in the firm where the training was taking place. In Britain, it is probably the greater employment experience that was encouraging the trajectory II respondents to look for opportunities elsewhere.

Politics

With respect to political participation and attitudes, we find both national and local differences. The British and German constitutions are fundamentally different, as are the electoral systems and the political parties which give different structures to the responses. Supporting the Green Party, for instance, represents something rather different in the two countries, and the major parties do not stand for exactly the same things. In Germany, the CDU is both a conservative and a confessional party; Catholic religious allegiance tends to be associated with support for the CDU. In Britain, on the other hand, Catholic confessional allegiance is, if anything, associated with support for the Labour Party, and this was certainly the case in Liverpool in the past, as we have seen earlier. Amongst our sample of young people in Liverpool, a surprisingly high percentage - 39% - gave no answer to the question on religious affiliation. Of those who did, the ratio of Conservative to Labour voters was 1:4 among Protestants and 1:32 among Catholics.

A sign of young people's entrance into full participation in the political system is expressed allegiance to a political party. One might assume that the German system of proportional representation would lead to less likelihood of respondents picking one of the two dominant parties than in Britain, where the 'first-past-the-post' electoral system is closely tied up with two-party politics. This was indeed the case for our respondents, even though their political preferences were not long-standing. Table 10.7 shows that the British respondents were more likely to express a preference than the Germans, and support for one of the two major parties (Conservative and Labour in Britain, CDU and SPD in Germany) was more common in Britain.

Table 10.7: Support for political parties

	Bremen %	Paderborn %	Liverpool %	Swindon %
Support for two major parties	43	58	88	77
Support for minor parties	37	32	21	18
No vote, DK etc.	80	70	51	65

Moving on from these national differences, there were also significant differences in the levels of support for specific parties in the different local areas. Taking the governing parties - CDU in Germany and Conservative in Britain - support was reported as Bremen (11), Paderborn (42), Liverpool (11) and Swindon (45). This result reflects the lower level of support for conservative governments in areas of high unemployment like Bremen and Liverpool. But lack of conservative support was probably not just a matter of individual assessment of national government action or inaction in relation to the local economies. Besides their longer tradition of 'left' political affiliations, in both Bremen and Liverpool there had been political campaigns on the particular issue of local finance. In Bremen there had been much public discussion about the level of federal funding to which Bremen was entitled, through the *Länderfinanzausgleich*. Similarly, in Liverpool, there had been a debate about the need for more central government financial support and controversy over restricting the freedom to raise local taxes ('rate-capping'). Such campaigns must have had at least some impact on the local populations, possibly making them feel they had been treated in a miserly fashion by the national governments.

When they were asked directly about their views on the central government, Liverpool youth seemed to be the most critical of all: two-thirds were dissatisfied. In Germany, there was marginally more dissatisfaction in Bremen (one-half) than in Paderborn (two-fifths); the same proportion as in Swindon. The Swindon respondents who expressed dissatisfaction with the government sometimes did so for 'middle-class' reasons:

'my political views are changing because of poll tax, inflation, dental charges and so on'.

'My parents are Conservative supporters, and I naturally thought I would follow their opinions, but now I have my own home my eyes have certainly been opened. My mortgage has risen £100 more a month due to the recent changes.'

In Liverpool, respondents tended to give 'working-class' reasons:

'this government needs to be thrown out. Mrs Thatcher only caters for her own class, and leaves the rest of us behind'.

Many pundits expect Green parties to increase in significance in European politics. Our study was undertaken just before the 1989 European Parliament elections in which the British Green Party won the highest of percentage of the vote of any European Green Party. It is of some interest, therefore, to look at support for the Greens in our samples (Table 10.8).

Table 10.8: Green Party support

	Bremen	Paderborn	Liverpool	Swindon	Total
Trajectory					
I	9	5	3	3	20
II	8	4	1	2	15
III	5	3	5	-	13
IV	3	5	-	3	11
Total	**25**	**17**	**9**	**8**	**59**

Of the small number who did endorse the Greens, we found more support in Germany than in Britain: probably a reflection of the longer history of the German Greens as a significant political force. There appeared to be greater support for the German Greens among girls than boys, which may have had something to do with the relatively high profile of women in the party. Surprisingly, there was only a weak relationship with trajectory, with marginally more Green supporters in trajectory I overall than in trajectory IV.

When asked which party was most active on behalf of young people, even a strong CDU supporter in Paderborn commented:

'probably the Greens side most strongly with the interests of young people because they are still a relatively young party, and they address young people with the important issue of environmental protection'.

In Bremen, a young man who claimed that he would vote for the neo-fascist NPD, as a protest against the major parties not doing enough for young people, said:

'if they weren't fighting one another all the time, the Greens could be the party most strongly in favour of young people's interests'.

Turning to the issue of how interested the young people were in politics, there was more expressed interest among the German sample: 69% of the Paderborn respondents and 55% of the Bremen respondents expressed interest, compared with 48% of the Liverpool respondents and 39% in Swindon. Overall, just under half of the sample stated that they did not have much interest in politics, with those in the lower trajectories and females showing the least interest of all (Table 10.9). Male-female differences in interest in politics are found in most studies of political preferences; but the national and trajectory differences may also reflect the educational component of the dual system and greater concern with citizenship issues. Barely any of the trajectory II young people in Paderborn, for example, expressed no interest in politics.

Table 10.9: Lack of interest in politics (numbers claiming to be not very interested or not at all interested)

Trajectory	Gender	Liverpool	Bremen	Swindon	Paderborn	Total	
I	Male	3	-	4	2	9)	
							}32
	Female	5	6	9	3	23)	
II	Male	9	8	12	4	33)	
							}77
	Female	15	13	13	3	44)	
III	Male	13	8	14	3	38)	
							}86
	Female	13	12	16	7	48)	
IV	Male	12	12	13	12	49)	
							}106
	Female	14	13	16	14	57)	
Total		**84**	**72**	**97**	**48**		**301**

Bremen and Liverpool showed a trend whereby those who claimed to be very interested in politics were the more likely to support right-wing parties. In Swindon and Paderborn, however, the reverse was the case, with those claiming to be very interested or quite interested being the more likely to vote for left-wing parties. Perhaps going against the local trend required greater political involvement. Half the respondents in trajectories III and IV in Germany said that they would not vote, or did not know how they would vote, or gave no answers at all. We need to recall again, though, that trajectory III young people were actually a much smaller proportion of the population in Germany than they were in Britain and were, therefore, much more outside the mainstream.

In relation to social class, the simplest way of looking at the data, given that our young people were generally against their governments, is to focus on those supporting the chief opposition parties - the SPD in Germany and Labour in Britain (Table 10.10).

Table 10.10: SPD and Labour Party identification and 'voting'

	Liverpool	Bremen	Swindon	Paderborn
Working-class background	83	40	38	21
Middle-class background	50	37	26	37

It is notable that support for the SPD was evenly spread between the classes in Bremen, but was rejected much more by the working-class than the middle-class young people in Paderborn. In the British cities, the more traditional picture of class political loyalties was evident, with higher levels of support for the Labour Party coming from working-class young people. This perhaps reflects the looser connection between class and politics in Germany than in Britain, and the interesting finding, noted earlier, of Catholic working-class support for conservative parties in Germany, compared with support for the (socialist) Labour Party in Britain.

Conclusion

It was difficult to detect any consistent or systematic pattern when considering the young people's views on family relations and life satisfaction. Perhaps the most significant finding is that the majority in both countries seemed to have positive attitudes to family life and personal relations, though it is interesting to observe that more of the German samples seemed to be rejecting the institution of marriage, and attached less importance to children within the family, despite the strong influence of Catholicism in Paderborn.

In response to questions about mobility and related matters, apart from their unwillingness to learn a new language, the British samples consistently tended to see themselves as the more likely to move elsewhere, and were the least satisfied with their existing circumstances. It might be argued that this signifies a greater flexibility of mind, a questing desire for improvement and a greater maturity, resulting perhaps from earlier initiations into the world of adult responsibility in employment. We must beware, however, of assuming that a greater propensity to move necessarily reflects expectations and values which are advantageous in the context of national economic development. It may simply be the case that young Germans have a greater degree of personal and professional commitment, having stronger ties to their employer and their locality. These feelings, combined with a higher degree of satisfaction with their home areas and the way they spent their free time, might have made it seem less desirable or necessary for the young Germans to move away than for their British counterparts, who felt dissatisfaction with youth opportunities and local circumstances more keenly.

This commitment among young Germans to their occupations and areas, may result from the longer, more formal and more thorough job training in Germany. The German training ideology still uses the concept of *Beruf*, with its connotation of a 'calling', and this connotation makes the concept substantially different from the British concept of a job. Reality, in the shape of local labour market pressures is, of course, liable to affect the relevance of the concept, and we do not know the degree to which such a value had been internalised by our young people. Only detailed biographical research could reveal this.

In looking at the young people's political participation, a number of factors appeared to be influencing them. Their trajectories, their transition experiences and probable occupational destinations and gender, all played a role, as did the national political cultures. Nevertheless, political identification and sympathies were also strongly related to the state of the local labour market. Taking the first two trajectories together, the Liverpool and Bremen samples were marginally more dissatisfied and displayed less identification with their national governments. This suggests that the young people there were not making judgements based only on their personal life experiences, but were also strongly influenced by their local political cultures. This is also shown by social class analysis. Social class is undoubtedly important in politics, in the sense that knowing family backgrounds enables one to to make predictions about the relative likelihood of left rather than right voting and party identifications, at any rate in Britain. In Germany, in our samples, it seemed more a matter of definite voting intention versus uncertainty, apathy or alienation associated with low trajectory. Neither social class nor religion appeared to operate with the same magnitude of effect on political participation in different localities. If we look at our young people's political choices, they reflected to a large extent those of their local communities. Liverpool and Bremen respondents, when not uncertain, apathetic or alienated, tended to be left-wing in their views. Swindon and Paderborn respondents were more right-wing. Thus, the young people were not cut off in their political views as a separate group from their communities: their views reflected the local political cultures. German youth were more interested in politics than their British counterparts, perhaps reflecting more attention to political education and citizenship in the dual system. But those German young people outside the occupational mainstream in trajectories III and IV were more likely to reject the idea of voting for any political party than those in the lowest trajectories in Britain.

The concept of a local political culture is complex and certainly not unproblematic. It may be built up from a number of elements. Reaction to local prosperity or depression is probably a key factor, but religion was important in Liverpool politics in the past, and is still of considerable significance in Germany. One may perhaps argue that our study justifies the investigation of young people's responses to the political systems in a cross-cultural perspective. Their interest and preferences cannot be explained wholly in terms of characteristics like social class background or age-based cultures. They are also influenced by national cultures, local communities, and the options and obstacles encountered during their transitions into adult life.

CHAPTER XI

Career trajectories in Britain and Germany

Introduction

In this chapter we return to the basic assumption underlying our comparative study of transition processes. Trajectories have been defined as the main routes for individual transitions from education to employment. This indicates that structural factors, individual attitudes and actions should be seen in reference to each other. Skills, interests and life plans result from the interplay of personal experiences and institutional requirements, like the ones differentiating our four trajectories. The transition processes of young people are embedded in opportunity structures that consist of various education, training and employment options. Furthermore, local labour markets define the range of job entry opportunities and thus influence the exchange value of the skills acquired and the future perspectives of young people.

Previous chapters have focused on particular aspects of transition as experienced by our respondents. In this chapter we draw together and refocus our findings on the concept of trajectories as sources of certain kinds of experience and outcomes. To what extent do similar trajectories involve the same kinds of participants and offer comparable learning experiences? How far do they produce similar outcomes in terms of work entry, life satisfaction and well-being, work values and citizenship?

In the early stages of the project, four broad trajectories were identified. Defining these trajectories was by no means a simple process. An initial notion, in which trajectory was defined by the 'jumping off' point at 16+ was rejected, as the activities engaged in immediately after leaving school were often transient, with little significance as indicators of longer-term direction, especially in Britain. Initial ideas about comparability of forms of provision were also overturned as the variations within and between them became apparent. The trajectories thus came to be defined by the broad equivalence of vocational preparation received, and by the expected or actual destinations of the young people.

Our findings now allow us to elaborate upon the trajectories, showing types of activity and their relative importance in each of the four labour markets. In general, we have found that the diversity of forms of activity increases though trajectories I to IV. Also, labour market and systemic effects have been clearly demonstrated. For example, various forms of regular paid employment appeared with the greatest frequency in Swindon, less frequently in Liverpool, and rarely featured at all in the German labour markets, while transitional vocational education schemes dominated the German scene at levels III and IV. The full range of main career routes in each country is illustrated by Figures 3 and 4. In-country differences in activity, experience and outcome will now be briefly reviewed, followed by a discussion of cross-country comparisons between the four trajectories.

Figure 3: School to work trajectories in Germany

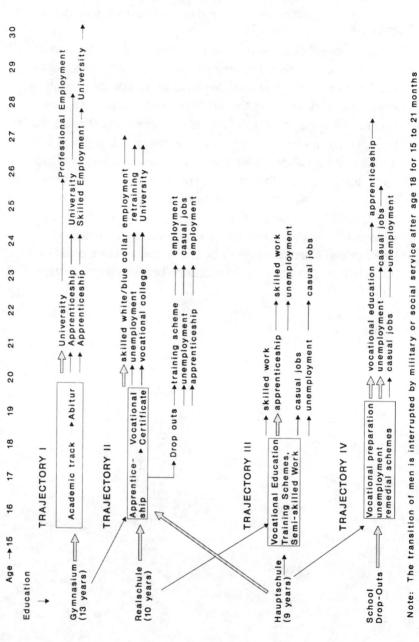

Note: The transition of men is interrupted by military or social service after age 18 for 15 to 21 months

208

Figure 4: School to work trajectories in Britain

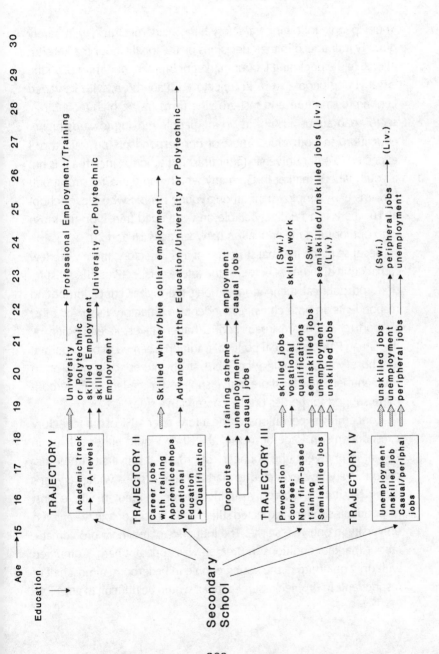

Trajectories in two German labour markets: Bremen and Paderborn

Young people following trajectory I, the academic track, were rarely directly influenced in their decisions by the local labour market situations. In the declining labour market of Bremen, one-third of all the city's young people were in trajectory I. Paderborn, with its varied economic structure and fast-growing firms in the high-technology sector, had about 20% of its young people moving towards higher education. In both cities, most of our respondents on trajectory I expected to enter university after finishing school. Since there is not a youth labour market in Germany which could exert a strong pull towards early employment among young people who leave school at 16, there is a relatively stable and extended transition for those who opt for full-time education between ages 16 and 20.

Because of the internal structure of this trajectory, there were few remarkable differences between the future perspectives, life satisfaction and political inclinations among the higher education-bound respondents. In both cities, respondents in trajectory I showed most support for non-mainstream political alternatives, as embodied by the Green Party, but local political traditions seemed to be important for those young people who were at all interested in politics: in Bremen there was far more active support for the left, in Paderborn more support for parties on the conservative side.

Concerning expectations for the future, over 40% of our trajectory I respondents in Paderborn said that they would either still be in school in one year (the younger cohort), or at university (the older cohort). Very few expected to start apprenticeships within a year's time. The situation was only slightly different in Bremen, where most respondents similarly expected still to be in school or to have entered university in one year's time. The influence of the more problematic labour market conditions in Bremen was apparent here. Compared with only one-third of the young people in Paderborn, almost half of respondents in Bremen assumed that it would be difficult to get a job.

In Bremen, the dominant training occupations in trajectory II were in business and administration, metal work, food and domestic services, and electrical engineering, which together accounted for about 70% of all apprentices. Young men were mainly trained in crafts and technical occupations, young women in clerical and service jobs. In Paderborn, there was a discrepancy between the occupations in which most of the young people were being trained (crafts and manufacturing) and the employment opportunities and qualifications required in high-tech companies. In both cities, it was mainly school-leavers from *Hauptschule* and *Realschule* who entered apprentice training after nine or 10 years at school. Many of them had problems in finding apprenticeships, and very few managed to find places in their desired occupations. Though the apprenticeship curricula were regulated by government laws, the quality of training, forms of control and employment prospects differed widely by economic fields, size of firms and labour markets.

Being in trajectory II and learning a trade seemed to provide more life satisfaction than continuing in school or being on temporary schemes. This positive attitude seemed to arise from the more independent status and the prospect of being able to enter skilled employment with a specific occupational identity. In both German cities, about 10% of respondents expected to be in full-time employment in a year's time. Two-thirds of our trajectory II cases in Paderborn expected still to be in apprenticeships; three-quarters in Bremen. This indicates that, in Germany, the apprenticeship track is a fairly secure passage; only about 15% of all apprentices drop out.

Young people who had neither entered apprenticeship training nor continued with general education were in trajectory III. It consisted of young people in public full-time vocational schools (*Berufsfachschulen*) and non firm-based programmes, ranging from a basic vocational year (BGJ) to local initiatives providing vocational qualifications. Most of these young people were hoping to use the trajectory III programmes as stepping stones for finally getting apprenticeships, thus connecting with trajectory II, although a sub-

211

stantial proportion of such individuals do not succeed in making this transition. Attending long-term specialised vocational schools was part of an extended transition process for girls who were being educated for traditional women's jobs, like kindergarten nurses, or in home economics. These occupations, however, had less than average employment prospects, even in an expanding labour market like Paderborn.

It did not come as a surprise that the young people on this track in Bremen and Paderborn were much less satisfied with their education and their future prospects than their trajectory I and II counterparts. Their attitudes towards employment were sceptical. This was reflected in their rather negative assessments of the usefulness of knowledge of modern technology like IT, compared to the respondents in trajectories I and II. Also, the young people in vocational schools and programmes were much less convinced that they would enter successful and stable employment, and only half of them felt that they would avoid unemployment in the future. In the two German cities, with the slow improvement in the training market, the basic vocational year (BGJ) was being selected by fewer and fewer school-leavers: there was a decline of about 50% in attendance between 1985 and 1988 in Bremen (partly due to the demographic trend).

In Bremen and Paderborn young people in pre-vocational, short-term or remedial training measures, and long-term jobless youth were categorised in trajectory IV. In both cities, unemployed young people under 18 were being placed on schemes mainly to keep them off the streets. Those who were on this track because of lack of qualifications or local labour market problems were trapped in a vicious circle: post-school transition started with unsuccessful applications for apprenticeships, followed by spells of unemployment. The young people were then referred to special schemes to improve their educational and vocational basics. This status then greatly reduced their chances of entering permanent employment or another apprenticeship scheme. Another vicious circle began with apprenticeships offering dim prospects of stable employment after completion (for example, hairdresser, waitress, baker). Realising that they were in dead-end training, and feeling exploited by the firms, some of these apprentices dropped out. Most of these had failed to find other training places and therefore shifted between unemployment and schemes.

Both circles could lead to a marginalised status in depressed labour markets which would not offer even unskilled jobs to such young people. A particular pattern reflects the transition problems of teenage mothers, who finally retreat from unemployment to 'domestic responsibilities'. Young people in trajectory IV belonged to a small youth underclass which seemed to be growing, especially in depressed areas. Recent figures show a sharper increase in poverty among the 17-25 year-olds in Germany, compared with other age groups (Hauser and Semrau, 1990). Despite their precarious situation, the expectations of eventual entry to apprenticeships among our respondents in trajectories III and IV signified the overwhelming importance of apprenticeship as the main non-academic route into employment.

Trajectories in two British labour markets: Swindon and Liverpool

Substantial differences in entry to, experiences in, and exit from, the trajectories were apparent in the contrasting labour markets of Swindon and Liverpool. A small minority of young people in Britain aim for, and gain, entry-level qualifications for higher education. Thus, trajectory I is confined to the highest academic attainers. Most trajectory I young people in the Liverpool sample intended to enter higher education or had already done so, while their Swindon counterparts more frequently entered employment. In both cities, nearly all those on the academic track had entered it without seeking jobs, apprenticeships or training places at 16. Learning experiences within the academic track were not closely linked with labour market conditions, and were similar in the two cities. They contrasted with the learning experiences of young people on the other trajectories, with the academic respondents being the most likely to report experiences of working in a team, taking group decisions, working to deadlines, and taking written tests. Swindon academic track young people appeared more likely to have had employment experience than their Liverpool counterparts. They were more likely to have access to IT through their homes, and were more likely to be 'courted' by employers and to proceed into jobs at 18+. Most of those entering higher education from both cities had middle-class backgrounds. In common with trajectory II respondents, they were more likely to express interest in politics and to vote (both left and right) than their lower trajectory peers. Overall, high academic achievement at 18 opened up a range of opportunities for both Liverpool and Swindon respondents. The local labour markets were mediating this, in that employment benefits would not accrue immediately for most Liverpudlians on this route, which was therefore part of a longer-term investment in education and skill development.

Trajectory II had typically been entered by middle-range achievers from mixed social class backgrounds in both cities. These were young people with significant educational achievements and a recognised capacity to benefit from systematic education and training leading to vocational qualifications. In Swindon, applications for training, usually through apprenticeships and jobs, had not generally involved substantial 'searching'. Small numbers of very selective applications were made. By contrast, Liverpool respondents had engaged in large-scale job applications, but were generally allocated to training schemes, YTS places being the main option for school-leavers at 16. Quality of training on this route appeared generally higher in Swindon, as poor-quality training was unlikely to attract participants when young people found themselves in short supply (and therefore in high demand) in the labour market. In both cities, young people following systematic training programmes, either full-time in college or through firm-based training leading to vocational qualifications, did not necessarily experience a close link between the theoretical and practical elements. 'Youth jobs with prospects' were a particular feature of the Swindon labour market, and advancement to supervisory roles by age 19 had not been uncommon for those who joined growing companies, or used the fluid labour market to change jobs when better opportunities presented themselves. In common with their trajectory I peers, respondents in this trajectory were more likely to express an intention to seek further qualifications than trajectory III and IV respondents. Attitudinally, where Liverpool trajectory II respondents had succeeded in gaining entry to skilled work or vocational qualifications, they were nevertheless more dissatisfied with the government than their Swindon counterparts, reflecting wider awareness of the local situation and politics, rather than individual circumstances.

Differences between Liverpool and Swindon, arising from the contrasting states of their labour markets, became increasingly marked as we moved downwards to trajectory III. Swindon young people had again found it relatively easy to obtain full-time employment, although the lower educational attainment levels typical of this trajectory meant that the level of labour market entry was usually semi-skilled, not requiring any form of vocational qualification or demonstrated educational capacity. Lower attainers in Liverpool, by contrast, had found it more difficult to gain direct entry to jobs than their more highly-qualified peers on trajectory II.

While obtaining semi-skilled work represented a degree of success in both cities, these jobs held out little prospect for advancement or training. The danger was that the initial attraction of a wage could blind lower achievers to the longer-term advantages of pursuing further training and skill development. In Swindon, pre-vocational courses, such as CPVE, in trajectory III tended to be followed by young people who wanted to improve their general employment prospects or create a 'bridge' into further education. It had usually been a positive choice. The courses represented a way of keeping options open or upgrading present positions, and were undertaken with these objectives in mind. In contrast, Liverpool young people tended to end up on these courses because no 'real' job opportunities presented themselves.

Many of the same difficulties beset the non-firm-based YTS schemes; the main form of trajectory III provision in Liverpool. Many, in practice, were 'warehousing' schemes, often providing a good grounding in basic skills and good-quality experiences of learning, but holding out little in terms of job prospects. They were substitutes for jobs, not significant pathways into jobs. Non-firm-based YTS schemes were not even considered to be an option by Swindon young people. Those schemes which did run in Swindon (other than the untypical ITEC scheme), were mainly special schemes for young people with learning difficulties. Jobs were usually found at the end of these special schemes, but were typically trajectory IV employment, in terms of skill level. Again, the schemes, although marginal, operated more successfully in Swindon because they held out real job prospects. A paradox was that prevocational schemes were making the most positive contribution where the labour market provided a range of choice and opportunity but, in practice, were most prevalent where labour market opportunities were least. Attitudinally, trajectory III and IV respondents showed less dissatisfaction with the government than their trajectory I and II peers in Swindon. In Liverpool, the position was reversed, in that greater dissatisfaction was apparent in trajectories III and IV. Young people in these latter trajectories were less likely to seek additional qualifications, less likely to see training in IT as potentially helpful to them, and more likely to perceive financial remuneration to be the most important aspect of a job.

In Britain, trajectory IV comprised unskilled, part-time and peripheral young workers, those involved in 'domestic careers', and the long-term unemployed. Those in trajectory IV were typically the lowest school attainers. Significant levels of participation in full-time unskilled employment were found only in Swindon, where the buoyant labour market presented many opportunities for such work (but relatively little job security or opportunity for advancement). In Liverpool, the very few young people who succeeded in obtaining full-time unskilled work found it in areas in which conditions were very poor and/or undesirable (work which no one else wanted). Long-term unemployment was, indeed, the dominant feature of the Liverpool sample on this trajectory, and the one which distinguished it most sharply from Swindon, where long-term unemployment was almost non-existent. Opportunities for peripheral or part-time work on a short-term basis abounded in Swindon, so even those experiencing spells of unemployment tended to intersperse them with periods of work. Young people with this type of profile, however, found themselves more sharply stigmatised in Swindon since the 'excuse' for non-employment was not present. The trajectory IV young people in Swindon were seen as being there because of personal inadequacy and lack of motivation, to a greater extent than their Liverpool counterparts. The long-term decline of Liverpool's labour market had built up an acceptance of, and community support for, the young unemployed. As expected, exposure to experiences relevant to adult and working life was lowest in trajectory IV. Young people on this trajectory were also the most likely to emphasise the importance of 'hanging onto a job', security and high wages, and were the least likely to express an intention to seek additional qualifications. More than one-quarter were dissatisfied or very dissatisfied with the education they had received.

Education to employment transitions in the two countries

Greater variation in patterns of experience leading to employment in Britain posed some particular problems of comparison as well as generating some significant findings. Greater uniformity and regulation of the German routes was reducing local labour market effects. In Britain, by contrast, on routes ranging from direct entry to jobs to full-time study for recognised vocational qualifications, the training arrangements were more closely tied to local labour market conditions and the requirements of particular employers than to anything resembling a national system.

In the German cities, centralised and regulated systemic factors determined the forms of vocational preparation available, mediated by local labour market conditions. In the British cities, the converse was true, in that local labour market conditions tended to dominate. In many respects, the Swindon phenomenon has emerged as unique in this study. It reveals the patterns and implications of unregulated market-led vocational preparation in a booming economy. In Liverpool, local labour market conditions necessitated an array of institutional transitional schemes designed to bridge the labour market gap for young school-leavers. In this respect, superficially at least, the vocational preparation in trajectories II, III and IV in Liverpool was more closely aligned with that in the two German cities. The distinctiveness of Swindon runs throughout the cross-country comparisons between the four trajectories. Those who stayed on the academic trajectory I could find themselves under pressure in Swindon because of the competing opportunities of entering a 'career job'. In Swindon, employment with career prospects was offered to, and taken up by, approximately half of the academic track respondents while, in Liverpool, Bremen and Paderborn, progression to higher education was the primary aim of the majority of young people on this track. Awareness of alternatives to higher education, however, was quite high in Germany, because many were considering opting out of this wider track. It was much more common for young people with an *Abitur* who did not proceed to university to start with an apprenticeship, while their Liverpool and Swindon counterparts tended to enter employment without such formal vocational training necessarily being part of it.

Young people in trajectory II in Paderborn and Bremen received theoretical and practical training which were usually well integrated. However, they were very unlikely to experience the degree of responsibility and remuneration afforded to many of their British peers. In

Paderborn and Bremen, young people experienced slower progression to responsibility, but greater depth of education and training, combined with the expectation of ongoing development through training into their early 20s.

Britain offered a variety of routes to vocational qualifications or competence on this trajectory, which were far less standardised than in Germany. Although firm-based YTS had become a two-year training period, it still seemed to be the second-best option for young people in Liverpool, who preferred to enter full-time employment right after leaving school. However, Liverpool employers were offering few opportunities for direct entry to skilled employment with prospects. Rather, they were using YTS as a probation phase for selecting prospective employees. While YTS was attempting to keep young people on the tracks towards employment, it has been criticised as an instrument of social control of young people who are kept out of the adult job market and off the streets (Coffield et al., 1986). The aspect of social control became even more pronounced with the government decision in 1988 that young unemployed persons lose their welfare benefits if they refuse to join the YTS (Rose, 1989).

Direct entry at the age of 16 to 'youth jobs with prospects', was strongly represented in the Swindon sample. This was a unique (in this study) feature of the Swindon labour market. Firm-based YTS training had not become established as an alternative to real jobs or full-time education. Where firm-based YTS schemes existed, they were usually embedded in existing apprenticeships or other well-developed company training programmes.

In Liverpool, most respondents on trajectory II expected to be in full-time employment in one year's time. This contrasted with their counterparts in Bremen, where only 10% expected to be in employment, while three-quarters thought they would still be in apprenticeships. About two-thirds of the British young people, but only one-third in Germany, expected that they would train for different occupations later on. This indicates that the apprenticeship fosters the idea of a stable occupational career, while the British system of labour market entry is less predictable, perhaps leading to more flexibility among young employees.

Young people in trajectory III who were in full-time pre-vocational education, semi-skilled employment, or on government training schemes, were acquiring qualifications by college- or school-based training, learning on-the-job, or by non-firm-based pre-vocational training. Most schools and programmes belonging to this track were temporary bridges of vocational education not leading to recognised vocational credit. Most of the respondents in Bremen hoped to use the training schemes as stepping stones towards apprenticeships while, in Britain, entering employment was the more attractive alternative. For most British young people and employers, de facto work experience seemed to be more important than vocational qualifications. This track was the entry port for semi-skilled jobs which required little systematic training. This distinction was obvious in the responses of our samples: while three-quarters of the Liverpool respondents expected to be in full-time work in a year, not even one-tenth of their Bremen counterparts expected to be in work, but two-fifths of them were looking forward to apprenticeships. Though this track was providing an alternative to unemployment, additional academic achievements were often proving difficult, and job prospects were not necessarily improving. Thus, young people on this track continued to apply for jobs in Liverpool and for apprenticeships in Bremen, but often without success.

If they could be kept in the educational system, supported with a stipend and counselling, there might be a chance for such young people to acquire credentials which would improve their self-conceptions. This strategy, however, is only likely to work where labour demand is strong. With little or no labour market improvement in Liverpool, it seemed very likely that young people on track III would try different routes, thereby extending their transition more and more, with declining chances of stable employment.

Pre-vocational courses tended to work better in Swindon than in the other labour markets. Presented with an array of opportunities, young people would enter pre-vocational schemes as a positive decision to keep options open, or to upgrade qualifications generally relevant to employment, only if the courses were really enhancing their prospects of obtaining the types of jobs they wanted.

Youth in trajectory IV were trapped in vicious circles in both countries. Entering unskilled work reduced their chances of obtaining the training experiences necessary for access to better employment. Furthermore, temporary and casual work created discontinuous employment patterns which became another barrier to gaining stable work. This particular type of circle was specific to Liverpool in our study, since the young jobless in Bremen and Paderborn were classified as 'youths without a training contract' and had to attend vocational schools until they were 18. In Paderborn, many of these young people were allocated to remedial schemes. But being in such schemes often led to stigmatisation. Young people could find themselves labelled as deficient or even handicapped, thus creating a different type of vicious circle.

Many trajectory IV respondents in Swindon had been successful in obtaining regular full-time unskilled employment. For those who did not find regular employment, an abundance of peripheral work opportunities meant that very few experienced long-term joblessness. Those who were unemployed tended to be more sharply stigmatised than their counterparts in the depressed labour markets. The structural effects on the transition to employment in this trajectory are summarised by Roberts et al. (1989b, p. 13), who argue that in Britain's depressed regions, 16 year-olds with low qualifications are confronted with a 'scope for choice which amounts to different ways of postponing their unemployment'.

In all the labour markets, the proportions of low-skilled jobs, underemployed, and unemployed youths had decreased in the late 1980s. However, there were still school-leavers who found employment only in unskilled, temporary jobs or switched between unemployment, short-term training schemes and casual jobs. Young people coping with a similar situation were studied by Coffield et al. (1986) in the north-east of England. These young adults, who were 'in and out of the labour market', exhibited two patterns: being 'on the dole', and having 'shit jobs and govvy schemes'. These case studies of working-class young men and women aged 16 to 28 demonstrate that, for these young people, becoming an adult meant leaving school and getting a job. For those who were unable to find a job, the transition to adulthood was severely strained:

'the period of transition of working class youth has been lengthened and has become much more fluid and uncertain' (Coffield et al., p. 199, 1986).

The young people in our Liverpool sample were in a similar situation of marginality, with severely limited options open to them in the labour market.

One of the few comparative studies of unemployment in a west German town (Augsburg) and an British town (Liverpool) was conducted several years ago, with small groups of unemployed men and women from various age groups (Guggemos, 1989). Though these case studies do not permit a general conclusion, it seems that unemployment was experienced rather as a collective problem in Liverpool, and as an individual fate in the German city. Most of the jobless in Augsburg saw unemployment as a temporary situation, compared to their Liverpool counterparts, who experienced joblessness as a way of life. The spread of poverty among the population of Liverpool had made more and more young people dependent on social welfare. Lack of confidence in government programmes like the YTS meant that family and friendship networks were seen as the main resort for support. In contrast, the experience of joblessness was attributed by the youths in Augsburg to individual causes, leading to a tendency to apply for jobs, to attempt further training and attend courses offered by the employment office.

Some of our results enable us to compare the two national 'transition cultures'. Irrespective of trajectory or labour market, the young people in the two British cities tended to be more satisfied with their family circumstances, but they were otherwise less satisfied with their present life situations. They displayed more readiness to move to other parts of their country to find work. Compared with the young people in Germany, most of the non-academic respondents in Britain had to cope with the requirements of the labour market directly after leaving school. In Germany, an extended and regulated period of vocational training not only meant staying in a more dependent status longer, but also developing a strong occupational commitment, often combined with hoping to be hired by the company providing the training.

In their future expectations, young people in the two British towns showed surprising optimism, compared with the Germans. While only about half of our respondents in Bremen and Paderborn felt that they would avoid unemployment, more than four-fifths in Liverpool and Swindon were convinced that they would not become unemployed in the future. This is corroborated by looking at the results on occupational self-confidence, which show that the respondents in the two British towns were more optimistic on all trajectories than the young people in the two German cities. There was a constant decrease in self-confidence by trajectory. However, self-confidence for respondents in trajectory IV in Britain was still higher than for those in trajectory I in Bremen and Paderborn. German young people seemed to be depressed by Germany's labour market situation in the 1980s. They were the more sceptical regarding their employment future, in spite of their generally high educational and vocational qualifications.

A surprising result was that the respondents in Paderborn were consistently pessimistic on all four trajectories. A very speculative explanation could be that this resulted from the crisis of the main computer company, Nixdorf, which culminated in 1989. As for Liverpool and Swindon, there seemed to be different motivations at work: the labour market in Liverpool could not get much worse, and only optimism allowed the young people to survive. In Swindon, the optimism was based on the reality of a booming local economy.

Trajectory membership in the two countries seemed to be exerting more influence on attitudes and future expectations than national characteristics and the condition of the labour market. Young people who were on the academic tracks were conscious of their relatively good prospects, regardless of where they lived. Young people in trajectory II, however, showed more differences between the two countries. In Britain, young people who had already entered skilled employment seemed to be less dependent ('junior employees with certain responsibilities') and earned much more than their German counterparts who were still apprentices. Thus, the experiences of young people on the skilled employment/apprenticeship track differed according to the overall dimension of 'independence' by nation: while many of the British respondents had already completed the status passage into adult employment, the Germans were still in a status transition towards qualified employment.

Looking at the context of experiences and future prospects of the young people in the precarious trajectories III and IV in both countries, the German provisions differed from the British ones. Full-time vocational education with different durations and little actual work experience was dominant in Bremen and Paderborn, thus producing an extended school-based transition phase while, in Liverpool and Swindon, there were more short-term combinations of vocational education and some practical work experience.

Trajectories revisited - extended and accelerated transitions

One of the most significant contrasts to emerge from the British-German comparisons is between extended and accelerated transitions. For German young people, the steps taken between 16 and 19 represent only the first stages in a transition process which continues to higher levels of training and qualification. In contrast, some British

students have completed first degrees by 21 years of age. Those pro-
gressing into jobs with prospects, or substantial vocational education
and training programmes, may well be employed not only with full
adult status and pay, but also with supervisory responsibilities by age
19, particularly in more buoyant labour markets. While transition
and progress towards maturity and responsibility is accelerated in
this way, is this at the expense of depth and breadth of vocational
preparation? What is the impact and effect at later stages of the life
course? Why are young people in Britain less interested in politics?
A full comparison of the relative benefits of different forms of provision needs to go beyond comparison by chronological age, and certainly beyond 19, since the time frames are substantially different
between the two cultures.

Compared to recent survey studies of the attitudes of young people
in post-industrial or 'service societies', which argue that there is a
decline of instrumental work orientations in favour of self-realisation
values (see Baethge et al., 1988), our research permits us to give a
more differentiated account. A major conclusion is that value orientations toward work, education and career depend on the actual experiences and perceived prospects which result from trajectory
membership. Work cultures and recruitment strategies of employers
in Britain and Germany are expressed in the different emphasis young
people place on training as a prerequisite for an employment career.
Thus, the proportions of young people entering the four trajectories
differ between the two countries. In Germany, most young people
(over 80%) are in highly organised transitions with good prospects.
In Britain, many more are in trajectories III and IV, and thus confront
uncertain routes and limited prospects for stable work careers.

While the academic route provides long-term prospects for entering a professional career in both countries, the three other routes
exhibit different relationships with the labour market, and lead to
variations in value-orientations and in scope for action. Trajectory II
is the pathway to skilled work in factories, office and service occupations. It provides experiences that support a positive orientation

towards a variety of aspects of work and the readiness to invest in further education in order to advance in the employment system. Especially for the apprentices in the German sample, there was the option to advance to the ranks of technician or white-collar employee status by a combination of further training and vocational schooling; some of them could finally move towards higher education. Being in trajectory III was seen by most respondents as a temporary detour, leading to full-time jobs in Britain, and to apprenticeships in Germany. These situations gave rise to work orientations which emphasised employment prospects and job security. Being trapped in unemployment or in provisions for 'problem groups' (trajectory IV) created precarious situations which seemed to foster materialistic and instrumental orientations towards work.

Our study also has implications for the ongoing debate on 'individualised youth biographies'. Most respondents in Germany were still in a formative period and on extended trajectories. Their work orientations reflected the status of trainee or student, rather than actual work experience. Thus, a mixture of individual and traditional orientations and scepticism about employment prospects predominated among the German respondents. Quite in contrast, most British respondents had more flexible job-orientations, combined with optimism about their future prospects. These orientations reflected their actual experiences in the labour market, and a general acceleration of the preparation for work. For some, however, this could have detrimental effects on their future prospects. It seems that early job flexibility among British young people is the result of a realistic assessment of labour market requirements. In contrast, young people in Germany seem to have more scope and time to find out about their interests and skills on entering the labour market. Their extended transition could provide more opportunity for an 'active mode of individualisation'.

One major conclusion is that national differences in the organisation of the transition from school to work, for example, in school-leaving ages, vocational education in colleges, apprenticeships, and other forms of on-the-job-training, create specific frameworks for experiences and attitudes. Trajectories thus mirror differential opportunities and cultural assumptions about how young people should proceed to adulthood via a combination of training, education and work. They seemed to have far more influence on the young people's future expectations and work attitudes than did their regional labour markets.

CHAPTER XII

Problems and solutions

Training for the future

Drawing useful policy conclusions requires relating our findings not so much to Europe's labour needs at the time of our research as to the twenty-first century's. There is general agreement that future workforces must be more skilled than their predecessors. The latest technological revolution associated with microelectronics is deskilling some jobs, but the more common net impact is an overall increase in firms' skill requirements. More and more routine manual and clerical operations are being automated. People are increasingly required to design, manage and maintain complex sociotechnical systems. As jobs become more demanding, the pressures on education and training increase accordingly. These trends are occurring in virtually all business sectors; public and private, manufacturing and services. Few of today's school-leavers will escape the consequences.

There are several aspects to the rise in skill requirements. The situation is not simply that an increasing proportion of jobs will be at skilled levels as traditionally defined. Skilled jobs themselves are becoming more skilled than in the past. The most rapid current growth in employment is not in traditional crafts, but in the technological, technical and professional occupations. Moreover, there are important qualitative differences between traditional and new skills. There is a heavier premium on adaptability and personal flexibility. This is a product of the hastening pace of technological change, which means that the size and shape of successful firms, and the requirements of specific jobs within them, change more rapidly than in the past. It is not new technology itself that imposes these requirements so much as competitive pressures which oblige firms either to exploit all the capabilities of the latest technologies, or to sink.

Throughout the world, simple bureaucratic hierarchies are being abandoned as too rigid and therefore dysfunctional. The most dra-

230

matic recent examples are in Eastern Europe. Business organisations are becoming more fluid. Employees are required to be creative and imaginative and to exercise discretion, but always 'responsibly', relating their own tasks and skills to internal and external company environments. Communicative and social skills are therefore being elevated to a new importance. Skilled workers are expected to address their specialist abilities and knowledge to ever-changing demands, as members of ever-changing work teams. Up to now, employment in large companies has been most affected by these trends. Hence big businesses' growing appetite for young people on the academic route who are believed to possess the desired qualities. Increasingly, however, small firms are seeking to harness the same kinds of skill.

The demographic downturn is another source of current pressure on vocational education and training. Throughout the postwar decades up to the 1970s, European countries' workforces were expanding. During the 1970s this was partly due to the increase in the number of school-leavers, a product of rising birth rates some years earlier. However, since the mid-1980s, the size of school-leaving cohorts has begun to contract in Britain and Germany, and this trend will continue into the 1990s. We already know that there will be no demographic upturn, unless large-scale immigration resumes, during the first decade of the twenty-first century. No one can be sure what will happen after that, but we know for certain that, for the next 20 years, businesses will have to recruit from smaller pools of beginners than were available in the 1970s and early 1980s. There will be fewer young people to educate and train up to the higher skill requirements of the future.

During the years preceding our research, the most sensitive question being asked of vocational education and training in Britain and Germany was whether all young people could be accommodated. During the 1980s, due to a rising gap between supply and demand for apprenticeships, the dual system not only had to be enlarged, but training schemes were introduced for socially deprived youth in

Germany, comparable in some respects to Britain's YTS. Even if these reforms met the needs of the time, it would be foolish to assume that they will match future requirements. According to our own and other evidence, both countries' young people seem prepared to follow the trends in the nationally prescribed way. In both Britain and Germany, increasing numbers have been enrolling in post-compulsory education, and in all our research areas most of the young people were obviously keen to obtain the best possible training and the highest-level employment. The key questions for each country concern whether its best will continue to be good or plentiful enough.

It would misuse and over-simplify the evidence in earlier chapters to try to conclude that one country's system was superior and should be emulated by the other. The value of international comparisons that delve to the level of individuals' experience is to raise questions about, and to probe strengths and weaknesses within, each system.

Questions for Germany

In terms of the system's ability to cope with the trends and pressures of the 1970s and 1980s, there can be no doubt that Germany's dual system proved superior to Britain's existing methods of vocational preparation. The main challenges in that period were posed by recessions and the growing size of school-leaving cohorts. Many of Britain's school-leavers floundered amidst high unemployment, so a new programme, the YTS, was introduced in 1983. In Germany, in contrast, virtually all young people could be accommodated through higher retention rates in education, some expansion of the apprentice system, and the creation of local training schemes. This solved the greater part of a threatening youth unemployment problem in Germany, though only, in some cases, by transferring joblessness to an older age group. But the system's ability to respond to the crises of the past is no guarantee that it will meet future challenges.

Indeed, the stresses of recession and the demographic upturn in the 1970s and 1980s could have concealed some longer-term problems in Germany. During the period of high unemployment rates among young people, there was a tendency for those from the academic track to enter an apprenticeship before taking up university studies. Today, however, this strategy has changed again: most young people with the *Abitur* continue on the route towards higher education and approximately 33% of all young people now follow this route. There has also been a steady decrease in the numbers attending *Hauptschulen*, the traditional base for a craft apprenticeship, and a corresponding rise in the number attending *Gymnasien and Realschulen*. The attractions of the more academic types of education are clear enough: the academic trajectory leads to the most rewarding jobs in terms of status, pay and promotion prospects. In response to the demographic downturn and increasing skill requirements, training curricula are being modernised in Germany. This meets with employers' appetites for highly-qualified recruits, including those with the *Abitur*.

Britain's YTS was originally unemployment-based. During the 1980s, the scheme's sponsors struggled to raise its status. They were battling against the reality that in economically depressed areas, such as Liverpool, many scheme places could perform little more than a warehousing role, merely postponing unemployment in many cases, rather than preparing young people for employment. In Swindon, the struggle at the time of our fieldwork was against employers' readiness to offer, and young people's willingness to accept, employment with or without systematic training. The near-adult wages available in the jobs on offer made it difficult for young people to refuse employment in favour of YTS.

Germany's system still commands tremendous domestic confidence and international admiration and, up to now, these have been among the system's special assets. Germany's employers have been, and remain, willing to train and to recognise the qualifications that apprentices gain. Trade unions wish to preserve and strengthen the system. For their part, German school-leavers from *Hauptschulen* and *Realschulen* continue to regard apprenticeships as a desirable route into working life. Many still regard it as the best of all possible starts. Parents similarly endorse it as a valued stepping stone to employment. Substantial numbers of *Abiturienten* still opt for apprentice training either prior to, or in preference to, entering higher education.

Apprenticeship has been, and is still, considered a necessary stage in the transition to adulthood for younger German school-leavers. This compares to the high regard for graduating from high school in America. Germans are no more dismayed when ex-apprentices do not obtain employment in the particular occupations in which they are initially trained than US citizens deplore high school courses with little direct vocational relevance. We suspect that this regard for formal training would survive in Germany even if all regulatory bodies and legal recognition of qualifications were scrapped. Our study, conducted at the end of the 1980s, shows that the standard response of Germans on reaching age 16 was still to seek an apprenticeship. Some of our respondents had returned to education only because they were unable to obtain apprenticeships of their choice. The prospect of gaining one made returning to vocational preparation at school for an extra year seem worthwhile. These attitudes have underpinned the West German training system. They have given it a solidity and resilience and blend into a training culture that is among the nation's assets.

However, our surveys tapped latent dissatisfaction, even frustration, much of it stemming from job search experience. Most of the young Germans who had sought apprenticeships had made multiple applications; far more on average than the British school-leavers had made for either jobs or YTS places. Many of the young Germans were eventually settling for training in occupations and with firms that the individuals considered second- or third-best. This was because many had lost out in the competition for high-grade apprenticeships with their more qualified contemporaries. It is true that very few apprentices voiced overall dissatisfaction with their training, but this seemed partly a product of a general willingness to come to terms with reality. Many of the German apprentices felt that their training allowances were unjustly low. Even so, in general, the Germans were more satisfied with their lives than were the British respondents.

'I want to become what I am trained for', is a familiar sentiment among German youth, which has no close equivalent in British popular culture. On reaching the end of their compulsory schooling, however, young Germans cannot be confident about their occupational destinies. They cannot rely even on obtaining the apprenticeships of their choice. In any case, many do not proceed to practise the occupations in which they are initially trained. The motivation to move through the training system depends on young people being hopeful that the system will deliver what they want. Up to now, they have been prepared to accept what they have been offered, usually the dual system, and have relied on this route to shape and deliver their future prospects. Will this continue?

One specific question that our evidence poses for Germany's dual system concerns the wide variations in the quality of training. Young Germans are well aware of these disparities. Hence the intense competition for 'good' apprenticeships. Training in a large company tends to be qualitatively different from what is on offer in a small firm, which will typically depend on the attitudes of the *Meister*, who may also be the employer. Some of the apprentices in Paderborn and Bremen complained that much of their time was spent performing unskilled tasks.

The fact that all the German apprentices in this survey were confident of completing their training successfully, demonstrates an awareness of the crucial importance of a vocational certificate for labour market entry. Germany is accustomed to foreign observers praising the training quality of the dual system. So it could be a surprise that in our surveys the British samples reported the greater number of vocational learning experiences. In both cohorts, higher proportions of the British respondents reported experience of information technology, learning new skills, being challenged or tested, using their initiative, and working co-operatively in groups. In many respects, the British samples appeared the more enterprising. For example, they were the more likely to envisage training for new occupations some time in the future, and migrating to different areas for better job prospects. These results mainly refer to the number of work-related experiences; they cannot tell us much about the quality of the experience or its context. Furthermore, British youth in trajectories II, III and IV were embarking on entry into the labour market proper two years before their German counterparts. Thus, they were probably bound to report a greater variety of work-related experiences.

Is Germany's education and training sufficiently demanding to satisfy future skill requirements? Certainly, up to age 16, German young people perform consistently better than their British counterparts on standard attainment tests. But is this superiority carried through equally into vocational training? There was as much, if not greater, variation in the quality of training reported by British respondents who were in employment and on the YTS. In Germany, there is stronger regulation of training by the 'social partners'. Young people have to master prescribed skills and pass examinations in order to qualify. This ensures minimum standards and quality control, and provides a generally recognised level of certified skills. But is the system sufficiently demanding above these baselines?

The extent to which vocational education and training in Germany are prescribed and controlled by regulatory bodies raises a further question: is the system too rigid? There could be an over-emphasis on specific skills at the expense of nurturing the flexible capacities that are increasingly required. This has been recognised through the recent redesign of training curricula for metal, electrical and business occupations. But there are many other areas, such as the building trades, where reforms have proved more difficult to achieve. The German emphasis on 'recognised' training and 'formal' qualifications could make the system vulnerable and provide access to occupations, even when they do not measure their holders' ability to perform competently. Meanwhile, individuals with uncertified talent are held back. This, of course, was one of the major criticisms of the craft apprenticeship system in Britain, which was often said to contain a large element of time-serving (DE, 1985).

Another question that our evidence directs at the dual system concerns apprentices' difficulties in changing track. In Britain, there was much more movement between jobs and training schemes, though rarely back to education. In our research it was relatively easy to see which trajectories the German samples were on, whereas in Swindon and Liverpool it was not just common, but perfectly normal, for young people to change direction. In Germany, the disadvantages stemming from dropping out were relatively harsh. Many respondents on trajectories III and IV in the German areas had arrived on these routes after failing to enter or stay in the dual system, having quitted apprenticeships or education prematurely. The fact that some German apprenticeships have high dropout rates, despite the penalties, is another indication of how the training and prospects vary in quality. In Britain, it was far easier for young people to move sideways, hopefully to build upon their existing experience, and to benefit from the better prospects elsewhere. Such a form of 'transferable credit' has not normally been available in Germany's dual system. Apprentices are expected to complete their training. If they fail to do so, they encounter barriers to employment. Therefore, most dropouts attempt to enter another, more promising apprenticeship. This, however, can be difficult, particularly in times of high unemployment, when dropouts may be forced into casual work or unemployment. Is the system penalising rather than rewarding the individual initiative and flexibility that future skilled workers are likely to need?

Another question for Germany concerns the absence of 'respectable' routes into non-skilled work. The routes where such jobs were the most likely outcome were filled by young people who were there not by choice, but as a result of failing on other trajectories, or their inability to obtain anything else. In Germany, such young people are a small minority, analogous to high school dropouts in North America. Rising skill requirements could leave this disadvantaged minority lagging further behind.

Yet even the most technologically advanced economies will continue to generate many unskilled jobs in manufacturing and, in particular, in consumer services. During recent decades, such jobs have been rejected by native-born adult males in most western countries. If locally-educated young people are to be channelled into these positions, both the routes and occupations may have to be upgraded. Britain has more young people on such routes - probably too many - but the individuals are not a class apart to the same extent as in Germany. On many of the measurements in our questionnaires, the contrasts between trajectories were much wider in Germany than in Britain because, in the former country, the samples in trajectories III and IV lagged well behind those on the more prestigious routes. Some of the young Germans who had been on trajectory III, though, had managed to climb back onto trajectory II.

Finally, the dual system is premised on a division earlier on in an educational career - between *Gymnasium*, *Realschule* and *Hauptschule*. The routes from these different secondary schools have become more blurred as pressures for access to a variety of post-16 routes have built up and traditional pathways have closed. It is difficult to see how any major reforms to the German dual system could take place without reviewing and, if necessary, overhauling what precedes it as well.

Questions for Britain

Some of our evidence gives Britain's education and training a better image than we have been led to believe it deserves. This applies particularly to the British samples reporting the broader range of vocational learning experiences, displaying the more enterprising attitudes, and expressing greater confidence in their own future employment options. Our findings have not repeated the now familiar story of all-round German superiority, though the indications of unexpected British strengths could be interpreted in several different ways. Were the samples unrepresentative of the countries' young people in each trajectory? Were the questions unintentionally biased so as to allow British respondents greater scope to report positive experiences, achievements and ambitions? Or had Britain's vocational education and training improved so dramatically during the 1980s as to catch up with and, in some respects, surpass Germany's achievements?

Our considered opinion is that at a certain level our findings are generalisable, and would probably have been similar had the study been conducted before all the changes of the 1980s. But the evidence must be set in context, rather than taken at its most obvious face value. A strength of comparative research that delves beneath macrostructures and captures individuals' experiences is to provide clearer evidence on exactly how countries differ. By asking young people to give us their appraisals of what they had learned and experienced, we can pinpoint the interactions of individuals with the content and processes of a training system. We did not test young people's vocational knowledge and skills, nor did we investigate the content of what they were taught. We do not know whether the words used to describe skills and experiences meant precisely the same thing in the two countries. Even an apparently unproblematic term like 'information technology' can have different national nuances. Nevertheless, the overall picture of greater breadth of experience and skill in the British system, and the more positive appraisals by the British young people of what they were learning, is sustained. At least as they saw it, their work-related training was covering a broader range of skills and work experiences than the dual system in the age group that we examined. Reasons for the difference are more difficult to come by, but it seems likely that one advantage of starting into the labour market earlier, and the employee status accorded to large numbers of 16-19 years-olds in Britain, is that their training is more closely integrated with their work.

In so far as Britain's young people are under-trained, the roots of this problem do not appear to lie in any general paucity of experience offered in training or employment. Indeed, the deeply-rooted British problem is more likely to lie in demanding that young people mature very quickly. At the age of 16, the majority have to make important choices like whether to remain in full-time education or to leave to seek a job or enter the YTS. Britain's 16 year-olds have little alternative but to display initiative and to act responsibly. By age 18, the majority are in regular employment. They must learn rapidly because the system demands that they grow up quickly. It also means that they detach themselves earlier than their continental counterparts from the educational process, thereby perhaps missing out on the benefits it may have for the wider aspects of preparation for adulthood. It is significant that more German young people in all the routes except trajectory IV expressed interest in politics, even though they were less certain as to which parties to vote for. The Germans were also generally more satisfied with their lives and where they lived. It seems likely that the relative stability of trajectory membership and the educational component of the dual system were fostering these attitudes and helping to develop active citizenship. On the other hand, good relations with parents and positive self-images were equally common in both countries.

One question for Britain that our evidence poses is whether even the country's new and reformed vocational courses and training demand too much too soon. Our samples were matched for age but, in terms of proximity to adult status in the labour market, the British respondents were at least two years ahead of their German counterparts. This applied on every career trajectory. On Britain's academic route, the transition to higher education is normally a year earlier than in Germany, and undergraduate courses are shorter. With the extension for national service for males in Germany, graduation typically does not take place until the late 20s, compared with the early 20s in Britain. When our British samples entered the YTS, it was a two-year scheme for 16 year-olds, and a one-year scheme for 17 year-old entrants. So, by age 18, all the individuals who followed this route were expected to hold their own in employment. In 1988, only 40% of British young people were still engaged in full- or part-time education at age 18, compared with 80% in Germany. Most members of our British samples who had left full-time education were already in employment at the time of the fieldwork, and very few anticipated being anywhere else in another year's time, whereas most of the Germans expected still to be apprentices or students. A typical problem in the British system could still be that vocational preparation finishes too soon and at too low a level for the individuals' or the economy's long-term good. The YTS releases large numbers of young people with low-level skills and qualifications that fall short of traditional craft standards, to say nothing of future requirements. As in Germany, the training available is of variable quality. Good YTS training is probably as good as that on offer in a comparable scheme in Germany; bad YTS training, because of its lack of regulation and paucity of educational content, is probably much worse.

A second question for Britain concerns the absence of the kind of training culture that is deeply rooted in Germany. In Swindon and Liverpool, the standard behaviour on reaching the statutory school-leaving age had been to search for a job. Only the academic high-fliers had taken staying in education for granted, and many of these at 18 were testing the labour market before entering higher education. Only if the typical 16 year-old school-leaver was unable to find a regular job would he or she consider the YTS, not least because the YTS allowance was about half the average teenage wage.

Such behaviour gives a clear signal that, in Britain, training is still not accorded anything resembling the status that it enjoys in Germany. Through the National Council for Vocational Qualifications the government has, of course, been trying to rectify this but, in comparison with Germany, Britain may still be setting its sights too low. In Britain, training has customarily been delivered on, rather than prior to, entering regular employment. Apprentices and other trainees are still usually employees and are remunerated accordingly. They have always regarded themselves as 'doing jobs', and have expected the offer of staying on, having served their time successfully. The YTS appears to have been assimilated into these ways of thinking, rather than changing them.

Young people continued to refer to YTS places as 'jobs', and judged schemes primarily according to the prospects of being 'kept on'. Employers have reciprocated these attitudes. Training is not a high-status function in most British companies. Investment goes into employment rather than training, and the progression from relatively low training allowances to much higher levels of pay later is absent from large areas of work. The *Meister* role, to which all skilled German workers can aspire, has no British equivalent. This is not a weak link so much as a wholly missing link in British vocational training (Rose, 1989). Training outside employment, and vocational qualifications that are not backed by on-the-job experience, carry little weight when most British employers sift applicants. The content of the training seems hardly relevant. Completing a college course or a YTS scheme will not guarantee British young people's acceptance as 'skilled' by employers, other employees, or the individuals themselves. It is fairly easy to alter the labels and content of training courses and schemes, whereas national attitudes seem far more resistant to change.

We queried whether Germany's dual system might be too rigid and might offer too few opportunities for individuals to change tracks. For Britain, in contrast, the relevant question posed by our evidence concerns whether the system veers too far in the opposite direction. The British respondents on trajectory II were following a variety of routes towards skilled employment. It was sometimes difficult to decide whether a particular career should be placed in trajectory II or III. There were no comparable difficulties in Germany, where routes towards skilled employment were defined more clearly. There are strengths in the less structured British system, and corresponding weaknesses. Beneath the professions, Britain has few occupations where vocational education and training must deliver prescribed learning experiences before individuals can practise. There are also few occupations for which particular entry qualifications are absolutely essential. There is usually a variety of routes towards an occupational goal, which makes it fairly easy for teenagers to change track without moving backwards. So, in an area such as Swindon where labour demand was strong, it was possible for young people to build careers into skilled employment by creating their own patterns of alternation between employment, training and further education. The British respondents in this research had often switched positions in an apparently haphazard manner. Courses and training schemes had been deserted before completion, usually not because the individuals were failing to make the grade, but so that they could seize better opportunities to progress and make more money. In Swindon, with its buoyant economy, any kind of post-compulsory education, training or work experience was likely to assist a young person to build a progressive career. Even without them, a job was not that difficult to find. The greater confidence in prospects shown by the British young people compared with those in Germany was undoubtedly reinforced by the relative ease with which employment could be achieved.

But there is a sense in which this was 'false confidence'. Whenever the economy contracts, people without training are usually the first to be squeezed out of the labour market. They can easily join a pool of unskilled under-trained labour, unattractive to the new businesses on which the regeneration of the economy depends. Even in booming Swindon, the main problem being faced by employers was finding recruits whose suitability was assured. And this problem was aggravated by the young people's skills, when they did have them, rarely being certified in ways that would allow potential employers to recognise the individuals' assets instantly. For their part, young people in Britain cannot rely on their qualifications and training being recognised by potential employers. The latter tend to have little confidence in the basic vocational qualifications that are within the majority's reach. Simultaneously, firms tend to be suspicious of 'mere' experience gained elsewhere.

It was the state of the local labour market in Swindon, not the intrinsic quality of the education and training on offer, that made it likely that young people would be able to build upon whatever qualifications and training they obtained. Liverpool's labour market was where young people faced all the problems. They were unable to rely on their experience, qualifications and skills being rewarded, or even recognised, by employers. Thus, the state of the labour market in Britain is critical in determining whether the diversity of routes will lead to adult employment. In Swindon, there was usually no real need, from a young person's or employer's point of view, for vocational preparation as envisaged in YTS. In Liverpool, it was more likely to be young people's only option for escaping joblessness.

A fourth question for Britain concerns the distribution of young people between the trajectories that we have distinguished. In virtually all parts of Germany, 80% or more of young people enter trajectories I or II, meaning that they either reach the higher education entry standard or become qualified for skilled employment. It is more difficult to say exactly how many of Britain's young people follow the equivalent routes, because the boundaries are less clear, but there can be no doubt that the proportion falls well short of Germany's. There are some benefits in this British situation. The fact that so many school-leavers are not trained up to skilled status means that they cannot be as stigmatised a minority as in Germany, though there is a danger of slipping into Britain's new underclass of permanently unemployed, marginalised people. In addition, the weaker boundaries between Britain's career routes create opportunities for individuals to ascend from trajectories III and IV. However, it may be useful to recall the rather different kinds of individuals who were on these trajectories in the two countries. Most of the Germans seemed to have dropped into these routes because they had lost touch with more promising passages towards work. Some had failed to obtain school-leaving certificates, while a larger number had left apprenticeships or jobs and had thereby literally descended from routes offering more attractive prospects. Most British respondents on the third and fourth trajectories had not dropped down: they had never been offered better opportunities. Many regretted not having worked harder at school. Nearly all deplored their obviously limited prospects. Unemployment was invariably detested. Most of those in unskilled jobs would have preferred something better.

Another common complaint, particularly in Liverpool, was about training schemes which the individuals had completed successfully but which had led nowhere. Many of the young people on trajectories III and IV in Britain complained that they seemed to have no immediate prospect of any further training. This response was also found among German youths on trajectories III and IV who had no realistic option to return to the mainstream by starting an apprenticeship. Most of these respondents were en route to unskilled jobs, or to nowhere at all, only because the transition systems in both countries had offered them too few structured and continuous passages to higher-level employment.

The British system of vocational training is now founded, for the majority of young people, on comprehensive secondary education up to age 16, and then a division between the academic and prevocational staying-on routes, and the variety of routes for leavers. But the decision about staying on is shaped earlier, in the light of the young person's school performance and the GCSE options arising from it. The educational route is thus curtailed for a sizeable proportion of young people and because, unlike the dual system, there is no mandatory requirement for continued contact with education after age 16, future prospects of 'returning to learning' are further weakened. In this sense, the British system departs perhaps further from the demands of a modern technological society than any other country in Europe.

The academic route

Most of our analysis and conclusions have been based on comparing and contrasting, but the design of this research rested on there being basic similarities between vocational preparation in Britain and Germany. It was possible to identify four similar routes in each country. The boundaries between these routes tend to be stronger, and the curricula within them are more likely to be uniform and prescribed in Germany. The proportions of all young people who follow each trajectory differ considerably between the countries. However, Britain and Germany have broadly comparable routes, which are arranged in the same hierarchy, headed by the academic trajectory.

This undoubtedly remains each country's most attractive route. Its prestige has survived successive waves of technological and occupational change. It is the longest and, in intellectual terms at least, the most demanding route into employment, yet its magnetism is undiminished. It attracts the bulk of each country's more educationally successful young people. This trajectory has not only survived but has become broader in both countries; the proportions of young people following the route have increased. Nowadays in Germany, approximately a third of all young people gain the *Abitur*. This growth has been more restrained in Britain, where all young people face a major examination hurdle at 16-plus, at which standards have been historically fixed so that, until recently, less than 25% have obtained the grades judged necessary to enrol for the two or more A-levels normally required for higher education. However, in Britain, there has been a strong and continuing trend towards 16 year-olds who do not quite reach this standard staying in full-time education to take various mixtures of less demanding academic and vocational courses. The net effect has been that nowadays, around half of each cohort in Britain enrols for some type of full-time post-compulsory education. A year later, however, the proportion drops to around a third.

A consequence of these trends has been that Britain and Germany's pools of statutory age school-leavers available for firm-based training or employment have diminished in size and quality. There-fore, many firms seeking recruits to train for higher-level occupations have switched their attention to 17-19 year-olds, or higher education graduates. These are the trends which, combined with the current demographic downturn, have pushed Germany's dual system into a process of modernisation. The same trends reduced the chances of Britain's YTS ever becoming a high-quality training programme. Em-ployers have been partly responsible for this situation. Their willing-ness to offer exceptional financial rewards to older, better-qualified entrants, encourages able 16 year-olds to remain in the academic mainstream. Yet many firms believe that they have no option but to follow the talent, and have mixed feelings about the consequences. Most employers, and many young people and their parents, see defi-nite advantages in firm-based training from age 16. This exposes young people to the culture of 'real work' in industry. It enables them to acquire practical skills, to apply their knowledge, and to spend their formative, late-adolescent years becoming incorporated into companies' workforces. Also, teenagers can be hired for sub-adult wages, thereby reducing firms' staff costs. However, employers also recognise the special value added by higher education. They ac-knowledge that it makes young adults independent and critical, and develops communication and other social skills, thereby laying the foundations for the kinds of occupational capability that are increas-ingly demanded. A principal challenge in training for the future in Britain, Germany and elsewhere, will be to strike the optimum bal-ance between the academic route into the workplace and the routes to skilled positions from firm-based training.

One recent response to this problem in both countries has been to vocationalise the academic routes by expanding courses based on science and technology, and by introducing work experience into student's programmes. Britain is probably more advanced than Ger-many in this particular area, partly because its academic mainstream is more difficult to enter, and its firm-based training weaker and there-fore less attractive. In both countries, however, the optimum balance is likely to require developing or maintaining near-equal status for firm-based routes into employment. The full development of human resources will depend on this, because some young people without exceptional academic interest flourish in work environments, just as some of the most academically motivated have little interest in translating their abilities into effective performance in the other 'real world' of work. The German dual system is undoubtedly the stronger base from which to build in this area. Britain's starting points are a contracting traditional system of apprenticeship and a low-status YTS. However, Britain has a strong tradition of employing young people which could make it sensible to promote education and training within, as well as outside, youth employment. In Britain, young people thus seem to have the better chance of avoiding the danger of upgraded firm-based training casting the majority, who cannot make the revised standards, further adrift. This, in our view, may become a serious problem in Germany, to which no easy solutions, short of starting apprenticeships for the less qualified, are in sight.

Building on national assets

A global perspective shows that there are alternative ways in which successful industrial economies have met their labour requirements. There has never been a close correlation between national industrial success and the proportions of young people proceeding through higher education. German-style apprentice training has never been a necessary condition for forming competitive industrial workforces. Sweden, the USA and Japan have been successful industrial economies without a dual system. Over 90% are still in full-time education beyond the age of 16 in each of these countries, and what is offered afterwards in terms of vocational training differs between them. Each organises the transition into employment in its own distinctive way. None of these countries is likely to break with the grain of its own history. Nor is Germany likely to abandon the dual system and the associated training culture. These are national assets which Germany will be ill-advised and most unlikely to cast aside in addressing the needs of the future. But what of Britain?

Our study has provided more evidence of now familiar problems, and has directed additional questions at Britain's vocational preparation. However, our evidence has also raised questions for Germany, which indicate that vocational preparation in Britain has some special strengths. If other impediments to economic success in Britain could be removed, time-honoured practices, such as the early exposure of teenagers to the realities of employment, might look positively effective. It is, perhaps, noteworthy that Britain's performance in agriculture, and in most service sectors, compares favourably with other advanced industrial societies. These British businesses rely on the same educational system, and have similar methods of assimilating beginning workers, as in manufacturing. At the same time, we have to consider why young people leave the education system early in Britain, and what could be done to make it more attractive and genuinely beneficial. The gulf between the academic and the practical, the 'varsity' and the workplace, the juvenile and the adult, are still perhaps too deeply entrenched to make post-16 full-time education a better option for many teenagers when compared with pay and adult status in the labour market. Only an overhaul of the whole 11 to 18 educational offer, and a radical shift in attitudes and expectations at all levels of education, are likely to make a difference.

We do not advise Britain or Germany to copy the other's vocational preparation slavishly, because neither has a ready-made system matching the needs of the present, let alone the future. Indeed, rather than looking to other lands, each country will probably be better-advised to focus on future requirements, and to seek to meet these by building upon its existing strengths. A country's heritage may sometimes create difficulties in addressing new problems and opportunities, but effective solutions are most likely to be developed within the existing culture's practices and modes of thought. Even countries which share much of the same European, scientific and industrial cultures can find it difficult to transplant specific practices. Methods that are imported from another society rarely work in exactly the same way elsewhere. There is ample evidence of this in recent British efforts to transplant two-step transitions into employment. At the same time, complacency can be equally dangerous and damaging. As well as making countries more aware of, and willing to question, their existing practices, an additional pay-off from cross-national research can be to make the participating countries more appreciative of their own special strengths. This should be taken as the starting point for reforms to improve the life chances of young people in both societies.

REFERENCES

Ashton, D., Maguire M., *The vanishing youth labour market*, Youth Aid, London, 1983.

Ashton, D., Maguire, M., *Young adults in the labour market*, Department of Employment, Research Paper No. 55, London, 1986.

Baethge, M., Hantshe, B., Pelull, W., Voskamp, U., *Arbeit und Gewerkschaften - Perspektiven von Jugendlichen*, Göttingen, 1985.

Baethge, M., Hantshe, B., Pelull, W., Voskamp, U., *Jugend: Arbeit und Identität*, Opladen, Leske & Budrich, 1988.

Banks, M., Evans, S., 'Employment and training orientation as a function of gender, careers and labour markets', *ESRC 16-19 Initative Occasional Paper* No. 9, City University, London, 1989.

BMBW (Bundesminister für Bildung und Wissenschaft), *Das soziale Bild der Studentenschaft in der Bundesrepublik Deutschland*, Bonn, 1986.

BMBW, (Bundesminister für Bildung und Wissenschaft), *Grund- und Strukturdaten 1988/89*, Bonn, 1989.

Brock, D., Friebel, H., Heinz, W.R., Otto-Brock, Eva-M., *Youth employment in the FRG*, paper presented to seminar on European research: young people and employment, Marseilles, 1987.

Bynner, J.M., 'Coping with transition: ESRC's new 16-19 Initiative', *Youth and Policy*, 22, pp. 25-28, 1987.

Bynner, J.M., Heinz, W.R., 'Matching samples and analysing their differences in a cross-national study of labour market entry in England and West Germany', *International Journal of Comparative Sociology*, 32, pp. 137-153, 1991.

Casey, B., 'The dual apprentice system and the recruitment and retention of young persons in West Germany', *British Journal of Industrial Relations*, 24, pp. 63-81, 1986.

CEDEFOP, *Description of vocational training systems in the Member States of the European Community*, CEDEFOP, Luxembourg, 1982.

CEDEFOP, *Employers' organisations and their contribution in developing vocational education politics in the European Community*, CEDEFOP, Luxembourg, 1987.

Clough, E., Gray, J., Jones, B., 'Curricular patterns in post-compulsory provision from the Youth Cohort Study', *Research Papers in Education* 3, pp. 27-41, 1988a.

Clough, E., Gray, J., Jones, B., Pattie, C., *Routes through YTS: the experiences of young people participating in the Youth Training Scheme*, Manpower Services Commission, Sheffield, 1988b.

Coffield, F., Borrill, C., Marshall, S., *Growing up at the margins*, Open University Press, Milton Keynes, 1986.

CBI (Confederation of British Industry), *Towards a skills revolution*, Interim Report of the Vocational Education and Training Task Force, London, 1989.

Corfield, P.J., *The impact of English towns 1700-1800*, Oxford University Press, 1982.

Dale, A., 'Part-time work among young people in Britain', *ESRC 16-19 Initiative Occasional Paper* No. 3, City University, London, 1989.

DE (Department of Employment), *Education and training for young people*, Cmnd 9135, HMSO, London, 1985.

DE (Department of Employment), *Working together, education and training*, Cmnd 9823, HMSO, London, 1986.

DE (Department of Employment), *Employment for the 1990s*, Cm 540, HMSO, London, 1988.

DES (Department of Education and Science), *HMI Report on aspects of the microelectronics education programme*, Department of Education and Science, HMSO, London, 1987.

DES (Department of Education and Science), *Statistical bulletin,* 14/88 and 1/89, Department of Education and Science, HMSO, London, 1988a, 1989.

DES (Department of Education and Science), *Education statistics,* Department of Education and Science, HMSO, London, 1988b.

Durrer-Guthof, F., Kazemzadeh, F., *Berufliche Ausbildung - Alternative im Studium?*, HIS, Hannover, 1984.

Engel, U., Hurrelmann, K., *Psychosoziale Belastungen im Jugendalter*, De Gruyter, Berlin, 1989.

Evans, K., Brown, A., Oates, T., *Developing work-based learning,* Manpower Services Commission, Sheffield, 1987.

Fitzgerald, A., *New technology and mathematics on employment,* University of Birmingham, 1985.

Flanagan, C., *Parents' work security and the young adolescent's development,* unpublished manuscript, University of Michigan, Dearborn, 1988.

Fothergill, R., 'The director's view', *British Journal of Educational Technology,* 18, 1987.

GEW (Gewerkschaft Erziehung und Wissenschaft), *Report to the International Federation for Free Teachers Unions,* Washington D.C., 1987.

Grimond, J., *Youth unemployment and the bridge from school to work,* Anglo-German Foundation, London, 1979.

Guggemos, P., *Bewältigung der Arbeitslosigkeit,* Deutscher Studien Verlag, Weinheim, 1989.

Haller, F., *Die Industriekonjunktur in Lande Bremen. Analyse ihrer gesamtwirtschaftlichen Beziehungen*, Bremer Ausschuss für Wirtschaftsforschung, Bremen, 1975.

Hamilton, S.F.,'Apprenticeship as a transition to adulthood in West Germany', *American Journal of Education*, 95, pp. 315-345, 1987.

Hauser, R., Semrau, P., *Polarisierungstendenzen in der Einkommensverteilung*, ISI, No .3, 1990.

Hayes, C., Anderson, A., Fonda, N., *Competence and competition*, National Economic Development Council/Manpower Services Commission, London, 1984.

Heinz, W.R., 'Between school and work: will compensatory training schemes solve the problem of youth unemployment?' In: Policy Studies Institute/Anglo-German Foundation, *Thinkers and makers: education for tomorrow's society*, London, 1985.

Heinz, W.R., et al., *Hauptsache, eine Lehrstelle*, Beltz, Weinheim & Basel, 1985 (second edition, 1987).

Heinz, W.R., 'The transition from school to work in crisis: coping with threatening unemployment', *Journal of Adolescent Research*, 2, pp. 127-141, 1987.

Heinz, W.R., 'Youth and labour markets: promises of comparative research on transition processes', in Ashton, D. and Lowe, G., *Making their way: school to work transitions in Britain and Canada*, Open University Press, Milton Keynes, 1990.

Heseler, H., 'Zu neuen Ufern? - Bremens Arbeitsmarkt zwischen Stagnation und Dynamik', in: Kooperation Universität-Arbeiterkammer Bremen (ed.), *Stadtstaat im Umbruch*, VSA, Hamburg, 1987.

Hurrelmann, K., *Social structure and personality development*, Cambridge University Press, 1988.

Inglehart R., *The silent revolution. Changing values and political styles among Western publics,* Princeton University Press, 1987.

Jones, I.S., 'Skill formation and pay relativities', in: Wordswick, G.D.N. (ed.), *Education & Economic Performance,* Gower, Aldershot, 1985.

Jones, I.S., 'Die Lehrlingsvergütung und die Kosten der Berufsausbildung in Großbritannien und West-Deutschland', in: *Soziales Europa,* Beiheft 8/85, 'Die Entlohnung der Jugendlichen und die Einstellungspraktiken der Arbeitgeber für junge Arbeitskräfte in der Gemeinschaft', Luxembourg, 1986.

Kieselbach T., 'Familie unter dem Druck der Arbeitslosigkeit. 'Opfer-durch-Nähe' und Quelle sozialer Unterstützung', in: Menne, K. und Alter, K. (eds.), *Familie in der Krise. Sozialer Wandel, Familie und Erziehungsberatung,* pp. 47-76, Weinheim, 1988.

Kieselbach, T., Lödige-Röhrs, L., Lünser A., *Die Kinder von Arbeitslosen - 'Opfer-durch-Nähe', Ergebnisse der psychologischen Arbeitslosenforschung zu den Auswirkungen von Arbeitslosigkeit auf die Familie.* Paper presented to the Social Democratic Party (SPD) conference: 'Gestohlene Kindheit - Verborgene Folgelasten der Langzeitarbeitslosigkeit', Bonn, 16 November 1989.

KUA-DGB, Kooperation Universität-Arbeiterkammer and Deutscher Gewerkschaftsbund Kreis Bremen (eds.), *Materialien zur Arbeitsmarktkonferenz,* 26. Mai 1988. Paper presented to the Labour Market Conference, 26 May 1988.

Lallade, J.P., 'Recent trends in vocational education and training: an overview', *European Journal of Education,* 24, pp. 103-125, 1989.

Laurance, J., 'Unemployment: health hazards', *New Society,* 1986.

Lenhardt, G., 'Youth unemployment in West Germany: trends and causes', in: Pettman, B.O., and Fyfe, J. (eds.), *Youth unemployment in Great Britain and the Federal Republic of Germany*, MCB Publications, Bradford, 1977.

Linn, P., 'Microcomputers in education: living and dead labour', in: Solomonides, T., and Levidow, L. (eds.), *Compulsive technology: computers as culture*, Free Association Books, London, 1985.

Liverpool City Council, *Past trends and future prospects*, Liverpool, 1987.

Liverpool City Council, *Population trends and prospects*, February, Liverpool, 1989.

Maier, C.S., *Changing boundaries of the political - essays on the economy, balance between the state and society, public and private,* Cambridge University Press, 1987.

Marriner, S., *The economic and social development of Merseyside,* London, 1982.

McLoyd, V.C., 'Socialization and development in a changing economy. The effects of paternal job and income loss on children', *American Psychologist,* 44, pp. 293-302, 1989.

Minford, A.P.L., et al., *The housing morass,* Institute of Economic Affairs, London, 1987.

Nabarro, R., 'The impact on workers from the inner city of Liverpool's economic decline', in: Evans, D.A., and Eversley, A. (eds.), *The inner city,* London, 1980.

Raffe, D., Smith, P., 'Young people's attitude to YTS', *British Educational Research Journal,* 13, pp. 241-260, 1987.

Raffe, D., *The status of vocational education and training; the case of YTS,* Research on Employment and Unemployment Workshops, ESRC/Department of Employment, London, 1988.

Roberts, J., 'Apprenticeships in West Germany', *Employment Gazette*, March/April 1986, pp. 109-115, 1986.

Roberts, K., ESRC, 'Young people in society', *Youth and Policy*, 22, pp. 15-24, 1987.

Roberts, K., Dench, S., Richardson, D., *The changing structure of youth labour markets*, Department of Employment Research Paper, No. 59, London, 1987.

Roberts, K., Parsell, G., 'Opportunity structures and career trajectories from age 16-19', *ESRC 16-19 Initiative Occasional Paper*, No. 1, City University, London, 1988.

Roberts, K., Parsell, G., Connolly, M., 'Britain's economic recovery, the new demographic trend and young people's transition into the labour market', *ESRC 16-19 Initiative Occasional Paper*, No. 8, City University, London, 1989a.

Roberts, K., Siwek, M., Parsell, G., 'What are Britain's 16-19 year-olds learning?' *ESRC 16-19 Initiative Occasional Paper*, No. 10, City University, London, 1989b.

Roberts, K., Parsell, G., 'The stratification of youth training', *ESRC 16-19 Initiative Occasional Paper*, No. 11, City University, London, 1989c.

Rose, R., *What's new in youth employment policy: from producing jobs to producing training*, Centre for the Study of Public Policy, University of Strathclyde, Glasgow, 1989.

Rose, R., Page, E.C., 'Searching and acting in diversity: a dissatisficing model of responses to unemployment in Britain and Germany', *Studies in Public Policy*, No. 174, Centre for Study of Public Policy, University of Strathclyde, Glasgow, 1989.

Rose, R., 'Prospective evaluation through comparative analysis: youth training in a time-space perspective', *Studies in Public Policy* No. 182, Centre for the Study of Public Policy, University of Strathclyde, Glasgow, 1990.

Rose, R., Wignanek, G., *Training without trainers?* Anglo-German Foundation, London, 1990.

Rosenberg, M., *Society and the adolescent self-image*, Princeton University Press, 1965.

Russell, R., 'A comparison of YTS in the UK with vocational foundation training in Germany', in: Wordswick, G.D.N. (ed.), *Education and Economic Performance*, Gower, Aldershot, 1985.

Sachau, C., *Berufsvorbereitende und berufsqualifizierende Maßnahmen im ausserbetrieblichen Bereich, Bewährungshilfe für Jugendliche und Heranwachsende*, Bremen, 1988.

Schmid, G., Baissert, B., 'Do institutions make a difference? Finance systems of labour market policy', *Journal of Public Policy*, 8, 1988.

Senator für Bildung, Wissenschaft und Kunst, *Vierter Berufsbildungsbericht Bremen*, Bremen, 1987.

Senator für Bildung, Wissenschaft und Kunst, *Schulstatistischer Dienst 2/88*, Bremen, 1988.

Social Europe, 'Recent progress made in introducing new information technologies into education', *EEC Supplement* 4180, Brussels, 1986.

Spruit, I.P., *Unemployment, employment and health*, University of Leiden, 1983.

Stegmann, H, Kraft, H., 'Erwerbslosigkeit in den ersten Berufsjahren', *Mitt AB*, 21. Jg., pp. 1-15, 1988.

Stokes, G., Cochrane, R., 'A study of the psychological effects of redundancy and unemployment', *Journal of Occupational Psychology*, 57, pp. 309-322, 1984.

Taylor, M.E., *Education and work in the Federal Republic of Germany*, Anglo-German Foundation, London, 1981.

Training Agency, *Training in Britain*, HMSO, London, 1989.

Walper, S., *Familiäre Konsequenzen ökonomischer Deprivation*, Psychologie Verlags Union, Munich, 1988.

Warr, P.B., Jackson, P., Banks, M., 'Duration of unemployment and psychological well-being', *Current Psychological Research*, 2, 1982.

Warr, P.B., 'Work and unemployment', in: Drenth, P.J.D., et al. (eds.), *Handbook of work and organisation psychology*, Wiley, Chichester, 1983.

Wellington, J.J., *Skills for the future*, University of Sheffield, 1987.

APPENDICES

Appendix I

Sampling and trajectory matching

Bremen sample

In order to elicit willingness to participate in the study, the Bremen team decided initially to use a short screening questionnaire. The city registration office supplied addresses of a representative sample of 1,200 youngsters aged between 16 and 19. The addresses of 19 individuals were incomplete, so 1,181 questionnaires were sent out. Because of data protection rules, it was impossible to retain the addresses once the questionnaires had been mailed, so no reminders could be sent out.

The result was rather disappointing: just 241 (20.27%) of the youngsters responded; 215 of them agreed to further participation in the project. The intense public discussion about the 1987 Census (especially in Bremen) and high sensitivity about data protection created by this discussion are possible reasons for the low response rate. Also, as we had expected, there was a big difference of responses between trajectories (Table 1).

Table 1: Response to screening questionnaire, by trajectory

Trajectory	I	II	III	IV
Participants	131	61	10	2

While we were able to fill trajectories I and II with respondents to the screening questionnaire, it was quite obvious that additional sampling had to take place in order to fill the other trajectories. So the Bremen team visited schemes and schools. Young people on all college-based, or otherwise non-firm-based, schemes providing training were considered to belong to trajectory III. Courses preparing for, and usually leading into, qualified training were put in this category too. Sampling in trajectory IV was even more difficult, because there was no co-operation from the labour administration. The educational authorities proved more helpful, however: all youngsters leaving secondary education ('*Sekundarstufe I*') without going into vocational preparation or training (the equivalent of unemployment in Britain) are obliged to attend 'general vocational school' up to age 18. With the help of school headmasters and teachers, it was possible to get unemployed youngsters to fill in the questionnaires at school. Additionally, the researchers approached the organisers of a variety of schemes mainly designed to keep the unemployed off the street (see chapter IV). Since their prospects, even after completing such a course, are still very bad, youngsters on the schemes were assigned to trajectory IV.

Due to the complexity of co-operating with all kinds of different institutions that run schemes or vocational schools, the sampling process was not completed before early May 1989. Altogether, by then, completed questionnaires had been received from 270 young people. Their distribution according to trajectory, sex and age is shown in Table 2.

Table 2: Response main questionnaire

Trajectory	I	II	III	IV	Total
OLDER COHORT					
Male	17	15	16	16	64
Female	22	16	25	15	73
YOUNGER COHORT					
Male	21	13	14	14	62
Female	21	15	17	18	71
Total	**81**	**54**	**72**	**63**	**270**

Paderborn sample

As the transition between school and the labour market in Germany does not usually start before the age of 17, the population for the survey in Paderborn was defined as all of those who were born in the years 1969, 1970 and 1971. In collaboration with the local registration authorities, a sample of every third female and male born in those years was selected for the survey. At this stage, the aim was to obtain a larger sample than 160, in order to be able to choose from a variety of cases in the twinning process with Swindon. Altogether, 1,750 questionnaires were distributed by post and the respondents were asked to return them to the university using stamped addressed envelopes. The number of questionnaires returned was 540, representing 30.85% of the number distributed.

These responses included sufficient numbers and a broad variety of occupations in trajectories I and II, and from the older cohort in trajectory III. To fill the remaining cells, young people were contacted in educational institutions. Additional questionnaires were sent out in batches to schemes run by church educational establishments, the local independent unemployment centre, the *Kreishandwerkskammer* (chamber of handicraft trades), and the local *Volkshochschule* (adult education centre) for distribution to their students. The papers were returned to the university in batches and an expansion by 106 cases was achieved (Table 3).

Table 3: Paderborn sample

	I	II	III	IV
OLDER COHORT				
Male	61	83	14	43
Female	85	71	32	39
YOUNGER COHORT				
Male	31	28	10	24
Female	67	23	19	16
Total = 646				

The sample of 646 cases created a satisfactory basis for the twinning process with the Swindon sample.

British samples (Liverpool and Swindon)

Because the British surveys followed on from the earlier ESRC 16-19 Initiative, the sample was drawn from the existing pool of respondents and, initially, allocation to trajectory was based on position in the six months following the compulsory school-leaving age. This information had been obtained from the earlier ESRC questionnaires. Forty people were needed from each area in each trajectory, 10 per cell by sex and cohort. An initial sample 50% greater was envisaged, to allow for loss. In the event, however, the response left gaps in some of the cells, which necessitated going back to the 16-19 pool. Trajectory II was also divided internally for the purposes of selecting the initial samples, so as to obtain a rough balance between those on firm-based YTS and those in full-time work.

The initial screening of the ESRC survey was for those who had completed questionnaires in both phases and were not already involved in additional investigations (this acted as a particularly severe constraint on those who had been unemployed).

In Swindon, a sample of 242 (intended 160 + 50% over to allow for non-returns) was drawn, with equal numbers by gender in each category. However, the initial categorisations were too wide and over-lapping, and the use of six months' post-16 experience (in two three-month intervals) to assign them to trajectories was too restricting and sometimes proved misleading. When the questionnaires started to be returned, and all the available information was considered, new criteria for allocation to trajectories were agreed. However, it became apparent that trajectories III and IV were seriously underrepresented. Hence, a fuller search of the ESRC sample was undertaken (including using the 1988 boost sample), and an additional 60 questionnaires were sent out to those identified as likely candidates for trajectories III and IV. At the same time, all those who

265

did not return the first questionnaire were sent a reminder and another copy of the questionnaire.

Between December 1988 and April 1989, 192 completed questionnaires were returned and from these the final 160 were drawn, after matching with Paderborn. In Liverpool, a similar process was followed, whereby initially 240 youngsters were approached and this was 'topped up' with a further 40. The final 160 were drawn by 'matching' with Bremen.

Matching

As noted earlier, the Bremen and Paderborn samples had to be selected to match as closely as possible the young people participating in Liverpool and Swindon in the British 16-19 Initiative. The critical factor in this selection was the career trajectory each young person was on. Only once sufficient numbers had been sampled in each country, representing each of the four career trajectories, could detailed 'twinning' at the level of individual occupational outcomes be achieved.

Detailed pen-pictures of the samples were drawn up using material from this survey, as well as quantitative and qualitative material from the 1987 and 1988 ESRC questionnaires as for the British pen-pictures. The next stage was to consolidate the information from the questionnaires, together with the contextual information we collected about employers, colleges etc., and the pattern of education, training and employment in and around the four towns. This information was then circulated to the other teams, together with possible implications for the process of allocation to trajectories I - IV. (Thus, category allocation was informed by the consideration of 'real' cases, as well as by specification according to stylised trajectories.)

The next stage involved discussions between the twin teams to select and match pairs as closely as possible, and to 'firm up' the trajectory allocation. This involved comparing the profiles, together with reference to the fuller pen-pictures if required. After completion of Paderborn/Swindon matching, Liverpool/Bremen undertook their matching, with a member of the former pair present to see that the same criteria and balance between the criteria were applied to their pairing. The criteria for matching varied between categories.

Trajectory I

All had done, or were doing, A-levels/*Abitur*. So each pair was then matched according to the higher educational field they had entered, or were intending to enter. If more detailed information about proposed or actual employment destinations was available, then this was also used.

Trajectory II

Where youngsters were undertaking formal apprenticeships and/or gaining relatively 'high-level' vocational qualifications, then the pairing was decided upon the type of apprenticeship and, if possible, upon the type of employer (size, type of work and whether public or private).

However, in Swindon and Liverpool (as elsewhere in Britain), there were 'tradesmen' who did not go through either formal apprenticeships, nor did they do much in the way of vocational qualifications. In Germany, such youngsters must be formally qualified, therefore they were on trajectory II, whereas they were 'cross-matched' with youngsters doing similar jobs, but who were on trajectory III in Britain. Generally, however, very close matches were obtained in this trajectory.

Trajectory III

A number of different criteria were assembled in this trajectory, and matching according to actual employment was only possible for some cross-matches (see trajectory II). The matching process was hindered by the constraint that, in Bremen and Paderborn, youngsters were much more likely still to be in full-time vocational education, whereas those in Liverpool and Swindon may already have had several jobs, so their careers were not very comparable. In some cases, youngsters were matched because of the type of training (e.g., non-firm-based training; special vocational school) rather than its content as such. However, it was still possible to produce sufficient directly comparable pairs to carry out the required analysis.

Trajectory IV

The youngsters allocated to this trajectory had an unstable career, unskilled work, significant spell(s) of unemployment, or had remained in remedial education. Their future occupational prospects were not good.

Again, the matching process was influenced by cultural differences. The majority of the German youngsters were mainly on compulsory remedial schemes (see chapter III), whereas the British young people had already entered the labour market as unskilled workers, or had experienced unemployment. Those engaged on domestic careers were also included here if they were looking for full- or part-time work.

Most cases were matched because of similarity of careers and the tasks they fulfilled, rather than on their formal occupational status.

Swindon-Paderborn matching

The potential pool to be drawn from Swindon was much smaller than Paderborn: 192:626. The key information about education, training and employment was abstracted so as to present brief profiles of the Swindon sample in order to facilitate the 'first stage' matching. An initial trajectory allocation was also made, although this was only tentative in some cases. The Bielefeld team were then able to produce similar profiles for the most likely candidates for matching.

The next step involved comparing the profiles, together with reference to the fuller pen-pictures, if required. The criteria for matching were applied and led to the following matches in the four trajectories.

Trajectory I
Older cohort: 16 of the 20 pairs represented the same former or present educational situation (both in school or higher education), together with matches on broad or specific employment destinations (depending on how focused these were for young people). Where a detailed match could not be found, the remaining eight cases were filled with those having typical careers for that category.

Younger cohort: all the younger cohort were at school or college, with expectations of going into higher education. (There was one exception to this, where one Swindon youngster had taken A-levels a year 'early' and was already in higher education.) Therefore, whole sub-sets were matched in a general sense, but more information about proposed higher education specialisation was not available.

Trajectory II
Older cohort: the 10 female pairs represented very close matches in relation to type of employment, education and training. Five male pairs were similarly matched, and five Paderborn youngsters were 'cross-matched' with those in similar occupations in Swindon, but the lack of formal training and vocational qualifications meant the latter were included in trajectory III. So the remaining five Swindon cases were filled with those having typical careers for that trajectory.

Younger cohort: five female pairs represented very close matches in relation to type of employment, education and training. The remaining cases, although typical of the category, reflected different patterns of employment in the two sub-sets (in Swindon, clerical employment predominated, whereas in Paderborn, as elsewhere in Germany, clerical apprenticeships are relatively low paid. This difference is exacerbated by different policies in the two areas on pay for young people. That is, in Swindon, it is possible to receive the full 'rate for the job' very early in their careers, rather than in Paderborn, where fixed national 'training rates' are paid).

For the male matching, the situation was the same as for the older cohort. Only this time, nine close matches and one 'cross-match' were obtained.

Trajectory III

The huge variety of criteria included in this trajectory influenced the possible number of matches.

Older cohort: five males from Swindon were 'cross-matched' with those in similar occupations in Paderborn, but the lack of formal training and vocational qualifications meant they were included here. One male pair was matched. The remaining four Swindon and Paderborn cases were filled with those having typical careers for this trajectory.

Two female pairs represented very close matches in relation to training. Both matches illustrate a situation where, in Britain, youngsters learn on the job and, in Germany, they attend a special vocational school in these occupational areas. The remaining eight Swindon and Paderborn cases were filled with typical careers for this trajectory.

Younger cohort: the occupational and training situation of the sample in the younger cohort was even more different in the two towns. Whereas most of the males from Swindon have already entered the labour market, or are on specific schemes, most of the Paderborn males are in the *Handelsschule.*

Three female pairs were matched because of the actual job description and the potential job description for those still in full-time vocational education.

Trajectory IV

Again, the variety of careers allocated to this trajectory influenced the number of possible matches.

In the *older cohort,* six pairs were matched with regard to the similarity of their career patterns rather than the content of the actual occupation as such. The remaining cases represent typical careers for this trajectory.

The matching process in the *younger cohort* was characterised by the fact that the Paderborn youngsters were in compulsory remedial schemes whereas, in Swindon, the young people were unemployed, in dead-end jobs, or domestic careers. The category was filled with those having typical careers.

Bremen-Liverpool matching

Having constructed profiles of the 160 respondents in each city, the Bremen and Liverpool teams did an initial matching based on training experience and general prospects. Then a second matching was carried out, based on close similarity of training and expectations about a specific occupational destination. The first matching achieved 99 pairs out of a possible 160, and the second matching left 41 pairs. Thus, only about a quarter of the samples constituted very close matches. The remainder of the sample consisted of the less closely matched pairs, or those of similar background but whose responses lacked statements of specific career intentions.

Trajectory I

There were 13 male pairs and 13 female pairs in the first matching process in trajectory I. On the tighter matching, there were two older male pairs, two older female pairs, no younger male pair and one younger female pair. The younger cohort, all still in education, showed a great degree of homogeneity. Thus, only one stricter match was possible for the younger females, based on a specifically business-oriented education.

Trajectory II

There were 14 male pairs and 10 female pairs from this trajectory in the first matching. On the tighter matching, there were three older male pairs, two older female pairs, four younger male pairs and three younger female pairs. The tighter matchings within this trajectory were based on respondents being on apprenticeships or in work in specific occupational fields. As five out of 20 of the younger cohort were still in school, further matching was not possible.

Trajectory III

In this trajectory there were 16 male pairs and 11 female pairs in the first matching. On the tighter matching, there were three older male pairs and one older female pair, five younger male pairs and five younger female pairs. Tighter matchings were based on close similarity of occupations. The Bremen young people were generally in some sort of training scheme. The Liverpool young people were on, or had completed, non-firm-based YTS, or were working in jobs, but of lower status and which were hence not in trajectory II. There were not many matches in the older cohort, because the Liverpool young people were working in a wide range of occupations, whilst their Bremen counterparts were on a limited number of schemes. In the younger cohort, there were more matches because the Bremen and Liverpool young people were more likely to be on comparable schemes.

Trajectory IV

There were 12 matched male and nine matched female pairs in the first matching in this trajectory, and four older male pairs, two older female pairs, one younger male pair and three younger female pairs in the second matching.

Trajectory V

In Liverpool, this category covered the unemployed and those in unskilled jobs with few prospects. Most of the Bremen young people in this category, having had a short spell of unemployment, were on 'warehousing' schemes, designed to improve basic skills and to keep them off the street, such as ABM-G3. Given this difference between the national situations, it was obviously difficult to make close matches, but we did make a few, based on similarity of unemployment experience and future career orientations, or similar attitudes to training and qualifications, such as expressing a desire to obtain further qualifications.

We made three cross-matches when people were doing very similar things, but due to national differences, these had to be put into different trajectories.

Appendix II

Profiles of young people

As much of the report is based on a qualitative analysis of matched individuals following similar career pathways, it is useful to present some brief profiles of respondents, illustrating the kinds of careers and views we encountered. A juxtaposition of German and British career patterns enables some broad contrasts to emerge. The names, of course, are not the respondents' real ones, but the initial letters are used to identify the towns, so Susan is from Swindon, Bertholt from Bremen, and so on.

Petra

Petra is at university, having left *Gymnasium* in the summer of 1988. Her father is a university professor and her mother a primary school teacher. She originally wanted to become an interpreter, but has now decided to become a physicist. Her academic performance at school was above average, and she seems to have had a positive experience of school in general. She regards young people's employment prospects in her home area as difficult, and considers it likely that she herself will have to move eventually. Petra is interested in obtaining further qualifications and learning another language. Work values seem important to her: she believes in getting on and that one's capacities can only be developed through work. In general, she has high self-esteem, although occasionally she feels useless and superfluous. Petra is generally very satisfied with her life and circumstances, although she has some doubts about how she spends her free time. The only aspect of her life with which she is dissatisfied is at home, where she sometimes has arguments with her parents about her friends. She expects to marry and have five children, is not interested in politics, but is doubtful about the present government and would vote for the SPD.

274

Susan

Susan is currently studying mathematics at university. Her parents wanted her to stay in full-time education and she obtained four A-levels with two A grades. She is ambitious, and values good career prospects and the opportunity to use her initiative. She has high self-esteem and is generally satisfied with her life, apart from some doubts about her health and standard of living. Susan is very satisfied with her local area. She is reasonably confident about the future, although she is very doubtful as to whether she will be able to avoid unemployment. She is not very interested in politics and does not know who she would vote for in a general election, although she has some reservations about the present government.

Luke

Luke is currently in a college of higher education doing a BSc degree, having left a further education college in June 1988 with four A-levels, though with rather poor grades. Originally he wanted to become a meteorologist, but now wants to become a geologist. Although his A-levels were in arts subjects, he feels that 'in this environment for jobs an arts degree would merely be a qualification rather than an automatic entry to a job'. He feels very strongly that a person must have a job to feel a full member of society, and believes that it would be important to hang onto a job, even if a person did not really like it. The main criteria he regards as important in a job are security, pay and a friendly atmosphere at work. In addition, Luke wants a job which will not interfere with his private life and leisure activities. In general, he has positive self-esteem and appears satisfied with his life, apart from dissatisfaction with his current standard of living. He is very interested in politics and would vote Conservative, although he actually expresses dissatisfaction with the present government. His father is a maths teacher in a secondary school and his mother a telephonist. Both parents were keen for him to stay in full-time education. He considers it very likely that he will go to live in another part of the country and, indeed, has already moved away from home to study.

Bertholt

Bertholt wants to be a geologist. He regards himself as having been average at school, and expects to be at university or *Fachhochschule* in a year's time. However, he is also prepared to take an apprenticeship if that does not materialise. He thinks that, in general, it is difficult for young people to get jobs in Bremen, but does not think it likely that he will move away from the area. Bertholt rules out going abroad, and considers it unlikely that he will learn a new profession, a foreign language or become self-employed. He regards security, pay and a friendly atmosphere at work as the most important aspects of a job, but also wants a job which will interfere as little as possible with his private life and free time. He has rather negative attitudes to family life. He does not want to marry or have children, and often quarrels with his parents over his occupational plans for the future. He expresses strong self-esteem but, despite this, seems rather apprehensive about the future and unsure of himself. Bertholt thinks it doubtful whether he will have a job he really wants in 10 years' time. He expresses an interest in politics and dissatisfaction with the government and would vote for the Greens.

Simon

Simon is a heating and ventilation technician, giving technical support in the installation and commissioning of heating, ventilation and air-conditioning units for a large company specialising in such systems. After leaving school at the end of the fifth form, he completed an ONC in electrical engineering at a college of further education and started a technician apprenticeship with the company for whom he has been working for the last 18 months. Besides applying for five apprenticeships, Simon also applied for three other jobs not involving such training. The latter applications were unsuccessful. He has gained a lot of experience of IT, obtained at home and at work. He is dissatisfied with his present job, has applied for three other jobs in the last six months, and thinks it quite likely that he will obtain additional qualifications and train to work in a different occupation in the future. Simon is also dissatisfied with the education he has received. He has generally high self-esteem and appears confident for the future, is satisfied with the government and would vote Conservative. He is also satisfied with his standard of living and has £450 (roughly DM 1,350) to spend each month. His parents always wanted him to stay in full-time education and, even now, Simon has frequent arguments with his parents about his job plans.

Patrick

Patrick is also a heating and ventilation technician, but in a small firm. He applied for about 20 apprenticeships after leaving school, and was offered two. In a year's time he sees himself in a full-time job, unemployed or in the army doing national service. He wants to finish his apprenticeship, but thinks that jobs are hard to come by in the area and that it is quite likely that he will have to move away. Patrick appears ambitious, agreeing strongly that the most important thing at work is to get ahead, and ranking possibilities to get further qualifications as one of the most important things to look for in a job. He is interested in politics, but is unsure who to vote for. He does not intend to marry, although he would like a couple of children. He has DM 450 (roughly £150) to spend each month.

Beate

Beate finished *Hauptschule* in the summer of 1987 and became an apprentice hairdresser right away, though both parents had wanted her to continue at school. Originally, she had wanted to become a florist. She made three applications for apprenticeships and was offered two places. At work she feels challenged, and has developed new skills. Beate feels that the opportunity to use initiative, good career prospects and a friendly atmosphere at work are the most important aspects of a job. Her educational aspirations are to finish her apprenticeship. She lives with her parents and wants to marry when she is 24 and have one child. Her father works as an electrical engineer (*Elektromeister*), while her mother used to work in the retail trade but is now a housewife. Beate seems to be satisfied with her life. She is not a member of a union, is interested in politics, but would not know who to vote for in a federal election. She has DM 400 (roughly £130) to spend each month.

Liz

Liz wanted to be a hairdresser and is now training to become one on a firm-based YTS. It was one of two schemes for which she applied. She expects to be kept on as a full-time worker when the scheme ends, and she considers the most important aspects of a job to be pay, job security, and a friendly atmosphere at work. She has high self-esteem and is satisfied with most aspects of her life, apart from her standard of living (£160 a month [roughly DM 480] to spend). She is not a member of a trade union, is not very interested in politics, and does not know who she would vote for at an election, although she is dissatisfied with the present government. She thinks it quite likely that she might obtain additional qualifications in the future.

Paula

Paula is currently at *Handelsschule* training to be a *Bürokauffrau* (office clerk), although originally she wanted to be a textile saleswoman. She regarded herself as above average at school, and both parents wanted her to continue in education. Since leaving school she has applied for some 10 jobs and training places, without success. Paula has some experience in IT, which she obtained at school and on a specialist course, which she believes will be helpful to her in the future. She hopes and expects to complete job training in a firm, and regards it as very likely that she will obtain further qualifications.

She is very satisfied with the local area, but rates the local job prospects for young people as very difficult, and thinks it likely that she will have to move away to get a job. She agrees strongly that one must have a job to be a full member of society, and that the most important thing is to get on, but Paula also wants a job which will not interfere too much with her private life, and believes that getting a job today is just a matter of chance. She has high self-esteem, apart from wishing that she could have more respect for herself. Her father was a machinist (turner) on the railway and her mother a dressmaker, but both have now retired. Paula regards herself as middle class, is quite interested in politics and would vote CDU. She hopes to marry at 25 but does not want any children.

Sally

Sally obtained five O-levels and spent two years in sixth-form colleges taking additional O-levels, one A-level (which she did not pass), and Stage 1 typing. She then started a low-level clerical job, has since switched employers, and is now working as a debt recovery assistant with a large fuel-card company. Ideally, she would like to become a supervisor in a large office. Sally claims a lot of experience in IT, obtained at work. The main things she regards as important in a job are security, good career prospects and responsibility. She has high self-esteem, is very satisfied with her life and future prospects, is not at all interested in politics, although she is not satisfied with the present government and would vote SLD in a general election. She earns £382 a month (roughly DM 1,150).

Len

Len is currently on an ITEC course and has obtained City and Guilds qualifications in electronics. He expects to be in an apprenticeship in a year's time. Before the ITEC course he had applied for five jobs. He is ambitious, believing that the most important thing at work is to get ahead, and ranks good career prospects, along with security and a friendly atmosphere at work, as most important when choosing a job. He is reasonably confident about having the kind of job he really wants in 10 years' time. Len has good relationships with his parents, high self-esteem and is generally satisfied with his life, but he is not sure about his standard of living (£160 per month training allowance, roughly DM 640), or about what the future holds for him. He is very dissatisfied with the present government, very interested in politics, and a Labour supporter.

Bernd

Bernd is currently on a BGJ training scheme in electronics. He claims to have a lot of experience in IT, obtained at home, at school and on his course, and believes that this will be useful to him in the future. He expects to be in an apprenticeship in a year's time and eventually would like to attend university or *Fachhochschule*. He does not believe that it is very difficult for young people to get jobs in the area, and considers it very unlikely that he will move away, although he expresses dissatisfaction with his home city. Bernd's main criteria for a job are the chance to apply his own ideas, good prospects and a friendly atmosphere at work. He has very high self-esteem and is confident about the future. Generally, he is satisfied with his own life, but is very dissatisfied with the present government and would vote for the neo-fascist NPD or DVU, although he says that he is not at all interested in politics. His father is a retired policeman, his mother a salesperson. Bernd regards himself as upper-middle class and has DM 300 (roughly £100) per month. He often has arguments with his parents about helping in the house, and has frequent arguments about his dress and hairstyle.

Steve

Steve left school without qualifications in 1985, worked during the summer, and then had a spell of unemployment before obtaining a job at the start of 1986 as a guillotine operator, cutting paper for a medium-sized local firm which makes pocket files. He applied for about a dozen jobs after leaving school. He did not apply for a YTS, but he did apply for an apprenticeship as a painter and decorator. He is dissatisfied with his present employment, and has applied for some seven jobs in the last six months. Steve feels that his present job does not stretch him in any way, use all his abilities, or give him any chance to act on his own initiative. He feels that it is important to hang onto a job, even if you do not really like it, but he also feel that good career prospects are among the most important factors in a job. He is very dissatisfied with the education he received, and feels that his lack of qualifications is hindering his prospects of training and finding a more interesting job. He believes that more training should be offered to the employed and those without O- or A-levels: 'as long as you have the determination and confidence and are also willing to learn, I don't see where the A- or O-levels come into it'. Steve doubts whether he will have the kind of job he wants in 10 years' time, but is very confident that he will avoid unemployment or dismissal because of unsatisfactory work. He often has arguments with his parents about his job plans. He is not very interested in politics and does not know which party he would vote for in an election.

Paul

Paul is currently training as a gardener on an ABM scheme. After leaving *Hauptschule*, he worked for some 15 months, and was then unemployed for three months, after which he entered the training scheme. He has already left a couple of apprenticeships, and thinks it is difficult to get jobs in the area, but regards it as very unlikely that he will move anywhere else to obtain a job or training place because, in general, he is very satisfied with his home town. Paul thinks it is necessary to have a job to be a full member of society, but wants one that will not interfere with his private life and free time. Security, pay and a friendly atmosphere are the most important aspects of a job to him. Paul is dissatisfied with his standard of living and how he spends his free time. He is not interested in politics, but would vote for the Greens.

Bettina

Bettina has been unemployed since October 1988. She attended *Fachoberschule* until June 1988, and did some jobs after she finished school. Originally, she wanted to become a veterinary auxiliary, but now she would like to be a designer. After secondary education, she applied once for an apprenticeship, but then stayed on at school (*Abitur*). Lately, she has been actively seeking work in a number of ways and has made 40 applications for jobs or apprenticeships. Bettina considers it very difficult for youngsters to find jobs or apprenticeships in Bremen. She thinks that job security, career prospects and the opportunity to use her own initiative are the most important things about a job. On the other hand, she does not want her private life to be affected too much by her work. She seems to be uncertain about her immediate future: in a year she expects to be at university/*Fachhochschule*, in a full-time job, or unemployed. She wants to finish a vocational training course, and considers it likely that she will obtain additional qualifications and learn another language. She is unlikely to move away from Bremen to find a job. Bettina is living with her parents, her father being a medium-level government officer (senior administrative inspector - *Verwaltungsoberinspektor*). Her mother, a former office clerk/secretary, keeps the house. She considers her family middle class, is interested in politics, and would vote for the CDU at a *Bundestag* election. She has DM 100 (roughly £35) to spend each month, which is not much for her age. She seems to get on fairly well with her parents; they seldom have arguments because of her unemployment, but very often because of her job plans. She does not know when she is going to move out, wants to marry when she is 22 and have two children. Bettina is satisfied with most aspects of her life, except her future prospects.

Linda

Linda has just become unemployed after working as a check-out cashier in a large supermarket for three years, which was the first job she applied for after leaving school. She lives with her parents and gets on fairly well with them. They left it up to her at 16 whether she stayed in full-time education or left. Linda is currently actively seeking work in a number of ways, believes that she is quite likely to obtain additional qualifications and to train to work in a different occupation, and she would like to go to university, but has no A-levels. She values good career prospects and possibilities of becoming better qualified, along with a friendly atmosphere at work, as the most important criteria in a job. She appears to be very confident about the future and believes that in 10 years' time she will have the kind of job she really wants. Linda feels that she has skills which are not recognised in formal qualifications: 'I have patience with children of all ages and handicapped children, and people come to me with problems'. She thinks that these skills might be useful in social work, or in a nursery. Linda is not at all interested in politics, although she is dissatisfied with the present government and would vote Labour in an election.

Appendix III

Family social class

Social class

This Appendix gives the breakdown of the sample by social class of father, derived from the British Registrar General's classification of occupations (applied to occupations in both countries). Table 4 shows the social class distribution in each town, and Table 5 the social class distribution for each career trajectory within each country.

Table 4: Father's social class, by area

Father's social class	Liver-pool	Bremen	Swindon	Pader-born	Bri-tain	Ger-many
Professional	4	20	11	5	15	25
Intermediate	14	10	23	21	37	31
Partly-skilled	12	7	23	6	35	13
Unskilled	8	7	2	12	10	19
Skilled non-manual	14	30	33	35	47	65
Skilled manual	66	67	43	72	109	139
Unclassified	0	2	0	0	0	0
No answer	42	17	25	9	67	2

Table 5: Father's social class, by career trajectory, by country

Father's social class	Britain					Germany				
	NA	Ac	Sk	Sem	Unsk	NA	Ac	Sk	Sem	Unsk
Professional	0	11	2	1	1	1	18	3	3	0
Intermediate	0	23	7	2	5	2	14	7	5	3
Partly-skilled	3	3	10	8	11	0	2	1	2	8
Unskilled	1	1	3	2	3	0	1	6	2	10
Skilled non-manual	3	15	15	8	6	4	27	16	12	6
Skilled manual	6	21	34	24	24	10	15	44	29	41
Unclassified	0	0	0	0	0	0	0	0	1	1
No answer	7	6	9	15	30	3	3	3	6	11

The distribution between countries is not dissimilar, except that the British samples had fewer in the skilled categories than the German samples, largely because of the smaller number of skilled manual fathers in Swindon. The main difference in the relationship between social class and trajectory is that more young people from skilled non-manual homes in Germany were on the academic trajectory than in Britain; otherwise the relationship was similar in both countries.

Appendix IV

Questionnaire

1. WE SHOULD LIKE TO KNOW WHAT YOU HAVE BEEN DOING SINCE OUR LAST SURVEY.

Please tick one box for every three months to let us know roughly what you were doing at each time. For each period pick the thing you were doing for all, or for most of the time.

	1988 April May June	1988 July Aug Sept	1988 Oct Nov Dec	NOW
1. Out of work, unemployed				
2. On Youth Training Scheme				
3. On Community Programme, Job Training Scheme, or Employment Training				
4. At school or sixth-form college				
5. Full-time at college of futher education, or tertiary college				
6. At university, polytechnic or college of higher education				
7. In a full-time job (over 30 hours a week)				
8. In a part-time job				
9. Something else, please say what:				

....

If you are currently in a full- or part-time job

2. What is the job called?

....

3. Are you an apprentice?   1. YES ☐   2. NO ☐

4. What kind of work do you do? What are your tasks and responsibilities?

....

....

5. What is the firm/organisation called?

....

6. What does the firm/organisation make/do?

....

7. How big is the firm/organisation? What is the total number of employees?

1-25 ☐   26-100 ☐   101-500 ☐   501 and over ☐

8. How long have you worked there?

.... Years .... Months

9. AFTER THE FIFTH FORM, DID YOUR PARENTS (STEPPARENTS, GUARDIANS) ENCOURAGE YOU TO STAY IN FULL-TIME EDUCATION, OR DID THEY THINK IT BEST FOR YOU TO LEAVE?

	Mother	Father
1. Wanted me to stay in education		
2. Wanted me to leave and enter training or employment		
3. Did not care		
4. Left it up to me		

10. AT THE END OF FIFTH FORM

Did you apply to take a full-time course at school or at a college?

1. Did not apply .... ☐

2. Applied but was not accepted .... ☐

3. Was offered a place, but did not accept .... ☐

4. Was offered and took a place .... ☐

11. Did you apply for an apprenticeship?

1. Yes ☐   2. No ☐

If YES, how many apprenticeships did you apply for? ....

What was the result?

1. I was accepted in, and started an apprenticeship .... ☐

2. There is a good chance I will be taken on soon .... ☐

3. I'm still looking .... ☐

4. I've given up the search .... ☐

12. Did you apply for any other jobs apart from apprenticeships?

1. YES ☐   2. NO ☐

    IF YES   How many jobs did you apply for? ....

                  How many jobs were you offered? ....

                  Did you take one of these jobs?

                                1. YES ☐

                                2. NO ☐

13. Did you apply for a YTS?

                            1. YES ☐   2. NO ☐

    If YES, how many applications did you make? ....

    How many places were you offered?

        0 1 2 3 4 More

    And did you accept one of these places?

            1. YES ☐

            2. NO ☐

14. SINCE COMPLETING THE FIFTH FORM, HAVE YOU CHANGED YOUR VIEWS AND WISHES ABOUT THE JOB OR PROFESSION YOU WOULD LIKE TO TAKE UP?

1. YES ☐   2. NO ☐

Originally, I wanted to become a ....

Now, I'm going to be or plan to become a ....

15. WHAT ADDITIONAL QUALIFICATIONS HAVE YOU GAINED SINCE YOU WERE 16, IF ANY? DO NOT LIST THOSE YOU OBTAINED IN THE FIFTH FORM

SUBJECT	QUALIFICATION	RESULT OR GRADE

16. HAVE YOU EXPERIENCED ANY OF THE FOLLOWING DIFFICUL-TIES?

	Never (1)	Once (2)	More often (3)
a. Had to repeat an examination			
b. Had to change a course because you couldn't meet the standards			
c. Been obliged to leave training scheme or apprenticeship before completing the training			
d. Been made redundant			
e. Been sacked from a job			

17. HAVE YOU BEEN LOOKING FOR WORK IN THE LAST 6 MONTHS?

1. YES ☐   2. NO ☐

If YES, how many jobs have you applied for? ....

In what ways have you looked for work? (Tick all those that apply)

a. Been to the careers office .... ☐

b. Visited Jobcentre .... ☐

c. Looked throght the newspaper adverts .... ☐

d. 'Phoned or visited employers .... ☐

e. Asked family .... ☐

f. Asked friends .... ☐

g. Asked people at work .... ☐

h. Any other way? Please say what .... ☐

18. WE WISH TO ASK ABOUT YOUR EXPERIENCE OF USING INFORMATION TECHNOLOGY (IT), WHICH INCLUDES MICRO-COMPUTERS, ELECTRONICS, MODERN OFFICE AND TELECOM-MUNICATIONS FACILITIES

(a) Do you consider yourself to:

1. - have little or no experience in the use of IT .... ☐

2. - have some experience in the use of IT .... ☐

3. - have a lot of experience in the use of IT .... ☐

(b) Where did you get most of your experience of IT? (Tick all that apply)

- Home .... ☐

- School .... ☐

- College .... ☐

- Training centre .... ☐

- Work .... ☐

- Somewhere else (please say where) ....

19. DO YOU HAVE ANY SKILLS WHICH HAVE NOT BEEN RECOGNISED IN FORMAL QUALIFICATIONS? FOR EXAMPLE, MENDING THINGS, HOBBIES, DEALING WITH PEOPLE ETC.

1. YES ☐   2. NO ☐

IF YES, PLEASE LIST

....

....

What do you think these skills are useful for?

....

20. SINCE THE END OF THE 5TH YEAR AT SCHOOL, HOW OFTEN HAVE YOU EXPERIENCED THE FOLLOWING?

	Never (1)	Rarely (2)	Sometimes (3)	Quite often (4)	Very often (5)
a. Discussed in a group the best way to perform a task					
b. Worked as a member of a team					
c. Been asked for advice by others on how to tackle a problem					
d. Felt a sense of achievement					
e. Had a chance to use your initiative					
f. Felt all your abilities were being used					
g. Been able to make decisions for yourself					
h. Been given responsibility					
i. Felt stretched/challenged					
j. Developed new skills and abilities					
k. Set your own goals/targets					
l. Had your skills tested					
m. Taken a practical test					
n. Taken a written test					
o. Taken some other form of test					
p. Had to work to a deadline					

**NOW WE WOULD LIKE TO ASK ABOUT YOUR PLANS AND EXPEC-
TATIONS FOR THE FUTURE**

**21. WHAT DO YOU EXPECT TO BE DOING IN A YEAR'S TIME (RING
THE ONE WHICH YOU ARE MOST LIKELY TO BE DOING)**

I expect to be:

1. At university/polytechnic

2. At sixth-form college

3. At college of further education

4. In full-time job (over 30 hrs)

5. In a part-time job

6. Out of work

7. On a training scheme

8. In an apprenticeship

9. In social or community service

10. Something else

**22. IN THE FUTURE, HOW LIKELY ARE YOU TO DO EACH OF THE
FOLLOWING? TICK ONE OF THE BOXES FOR EACH ACTIVITY:**

	Very likely (1)	Quite likely (2)	Possibly (3)	Unlikely (4)	No chance (5)
a. Become self-employed					
b. Obtain additional qualifications					
c. Train to work in a different occupation					
d. Go to live in a different part of the country					
e. Go to live in a different country					
f. Learn a new language					

YOUR VIEWS ABOUT JOBS AND TRAINING

23. PEOPLE HAVE VERY DIFFERENT OPINIONS ABOUT MANY THINGS. HERE IS A LIST OF OPINIONS. READ EACH OPINION AND PUT A TICK IN THE BOX THAT DESCRIBES YOUR OPINION.

	Strongly agree (1)	Agree (2)	Uncertain (3)	Disagree (4)	Strongly disagree (5)
a. A person must have a job to feel a full member of society					
b. The most important thing at work is to get ahead					
c. Only at work can you develop your skills					
d. It's important to hang onto a job even if you don't really like it					
e. Earning high wages is the most important thing about a job					
f. I'd rather have a job which does not interfere with my private life and leisure activities					
g. Getting a job today is just a matter of chance					
h. I think a training in new technology will help me in the future					

24. PLEASE TICK THE THREE ITEMS FROM THE LIST BELOW WHICH YOU WOULD REGARD AS THE MOST IMPORTANT WHEN CHOOSING A JOB:

1. Good job security ☐

2. Good pay ☐

3. Opportunity to use initiative ☐

4. Responsibility ☐

5. Good career prospects ☐

6. Possibility of becoming better qualified ☐

7. Friendly atmosphere at work ☐

25. YOUR VIEWS ABOUT YOURSELF :
HOW DO YOU THINK ABOUT YOURSELF?

	Strongly agree (1)	Agree (2)	Disagree (3)	Strongly disagree (4)
a. I feel that I'm a person of worth, at least on an equal plane with others				
b. I feel useless at times				
c. I feel that I have a number of good qualities				
d. All in all, I am inclined to feel that I am a failure				
e. I am able to do things as well as most other people				
f. I feel I do not have much to be proud of				
g. I take a positive attitude towards myself				
h. On the whole, I am satisfied with myself				
i. I wish I could have more respect for myself				

26. YOUR SATISFACTION WITH LIFE

WE WOULD LIKE YOU TO CONSIDER SOME ASPECTS OF YOUR LIFE AT THE PRESENT MOMENT. FOR EACH ONE, PLEASE INDICATE HOW SATISFIED YOU FEEL ABOUT IT.

	Very satisfied (1)	Satisfied (2)	Not sure (3)	Dissatisfied (4)	Very dissatisfied (5)
a. The work you are doing now (including school work)					
b. The local district you live in					
c. Your standard of living: the things you can buy and do					
d. The way you spend your leisure time					
e. Your present state of health					
f. The education you have received					
g. What the future seems to hold for you					
h. Your friendships					
i. Your family life					
j. The present government					

YOUR ACTIVITIES AND VIEWS

27. Are you a member of a Trade Union?

1. YES ☐   2. NO ☐

28. How interested are you in politics? (TICK ONE)

1. Very interested .... ☐

2. Quite interested .... ☐

3. Not very interested .... ☐

4. Not at all interested .... ☐

29. If there were to be an election shortly, which party would you vote for?

1. Conservative .... ☐

2. Labour .... ☐

3. Social and Liberal Democrats (Democrats) .... ☐

4. Social Democratic Party .... ☐

5. Green Party .... ☐

6. Wouldn't vote for any party .... ☐

7. Other (specify) ....

8. Don't know .... ☐

30. How confident are you about each of the following?

PUT A TICK IN THE BOX WHICH IS RIGHT FOR YOU

	Very Confident (1)	Reasonably Confident (2)	Fairly Doubtful (3)	Very Doubtful (4)
a. In 10 years' time I will have the kind of job that I really want				
b. I will be able to impress an employer in a job interview				
c. I will be able to get on with the people I work				
d. I will avoid unemployment				
e. I will never be dismissed from a job for unsatisfactory work				

YOU AND YOUR FAMILY

31. AT WHAT AGE DID YOUR PARENTS LEAVE FULL-TIME EDUCATION?

	a. MOTHER	b. FATHER
1. Under 16		
2. 16		
3. 17		
4. 18		
5. 19		
6. 20		
7. 21 or above		

32. WOULD YOU SAY THAT, GENERALLY SPEAKING, YOU ARE FINANCIALLY BETTER OFF, WORSE OFF, OR ABOUT THE SAME AS A YEAR AGO? (PLEASE TICK ONE.)

1. Better off ☐ 2. Worse off ☐ 3. Same ☐ 4. Don't know ☐

33. HOW MUCH EACH WEEK DO YOU CURRENTLY RECEIVE FROM THE FOLLOWING SOURCES (WRITE IN THE AMOUNT TO THE NEAREST £). IF YOU DO NOT GET THE MONEY EACH WEEK, HOW MUCH DO YOU GET AND FOR WHAT PERIOD?

	AMOUNT	PERIOD COVERED
a) Main job (please give the net amount, that is, after tax and national insurance deductions, but include any overtime or bonuses that you normally earn)	£	....
b) Any other job or jobs	£	....
c) Training allowance (including any travel allowance)	£	....
d) Social Security benefits, e.g., unemployment or income support	£	....
e) Education grant or bursary	£	....
f) From parents or other members of your family	£	....
g) Any other sources (please write in the source)	£	....

34. DO YOU SOMETIMES OR OFTEN HAVE ARGUMENTS WITH YOUR PARENTS?

	Never (1)	Seldom (2)	Sometimes (3)	Often (4)	Very often (5)
a. Because of your performance at school or work					
b. Because you don't help in the house					
c. Because of your job plans					
d. Because of your friends					
e. Because of your unemployment					
f. Because of your dress/hairstyle					

35. AT WHAT AGE DO YOU EXPECT TO LEAVE YOUR PARENTS' HOME?

1. Already left at age ....
2. Expect to leave at age ....
3. Don't know ....
4. Do not expect to leave ....

302

36. WHAT IS YOUR NATIONALITY?

1. British ....

2. Other (say what) ....

37. Thank you for completing the questionnaire. If there is anything else you would like to tell us, please write it in below. We shall be most interested to read what you have to say.